SOUTH KOREA'S WEBTOONIVERSE AND THE DIGITAL COMIC REVOLUTION

Media, Culture and Communication in Asia-Pacific Societies

The Asia-Pacific region houses some of the richest and most diverse cultural, media and social practices in the world, with much of it yet to be analysed or uncovered. At the same time, there is a growing scholarly interest in understanding the breadth and depth of culture and media/communication practices in Asian societies. The aim of this series is to support this quest by enabling high-quality accessible and emergent scholarship on culture, media and communication in the Asia-Pacific to be published. It showcases innovative research produced in the region to a global readership with an eye to generating dialogue that will spark new ideas and enhance social and cultural understandings.

Series Editors:

Terence Lee, Associate Professor, Communication & Media Studies at Murdoch University, Australia

Susan Leong, Research Fellow, School of Media, Culture and Creative Arts, Curtin University, Australia

Titles in the Series:

Media Power in Indonesia: Oligarchs, Citizens and the Digital Revolution, Ross Tapsell

Activism and Digital Culture in Australia, Debbie Rodan and Jane Mummery

The Tastes and Politics of Inter-Cultural Food in Australia, Sukhmani Khorana

Willing Collaborators: Foreign Partners in Chinese Media, Edited by Michael Keane, Brian Yecies and Terry Flew

Transnational Migrations in the Asia-Pacific: Transformative Experiences in the Age of Digital Media, Edited by Catherine Gomes and Brenda S. A. Yeoh

Digital Media in Urban China: Locating Guangzhou, Wilfred Yang Wang

Remaking Red Classics in Post-Mao China: TV Drama as Popular Media, Qian Gong

South Korea's Webtooniverse and the Digital Comic Revolution, Brian Yecies and Ae-Gyung Shim

SOUTH KOREA'S WEBTOONIVERSE AND THE DIGITAL COMIC REVOLUTION

Brian Yecies and Ae-Gyung Shim

ROWMAN & LITTLEFIELD
Lanham • Boulder • New York • London

Published by Rowman & Littlefield
An imprint of The Rowman & Littlefield Publishing Group, Inc.
4501 Forbes Boulevard, Suite 200, Lanham, Maryland 20706
www.rowman.com

6 Tinworth Street, London SE11 5AL, United Kingdom

British Library Cataloguing in Publication Information Available

Library of Congress Cataloging-in-Publication Data
Names: Yecies, Brian, 1967- author. | Shim, Ae-Gyung, 1973- author.
Title: South Korea's webtooniverse and the digital comic revolution / Brian Yecies and Ae-Gyung Shim.
Description: Lanham : Rowman & Littlefield Publishing Group, 2021. | Series: Media, culture and communication in Asia-Pacific societies | Includes bibliographical references and index. | Summary: "This book investigates the meteoric rise of mobile webtoons-also known as webcomics-and the dynamic relationships between serialized content, artists, agencies, platforms, and applications, as well as the global readership associated with them"-- Provided by publisher.
Identifiers: LCCN 2020057519 (print) | LCCN 2020057520 (ebook) | ISBN 9781786606358 (cloth) | ISBN 9781538153383 (pbk) | ISBN 9781786606365 (epub)
Subjects: LCSH: Webcomics--Korea (South)--History and criticism. | Webcomics--Publishing--Economic aspects--Korea (South) | Webcomics--Social aspects--Korea (South)
Classification: LCC PN6790.K6 Y43 2021 (print) | LCC PN6790.K6 (ebook) | DDC 741.5/95195--dc23
LC record available at https://lccn.loc.gov/2020057519
LC ebook record available at https://lccn.loc.gov/2020057520

CONTENTS

LIST OF TABLES

LIST OF ABBREVIATIONS

ACA	Australian Cartoonists' Association
AR	augmented reality
ARMY	Adorable Representative MC for Youth
BBS	bulletin board system
BL	boys' love (genre)
BTS	Bangtan Boys (K-pop group)
BU	BTS Universe (aka Bangtan Universe)
CESA-KCSC	Cartoonists Emergency Committee Against the Korea Communications Standards Commission
CIC	company in company
CTO	chief technology officer
DMB	digital multimedia broadcasting
DSL	digital subscriber line
EP	extended play (extended play album)
GDP	gross domestic product
GL	girls' love (genre)
HD	high definition
ICT	information and communication technology
IP	intellectual property

ISP	Internet service provider
IT	information technology
ITU	International Telecommunication Union
KCA	Korea Cartoonist Association
KCSC	Korea Communications Standards Commission
KISA	Korea Internet & Security Agency
KOCCA	Korea Creative Content Agency
KOFIC	Korean Film Council
KOMACON	Korea Manhwa Contents Agency
K-pop	Korean popular music
KRW	South Korean won (currency)
LGBTQ	lesbian, gay, bisexual, transgender, and queer/questioning
LitRPG	literary role-playing game
MCST	Ministry of Culture, Sports and Tourism
MG	minimum guarantee
MMORPG	massive multiplayer online role-playing game
MOU	memorandum of understanding
MR	mixed reality
MSIT	Ministry of Science, ICT and Future Planning
OECD	Organisation for Economic Co-operation and Development
OSMU	one-source-multi-use
OTT	over-the-top (content streaming)
PPL	product placement
PPS	page profit share
RPG	role-playing game
SALUT	Solidarity Against Lezhin's Unfair Treatment
SBA	Seoul Business Agency
SNS	social-networking service

TXT   Tomorrow X Together (K-pop group)

UGC   user-generated content

UNCTAD   United Nations Conference on Trade and
                 Development

UX   user experience

VR   virtual reality

ACKNOWLEDGMENTS, METHODS, AND SOURCES

The authors wish to acknowledge funding from the Australian Research Council for Discovery Project grant DP180101841, Mobile Webtoons: Creative Innovation in a New Digital Economy. This work was also supported by the Laboratory Program for Korean Studies, through the Ministry of Education of the Republic of Korea, and through the Korean Studies Promotion Service of the Academy of Korean Studies, AKS-2018-LAB-2250001, as well as by Korea Creative Content Agency (KOCCA) project funding for the 2019 Corporate Driven Webtoon Overseas Promotion Supporting Program: Korea-Australia Webtoon Forum and OZ Comic-Con Participation, Project 1-19-H233-007, Application #A0080322000377.

In writing this book, we have utilized multiple research methods, including the collection and analysis of industry data, gleaned directly from webtoon platforms and key online database resources such as *WebtoonGuide* (https://www.webtoonguide.com/ko/) and *Webtoon Insight* (https://webtooninsight.co.kr). Examinations of pertinent government policies and industry legislation were achieved through major Korean policy repositories like *POINT* (https://policy.nl.go.kr) and KOCCA (http://eng.kocca.kr/cop/main.do), and invaluable technical facts and other comparative details concerning industry websites and mobile apps were harvested from analytical sites such as *SimilarWeb* (https://www.similarweb.com), *Statista* (https://www.statista.com), *AppBrain* (https://www.appbrain.com), and the World Intellectual Property

Organization (https://www.wipo.int/portal/en/). Searching the gamut for relevant details and viewpoints in Korean and English, we conducted painstaking reviews of fan blogs and websites, articles in the trade and popular press, industry press releases, government studies (e.g., by KOCCA, MCST, KOMACON, etc.), and corporate annual reports. This diverse collection of materials has enabled us to achieve the dual purpose of documenting and analyzing the rise of Korean-born webtoons while also deciphering the ways in which this history has been shaped by both domestic and international perspectives that have transformed over time. That is, we have immersed ourselves in the historiography of webtoons while also contributing to the writing of its history. With this in mind, the present work is a companion to other studies on comics and the creative industries more broadly, such as *Screen Distribution and the New King Kongs of the Online World* (Stuart Cunningham and Jon Silver, 2013), *The Routledge Companion to Comics* (edited by Frank Bramlett, Roy T. Cook, and Aaron Meskin, 2017), *New Korean Wave: Transnational Cultural Power in the Age of Social Media* (Dal Yong Jin, 2016), and *Social Media Entertainment: The New Intersection of Hollywood and Silicon Valley* (Stuart Cunningham and David Randolph Craig, 2019), to name only a few.

Between 2016 and 2020, we conducted exhaustive secondary-source desk research and also completed multiple field research trips to Korea, China, and the United States in order to conduct semistructured industry interviews and participant observation at major events, such as the Seoul International Cartoon & Animation Festival, Comic World, the Bucheon International Comics Festival, and KOCCA international forecast and emerging market strategy fora and symposia, as well as San Diego Comic-Con International, Amazing Las Vegas Comic Con, and Anime Expo Los Angeles. We also examined the large collection of archival print comics materials held at the Bucheon Manhwa Museum and at San Francisco's Cartoon Art Museum. In Australia we attended and also spoke at multiple annual awards and conference events hosted by the Australian Cartoonists' Association (ACA), as well as OZ Comic-Con, Supanova Comic Con & Gaming Expo, and Wollongong's own Comic Gong. Lengthy consultations with Jules Faber (ACA president) and active ACA members, including Mal Briggs (director/manager at Impact Comics, Canberra), Jim Bridges (president of the Australian Cartoon Museum, Melbourne), and Paul Caggegi (producer of webcomic *Homebased*), as well as other practitioners, consisting of Dan Gilmore (creator of *Kun-ghur*), Milan Ilich, and Aaron Sammut (creator of the comic book series *Maurice and the Metal*), exposed some of the nuanced cultural and technical aspects of webtoons (and digital comics more generally) and their potential for expansion in Australia.

In addition editorials, news articles, reviews, and advertisements in newspapers, as well as webzines, were examined to gain a better understanding of how industry issues were discussed and how particular webtoons (and webcomics and comic books) were marketed and reviewed by the press and fans. These media sources include *10Asia, Billboard, Bloter, Business Post, Channel Yes, ChosunBiz, Chosun Ilbo, Cine21, The Comics Journal, Crunchbase, Deadline Hollywood, Digital Daily, Digital Manhwa Gyujanggak, Donga Ilbo, Economic Review, eMarketer, ETnews, Forbes, Hankook Ilbo, The Hankyoreh, The Hollywood Reporter, International Business Times, IMDb, iZE Magazine, Japan Times, Joongang Daily, Korea Herald, Korea Times, Kyunghyang Shinmun, Maeil Kyungjae, Media Today, Naver Corp. Blog, Newsen, Observer, Oh My News, Platform, PPSS, SBS, Seoul Newspaper, SisaIN, Slow News, TechCrunch, Tech in Asia, Time, Variety, Wired, Yonhap News,* and *ZDNet.* Secondary literature was also consulted; journal articles and books in both English and Korean on comic books and webcomics, albeit few in number (but now slowly expanding), helped to broaden the scope of our investigation and arguments. Finally, studying some of the most important genre webtoons (and webtoon platforms) developed and published since 2003—often seen with the assistance of the Internet Archive Wayback Machine (https://archive.org/web/), served as a critical aspect of our research, revealing the distinctive narrative strategies and aesthetics developed by both platforms and owner-creator practitioners, as well as a range of user experiences and fan reactions evidenced by conspicuous user-generated content (i.e., comments, likes, and readership statistics, etc.).

Additionally, the book uses qualitative-forms data collection: the semistructured interview and (webtoon) content analysis. Although these two approaches might seem to produce divergent findings, they were purposefully chosen as an illuminating strategy of linking the reflections and experiences of representative content creators (i.e., writers and illustrators), producers, and other practitioners from multiple sides of the webtoon industry to a detailed consideration of their work.

Combined, these mixed approaches offer deep (and sometimes contrasting) insights into the webtoon ecosystem, more so than could be derived from articles in the trade and popular press alone—not just as responses to the various influences that have shaped Korea's (and now the international) webtoon industry but also in terms of the broader social, cultural, and industrial settings. As each week passed, it became challenging to keep up with all the rapid transformations the industry was undergoing.

Having said this, we are indebted to all of the industry experts, content creators, scholars, researchers, policy makers, producers, and other practitioners with whom we spoke informally or interviewed for this study—in Korea, China, Australia, and the United States. While this approach was time-consuming, and while it was often a challenge to synthesize the full range of people's attitudes and viewpoints about webtoons (and webcomics and comic books more generally), their first-hand experience and diverse perspectives enabled us to gain a multifaceted understanding of the industry before and during its domestic and international development. Creators Karl Altstaetter (*Mirror*), Ryan Benjamin (*Brothers Bond*), HWANG Sun Tae, JI Gang Min, James Gilarte (*The Misfits*), KANG Full, Dave Kellett, KIM Dae-ho (aka NOTZ), KIM Tae-hee (*The Black Label*), Luke Lancaster (*The Badguys*), LEE Jong Beom (*Dr. Frost*), LEE Narae (*Bloody Sweet*, aka *Honey Blood*), PARK Jong-won (*Midnight Rhapsody*), Waraporn Sirilai (*Dream Come True*, Thailand), and YOON Tae-ho shared their invaluable knowledge and personal views of the industry's development. Discussions with a range of platform founders and producers elicited commentary on Korean webtoons from competing creative/cultural and economic agendas. Sun BANG (founder of Tappytoon), Didier Borg (founder of Delitoon, France), Dennis CHA (Mr. Blue), Grace CHONG and James KIM (former president and head of US Business Development and Marketing at Lezhin Entertainment)—both from Lezhin, Heewoon CHUNG (Netcomics), LEE Gayoung (Naver Corp.), LEE Se-in (founder of Webtoon Insight), Steve Edwards and Warren KWON (CEO at Rolling Story)—both from Spottoon, David Lee (Head of Content) and Kim Estlund—both from Webtoon US (formerly Line Webtoon, before September 2019)—Akira Phattanakul (content manager at Line Webtoon-Thailand), WON Dong Yeon (producer of *Along with the Gods: The Two Worlds* and its sequel, *Along with the*

Gods: The Last 49 Days), YANG Byoung Seok (CEO at ComixV), and Andy YOON (CEO at Moonwatcher) affirmed the fluidity and unevenness of the domestic and increasingly transnational webtoon platform conditions. We are especially grateful to industry veterans LEE Jae-sik (CEO at C&C Revolution), PARK Jeong-seo (CEO at Daum Webtoon), and master creator YOON Tae-ho, as well as insiders TJ Kang (CEO at WebtoonGuide) and LEE JaeMin (Webtoon Insight) for generously explaining some of the industry's pointy ends. Interviews with policy officers, such as KIM Suk (KOCCA), KIM Yu-chang (chairperson at Korean Webtoon Industry Association), AHN Jiheon and JUNG Jaeson—both from Seoul Business Agency (SBA) Webtoon Contents Agency—as well as KIM Seon-mi/Can, KIM Bo Geum, Shim Rina, and BAEK Su-Jin—all from Korea Manhwa Contents Agency (KOMA-CON)—corroborated the significant role that cultural policy played in the process of industry development and international expansion, thereby shedding light on politicoeconomic perspectives. Finally scholars such as HAN Chang-wan (president of the Animation Society of Korea and professor at Sejong University) and PARK Seok-hwan (professor at the Korea University of Media Arts) pinpointed gaps in the conventional history of webtoons and their development in Korea. We were extremely fortunate to absorb a great deal of knowledge from the above-mentioned and other people too numerous to mention, which bestowed critical information unavailable in either Korean- or English-language published sources. Amalgamated, this unique corpus of information expands on and often questions conventional interpretations of the industry's transformation found in limited published materials. Our only regret is that we were unable to include direct quotes from many of the people that we encountered during the research process. Nonetheless, this final version of this book was only made possible after having synthesized all of the knowledge drawn from this plethora of sources. Many thanks go to Terence Lee and Susan Leong, the series editors of *Media, Culture and Communication in Asia-Pacific Societies*, for believing in this project (and in us). Finally we are grateful for the friendships with and mentoring received from colleagues Adrian Athique, Luke Buckmaster, Dal Yong Jin, Steinar Ellingsen, Terry Flew, Ben Goldsmith, Gil-Soo Han, Michael Keane, Terence Lee, Tom O'Regan, and Doobo Shim.

For the romanizing of Korean words and names, the book generally follows the Korean government's Revised Romanization System, except where an alternative system was already established, such as for the term *chaebol*, the name of president KIM Dae-jung, creator YOON Tae-ho, and other webtoonists whose names have been popularized through the popular press or KOMACON/KOCCA publications. When referring to personal Korean and Japanese names, including those of industry practitioners, the family name appears capitalized (our choice), and it usually precedes the given name, following established convention. All translations into English from Korean materials and interviews are our own work. The titles of Korean and other country's webtoons and all figures cited in this book are identified faithfully from the sources indicated in the text and/or the endnotes.

By pooling and analyzing the details and insights extracted from these diverse sources in both Korean and English, we hope to offer readers a previously overlooked understanding of the complex development of Korean webtoons and particularly what we call the "webtooniverse." The various carefully selected developments included in our investigation represent the latest interventions to enrich the webtoon ecosystem, which in our analysis has passed through four distinctive stages: first (1998–2002), the emergence of amateur web comics and experiments with distributing digital comics via the Internet (i.e., N4 and Comics Today); second (2003–2009), the online birth and early transmedia adaptation of webtoons; third (2010–2013), the creation of a mobile-centered ecosystem launched via the rapid proliferation of smartphones and novel monetization strategies; and, fourth (2014–present), an accelerating internationalization push through globally facing platforms. Put together, these transformations amount to a golden age of Korean webtoons and a digital comic revolution.

I

INTRODUCING WEBTOONS AND THE EXPANSION OF KOREA'S CREATIVE INDUSTRIES

Since the late 1990s, South Korea's popular culture and media products have flowed out of the country to other neighboring countries; this phenomenon, known as Hallyu, or the Korean Wave, continues nearly unabated today. One of the most far-reaching examples of the global spread of popular South Korean (hereafter Korean) culture is the award-winning black comedy thriller feature film *Parasite* (2019). Directed by critically acclaimed Korean writer-director BONG Joon-ho, Korean-language *Parasite* dominated the popular and social media press and industry and trade paper headlines between late 2019 and early 2020, after winning over 180 major domestic and international awards, including the Palme d'Or at the 2019 Cannes Film Festival and Best Picture, Best Director, Best Original Screenplay, and Best International Feature Film at the 92nd Academy Awards. *Parasite* is the first Korean film to receive the Palme d'Or and also the first foreign-language (non-English-language) film to win the Academy Award for Best Picture. These accolades demonstrate the global appeal of Korean cinematic culture and have also boosted international awareness of the Asian film industry. While Director BONG's film is not based on a particular webtoon, it has clear links with other media. In an interview recorded around the time of the film's initial release in Korea—prior to the flood of international publicity—BONG stated that he had been influenced by comics (*manhua* in Korean): "I draw my storyboards myself as well, and when I work on the storyboard I consider myself a cartoonist. In my next life I want to be a cartoonist, because I love Manga" (Wise 2019).[1]

The success of blue-chip media products such as *Parasite* is encouraging the Korean government to increase the global competitiveness of its national creative industries by investing more than $840 million USD in them (Yonhap News Agency 2019). Along with other information and communication technology (ICT), this funding surge is expected to benefit a plethora of webtoon enterprises and apps, as well as the diverse spectrum of genres—action, comedy, drama, educational, fantasy, horror, thriller, science fiction, sports, slice-of-life, and superhero—associated with them.

According to reports released by the Organisation for Economic Cooperation and Development (OECD 2017 and 2019), the International Telecommunication Union (ITU 2019a and 2019b), and the United Nations Conference on Trade and Development (UNCTAD 2019), South Korea is a leading region of innovation in ICT. Korea's creative industries are attracting global attention for their vibrant ICT content, as well as for the economic and cultural heft of their internationalization strategies (see Jin 2016; Yecies 2017a and 2017b; Yecies, Shim, and Yang 2019). However, Korean-originated webtoons—a relatively new open online and mobile media platform that blends aspects of digital storytelling, social media entertainment, and serialized digital comics—have yet to be studied and understood as a key energizer of Asia's globally oriented creative industries and their distinctive brands of popular culture. Major creator-centric platforms include Naver Webtoon, Daum Webtoon, KakaoPage, Lezhin Comics, Toptoon, Bomtoon, Comico, Toomics, One Store, and Justoon—to name a few. These enterprises, some of which are explored in depth throughout this book, are now hosting, coproducing, translating, licensing, and investing in multilanguage webtoons as a major source of transmedia content for global audiences. As a vehicle for transmedia IP—a network of interconnected media, popular culture, and merchandise emanating from a single creative source—webtoons are cultivating new audiences and participatory cultures beyond Korea's national border.

This unprecedented turn for Korea's creative industries—driven by the genre-bending and diverse story lines of webtoons and their expanding potential for transmedia adaptation—differs radically from earlier technological developments, such as Japanese keitai novels (i.e., digital texts accessed on a cell phone through text messaging) studied by Hjorth (2003), Nishimura (2011), Rebagliati (2016), and Nagaike and Langley (2019). By 2020 webtoons had far outstripped the potential of the digital comics promoted by Marvel, DC, ComiXology, and Madefire, particularly in terms of numbers of individual series and creator-owners of content. Furthermore, unlike these abovementioned platforms, webtoon enterprises have been expanding the potential of user-generated content (UGC), which in turn is contributing to the explosive growth of digital and social media entertainment across the region's creative sectors. This activity has generated almost $17 billion USD in revenues across Australia, Korea, and Japan between 2012 and 2014 (Bhargava and Klat 2016) while playing a significant role in the $2.25 trillion USD (3 percent of global GDP) that the broader cultural and creative industries generate annually (EY 2015).

Remarkably, as far as one can tell, *The Korean Popular Culture Reader* (Kim and Choe 2014) seems to have overlooked webtoons completely, as well as the "digital revolution" that they have created for comics more widely.[2] Yet since 2016 a gradually increasing number of English-language studies (including Lynn 2016; Jang and Song 2017; Park, Lee, and Lee 2019; Kim and Yu 2019; Jihoon Kim 2019; and Jin 2020) have begun to explore the webtoon industry from various media industry, cultural studies, and political-economic perspectives. Other Korean-language investigations on the technological infrastructure of webtoon platforms and the range of UGC that they facilitate have been dominated by scholars working across universities in South Korea, including Korea Advanced Institute of Science and Technology (KAIST), as well as a small number of researchers working among the many R & D clusters at Naver (aka "Korea's Google"). Examples of these studies, which mostly sit within the fields of computer science, appear in two broad categories: (1) neural networks for story analytics and image processing (i.e., Chan-Ik Park 2016; Cinarel and Zhang 2017; Song et al. 2018; and Lee and Jung 2020) and (2) platform infrastructure linking content producers and users via cooperative two-way communication features (i.e., Kim et al. 2016; Lee, Park, and Jun 2019). Apart from the brief case studies appearing in these informative studies, the general history of webtoons and webcomics more widely remains fully underexplored. Even the self-purported cutting-edge, all-faceted, and up-to-date 450-plus-page "authoritative" *Routledge Companion to Comics* (Bramlett, Cook and Meskin 2017), featuring some of the most knowledgeable scholars in the field and covering a truly global approach, contains little if any attention to web or digital comics, let alone webtoons. This is strange, since webtoons and webtoon platforms had well and truly made a name for themselves by 2014.

With these former studies in mind, the present chapter introduces the reader to webtoons and establishes the nuanced and detailed context for our investigation of the transformation of Korea's digital economy. It sketches the meteoric rise of Korea's online and mobile webtoon industry and explores how this new digital entertainment medium is transforming Korea's legacy media and creative industries, including film, television, music, online and mobile video gaming (aka e-sports), web series, video-sharing and -streaming platforms, and digital publishing (webnovels in particular). The authors trace webtoons' dynamic links to cross-media storytelling, styles, and technologies as well as the production, localization, and reception of innovative smartphone apps and platforms. While the "Korean Wave" of popular culture has enjoyed striking global success since the 2000s, limited attention—at both popular and scholarly levels—has been paid to the complex relationships between webtoon artists, platforms, agencies, policymakers, translators, and readers—all elements of what we call the "webtooniverse."

THE WEBTOONIVERSE: A NEW ERA FOR THE DIGITAL KOREAN WAVE

One of the most exciting and dynamic aspects of Korea's creative industries—one set to lead the next generation of the mobile Korean Wave, or m-Hallyu, as it is becoming known—is taking shape in the cartoon sectors. Online and mobile webtoons are forming the "webtooniverse," a phenomenon that is swiftly becoming the most visible and profitable aspect of the Korean Wave, albeit in an evolving digital environment of their own.

Webtoons are comics published on online or mobile platforms; the term was coined in Korea in the early 2000s as an amalgam of "web" and "cartoon." Webtoons use a revolutionary content-delivery method that takes advantage of the high-speed broadband capability well established in Korea. As with K-pop, webtoons represent a convergence culture, a place where media producers and consumers actively engage with one another and where participatory culture plays a large role (Jenkins 2006, 2–3). Webtoons differ in many regards from webcomics familiar in the West, for instance, which are mostly digitalized (scanned) versions of paper comics published online (e.g., ComiXology, Marvel.com). While the term *webcomics* originated in the 1980s, referring to the practice of "posting strips online for free and monetizing [them] once an audience formed,"[3] webtoons took a further twenty years to be realized as a unique vertical-scrolling format. In 2000, the term *webtoon* was first used in conjunction with published webcomics by Korean telecom carrier Dacom's web portal Chollian, but it was not until 2003 and 2005, respectively, that the Daum and Naver search engines commercialized webtoons in the format with which we have become familiar. Today Naver and Daum are Korea's first and second largest portal sites, and the current webtoon ecosystem was largely a result of their efforts. They established this pioneering online digital comics–viewing model initially for free, expanded the market, found various ways of using intellectual property (IP), and devised the micropayment funding model for viewing.

Webtoons take advantage of online publishing platforms not only for distribution and consumption but for two-way communication with readers as well. Unlike digital comic sites, which offer previously published content, webtoon sites like Daum Webtoon and Naver Webtoon (discussed in chapter 4), as well as KakaoPage and Lezhin (discussed in chapter 5), offer dynamic serialized content that is mostly creator-owned. Generally speaking, each episode is uploaded on a weekly basis, and reader feedback is instantaneous (except on the platforms that disable the user-feedback function), allowing artists the potential to enrich the details of their story lines and aesthetics over time. The means of viewing—scrolling down a vertical strip—allows readers to take in a single episode in a couple of minutes. Similar to the open nature of YouTube and other video- and image-sharing sites that generate profits from user clicks and ads, webtoon creators too can upload content to webtoon platforms, such as Naver Webtoon or Daum Webtoon, which strongly encourage amateur content creation.

Transmedia adaptation, or *transmediality*, is another feature distinctive of webtoons (Cho 2016). Their origin was digital, and webtoon artists have been eager to use and develop a variety of digital technologies in creating their series. Thus, as this book explores in great detail, webtoons have been enhanced with color, vibration, music, sound effects, animation effects, and, most recently, infusions of augmented-reality (AR) images. One offshoot, the *smart-toon*, is designed for smart-device screens, utilizing a touch-screen function for viewing, and offering novel ways of framing each panel. One representative example is the series *Distant Sky* (2014). This smart-toon—discussed in detail in chapter 6—was produced by YLab (story by YOUN Inwan and illustrated by KIM Sunhee) and released by Naver.

According to one report by the Korea Creative Content Agency (KOCCA)—a quasi-government agency under the auspices of the Ministry of Culture, Sports and Tourism (MCST)—at least one in three Koreans reads webtoons on a smart device each week, and many are paying fees to read episodes. Distinctive for this format, this payment model offers either all free content or a range of micropayments for continued access to paid content. The high consumption rate of webtoons, which has increased steadily over the last decade, is keeping creator-owners busy to the point where (depending on contract conditions) a rookie practitioner can earn somewhere between 500,000 to 900,000 KRW (approximately $410 to $750 USD) per serialized episode. Normally, established webtoonists can earn 1,000,000 KRW ($825 USD) per episode. On average, these payments are quadrupled each month because one episode is usually released each week. As of 2020, over 8,500 domestic artists were working in the field, and 12,291 individual series had been published (since 2010) on webtoon platforms based in Korea.[4] The figures are even larger when translated and localized versions for international markets produced by such platforms as Line Webtoon (renamed "Webtoon" in September 2019), Tapastic, Spottoon, and Lezhin Comics are taken into account; these sites are all growing in popularity on a daily basis. New talent, both amateur webtoonists and established comic artists, are constantly entering the webtoon market, pushing standards steadily upward. Korea's comics industry is being rapidly reshaped with a focus on webtoons, which are designed specifically for the Internet and, especially, mobile services. Little wonder that webtoon platforms have been dubbed "the YouTube of comics."[5]

In mid-2020, according to Webtoonguide's Webtoon Analysis Service, sixty-five companies were competing on the domestic market in Korea, with seventeen rated as highly active.[6] Average monthly page views on the top ten platforms were Naver Webtoon (four million), Toptoon (2.5 million), KakaoPage (1.5 million), Lezhin Comics (1.4 million), Bomtoon (812,000), Daum Webtoon (754,000), One Store (525,000), Toomics (480,000), Comico (356,000) and Justoon (277,000). These figures leave the statistics for monthly comic book sales to comics shops—available on Comichron's website[7]—in the shade. Most of these leading platforms (which now include both websites and mobile apps) showcase "creator-owned" content, which has always differentiated the webtoon format from most other types of commercial digital comics. As a now-standard practice—innovated by Daum in 2003 and then adopted by Naver in 2005—this feature has attracted a new generation of creators, writers, and illustrators to publish on webtoon platforms which, in turn, has fueled the expansion of Korea's creative industries as a whole.

In May 2020 domestic statistics recorded some astonishing totals: 2.2 billion total monthly page views by 262 million unique monthly visitors across 1,798 serialized titles featuring over 15,330 episodes (normally uploaded on a weekly basis).[8] As a rough comparison, there are currently 64,510 comic book series published by 4,768 publishers in United States alone.[9] Table 1.1 provides some insights into the commercial activities and scale of the webtoon platforms dominating Korea's domestic and international markets. The table sets out some of the major differences and similarities between each platform, including "exclusive" arrangements whereby a single platform hosts a particular series in a given language; a "nonexclusive" status means that a title is licensed across several different platforms. These are the major domestic platforms contributing to the inner ring of the webtooniverse.

The auxiliary market for webtoon content embraces a large variety of media. In Korea a number of webtoons have become the basis of television shows and feature films. Webtoon-originated television dramas include *Full House* (2004), *Flower Boy Next Door* (2013), *Misaeng* (2014), *Awl* (2015), and *Cheese in the Trap* (2016). Film adaptations include *Moss* (2010), *The Neighbours* (2012), *Secretly, Greatly* (2013), *Inside Men* (2015), and *Along with the Gods* (2017, and its 2018 sequel). As a representative example, the twenty-episode Korean television series *Misaeng* (2014), based on an original webtoon story, is especially worth noting here. *Misaeng* concerns an everyday man who reluctantly pursues a career as an office worker after failing to become a professional *baduk* (Chinese Go) player. The protagonist's harsh experiences in the corporate world and the exploration of the human condition resonated with so many viewers that Japan's Fuji TV and China's Dragon TV, Jiangsu TV, and Zhejiang TV decided to produce localized versions titled *Hope* (2016) and *Ordinary Glory* (2018), respectively. Numerous other and more recent transmedia adaptations are discussed below. Through such transmedia adaptations, content flowing between Korea's creative-industry sectors is continuing to make fresh inroads at home and abroad.

Other auxiliary markets for webtoons include e-gaming-inspired transmedia adaptations. Korea is well known as one of Asia's largest gaming hubs; this sector of the industry is linked closely with webtoons, as a number of gaming companies own and/or create their own webtoon platforms. When it comes to size—excluding industry leader Naver Webtoon—the webcomic portal Bufftoon and its parent gaming company NCSoft operate one of the largest potential webtoon enterprises, containing the biggest archive of exclusive content featuring e-gaming IP-comprising characters, artwork, and stories.[10]

An increasing number of webtoon series, such as *The God of High School* (2011–present) and *Tower of God* (2010–present), are developing synergistic connections with domestic and international online and mobile games. This recent trend, led by Naver and its partners, demonstrates a newfound expertise in mixing digital-media formats and using original webtoon content as a way of expanding Korea's digital economy. In 2016 Naver and YD Online released *The God of High School* as a mobile online game. Similar to the fighting video games that were popular in the 1990s, *The God of High School* role playing game (RPG) provides users with more than four hundred character variations from the original webtoon series. The aim is to challenge competitors in an intensifying tournament, with the ultimate winner becoming the "God" of high school. Similarly, *Tower of God* is a RPG mobile game that was released in 2016 through a partnership with Naver and Neowiz Able Studio.

Table 1.1. Overview of Korea's Most Active Webtoon Platforms

Platform (year established)	Sales figure in billion KRW			No. of webtoon creators as of October 2019	Total no. of exclusive webtoon series as of October 2019	Total no. of nonexclusive webtoon series as of October 2019	Traffic: Total visits on desktop and mobile apps in July 2019 (millions)	Percentage of adult webtoons as of October 25, 2019
	2017	2018	2019					
Daum Webtoon (2003)	164.80	n/a	n/a	171	781	264	10.00	3.0
Naver Webtoon (2005)	34.00	72.2	161.0	353	1,033	30	92.20	4.2
KakaoPage (2013)[1]	39.50	55.2	77.1	166	229	241	2.25	n/a
Lezhin Comics (2013)	44.80	37.4	34.5	170	910	76	10.00	37.2
Ktoon (2013)	6.66	n/a	n/a	63	60	353	1.40	13.5
Mr. Blue (2014)	30.20	31.0	63.8	95	169	440	1.30	45.9
Toptoon (2014)	22.50	40.4	53.7	121	405	520	6.15	65.9
Toomics (2015)	17.50	17.5	15.3	160	468	327	8.20	49.3
Bomtoon (2015)	11.90	19.6	25.2	134	404	487	1.30	39.3

1. Sales of content via the KakaoPage brand in 2017 include Daum Webtoon and Piccoma (from Japan). KakaoPage's total revenue in 2017 is 131.8 billion KRW, of which webtoon sales account for 30 percent of this share (39.5).

To set the wider context for these transmedia developments and the ways in which webtoons and major enterprises are shaping them, we next describe the key pillars of Korea's creative industries, of which webtoons are the newest member.

THE EVOLUTION OF DEMOCRACY, ICT, AND KOREA'S SOFT-POWER STRATEGIES

Since the election of the KIM Dae-jung government (1998–2003), the transnational dissemination of Korean popular culture—aka the "Korean Wave" (or *Hallyu* in Korean)—has gradually transformed Korea from an Asian backwater into a vibrant, ultramodern trend-setting society. Through their transnational ebb and flow into China, Taiwan, Vietnam and Japan, among other countries in Asia and across the globe, Korean firms, practitioners, policymakers, and audiences have witnessed the rapidly evolving soft-power expansion of the Korean Wave. During this period, the KIM government began aggressively steering the nation in the direction of a "knowledge-based economy," in which cultural products were valued for their commercial viability and economic value. As noted by other studies (such as Yim 2002; Otmazgin 2011; and Kwon and Kim 2014), cultural products such as feature films, television programs, and radio broadcasts were utilized by successive military governments to advocate national policies and as vehicles for progovernment messages, as well as to promote themes of hard work and loyalty to the nation. Korea's major family-run conglomerates (or *chaebols*), as well as other minor industry players, began exploring innovative globalization strategies as they became increasingly aware of international cultural products, trends, and markets. Korea's cultural industries—primarily drama, film, music, and gaming—received escalating financial support from the government, which in turn assisted the growth of numerous related sectors. These reforms coincided with the 1996 ruling of the Constitutional Court that made film censorship illegal and with the promulgation of the 1996 Sound, Record, Video and Game Products Act, which protected the manufacture of sound records and video products under the umbrella of freedom of speech and the press. Under Korea's new civilian administrations and newly shaped policy instruments, the cultural sector braced itself for an explosion of creativity under the banner of the Korean Wave.

The slogan "support without intervention," promulgated in 1999 under the KIM Dae-jung administration, signaled a significant turning point in the government's approach to the creative and cultural industries. This "hands-off" approach would soon drive the new Culture Industry Promotion Law and its spinoff, the Culture Industry Promotion Fund. The Korean government now committed itself to allocating approximately 1 percent of the nation's annual budget to the cultural industries in order to promote and expand Korean cultural products internationally. The Ministry of Culture and Tourism (later renamed the Ministry of Culture, Sports and Tourism) acquired the means to promote the production of Korean creative and cultural content at home and abroad. In turn, Korea's creative industries have benefitted from a series of economic boosts. The government has increased its financial commitment to the arts and culture in general, directly supporting the promotional work and industry-networking activities of organizations such as the Korea Creative Content Agency (KOCCA), the Korean Film Council (KOFIC), and the Korea Manhwa Contents Agency (KOMACON), with a view to generating significant profits on the international stage. Today KOCCA and KOMACON—which is discussed in more detail in chapter 3—remain strong allies for the webtooniverse.

In a wider context, Korean webtoons—along with Japanese popular culture, represented by manga, and China's rapidly rising pop culture—are part of a regional push to assert Asian "soft power," a term coined by Joseph Nye in his landmark book *Bound to Lead: The Changing Nature of American Power* (1990). Other scholars, notably Beng Huat Chua in *Structure, Audience and Soft Power in East Asian Pop Culture* (2012), have applied Nye's theories to Asia's creative industries and their competitive character. Borrowing these concepts from Nye and Chua, we argue that the soft-power dynamics embodied in the Korean Wave in general, and webtoons in particular, reflect an inherent appeal and charisma that draw audiences to its products. Although most countries would like their creative industries to generate soft power, only a few succeed—usually as a result of a serendipitous combination of proactive policy support, freedom of expression, genre experimentation, international collaboration, awareness of audience tastes, and good timing.

Underpinning the vitality of Korea's creative industries is the country's advanced technological infrastructure, a key phase of which was launched in 1999 by the KIM administration as the Cyber Korea 21 policy—the government's vision statement for leading the country into the new century as a superpower in terms of ICT. This policy was intended as a blueprint for building a public infrastructure that in a few short years made Korea the most wired and computer-savvy nation in the world. The factors that specifically favored Korea in this endeavor were the innovation of a state-of-the-art telecommunications and Internet infrastructure and the subsequent development and dissemination of revolutionary "smartphones," as well as hardware, devices, and services for mobile free-to-air television digital multimedia broadcasting (DMB) since the mid-2000s.

The rapid transnational take-up of Korean popular media and cultural content is an integral part of this ICT revolution. As is widely known, Korean television drama has become a key energizer of what is officially known as "global Hallyu"—the worldwide spread of Korean popular culture led by the nation's creative and cultural industries from the late 1990s. Beginning with the unexpected success of the blockbuster action-drama *Shiri* (1999), and continuing all the way up to the critically acclaimed *Parasite* (2019), Korean cinema has earned the sobriquet "Planet Hallyuwood," infusing local sentiment with a globalized and thus more accessible suite of universal story lines, genre choices, high production values, and vertical integration across the production and distribution sectors (Yecies and Shim 2011).

WEBTOONS AND PLANET HALLYUWOOD

Since the late 1990s, Korean cinema has become one of the most exciting and dynamic national cinemas in the world. This remarkable surge was fueled by the unexpected and extraordinary success of KANG Jegyu's blockbuster action-spy drama *Shiri* (1999), which exceeded $25 million USD at the local box office and outsold Hollywood's megablockbuster *Titanic* (1997, released in Korea in February 1998). Making a successful Hollywood-style blockbuster with a Korean inflection—at a time when few people expected such an achievement in this part of the world—put the local film industry on the pathway toward its current international acclaim. Around this time many Asian countries began looking for entertainment products from countries other than Japan, whose exports were expensive compared to those from Korea (Chua and Iwabuchi 2008, 4). *Shiri* and its international reception eventually gave rise to what the authors have elsewhere called "Planet Hallyu-wood" (Yecies 2008; Yecies and Shim 2011).

After the Korean Constitutional Court eliminated film censorship in 1996 under KIM Young-sam (1993–1997), the nation's first civilian president, conditions were ripe for the production and exhibition of an increasing number of domestic films.[11] New spaces for freedom of expression—held shut by decades of military dictatorship, preceded by three years of occupation by the US Army and thirty-five years of Japanese colonial rule—began to open. Creative and cultural practitioners immediately set about developing one of the world's fastest-growing film industries. Filmmakers began telling new and arresting stories that quickly gained a following at international film festivals. This surge of media and popular culture has been covered in great detail elsewhere. Suffice it to say that after the domestic and regional readership of webtoons began to build, feature-film adaptations of some of the sector's more provocative series started to fuel the further expansion of Korean cinema.

For instance, as early as 2005 webtoons created by high-profile artists such as KANG Full and YOON Tae-ho launched an increasing flow of film adaptations and television remakes. The 2012 action-thriller feature film *26 Years*, based on KANG's 2005 webtoon of the same name, deals with the traumatic events of the 1980 Gwangju Massacre. With the aid of fantasy elements, *26 Years* imagines how the children of four massacre victims seek revenge on the primary figure responsible for the historical incident (President CHUN Doo-hwan, 1980–1988). Set in Seoul on the twenty-sixth anniversary of the massacre, the film adaptation builds suspense through the characters' plans to assassinate the chief perpetrator—a bold project that would have been inconceivable in the pre-1996 censorship era.

Other webtoon series such as *The Neighbors* (2008), *Covertness* (2010), and *The Insiders* (2010) have also been remade as feature films. In 2012 director KIM Hwee adapted KANG Full's *The Neighbors* into a horror-thriller film set in a grungy urban apartment complex. In this story a serial killer kidnaps a middle school student, and her neighbors attempt to save her by carrying out a vigilante-style revenge on a suspicious individual living in their apartment building. Artist HUN's (CHOI Jong Hoon) spy webtoon series *Covertness* was remade as the spy-action-comedy-drama *Secretly, Greatly* (2013). Three young North Korean spies infiltrate the South and attempt to assimilate with the locals by pretending to be a fool, an aspiring singer, and a high school student. Their adventures culminate in a ruthless battle against their commanding officer, who has been sent from North Korea to kill them. Novice writer-director WOO Min-ho made a name for himself by remaking YOON Tae-ho's *The Insiders* as a political thriller renamed *Inside Men* (2015), which won numerous awards and became the top-grossing R-rated movie of all time in Korea. YOON's webtoon depicts deep-rooted political corruption while also scrutinizing the complex relationships between journalists, *chaebols*, politicians, prosecutors, and gangsters. The narrative transformations that mark these and many other transmedia adaptations explain how webtoons are sources of inspiration for both seasoned and emerging Korean directors.

As in the United States, where numerous superhero films are made based on Marvel and DC Comics, in Asia webtoons have become a significant source for films, television dramas, and mobile games. The film and television industries have been active in using webtoons not only in adaptations but also for promotional branding purposes—for example, using "branded webtoons" (discussed in chapter 7) as a transmedia prologue or epilogue tool for drama productions. The crossover potential of webtoons is well understood by Hollywood companies such as Lucasfilm and Marvel Studios. Daum has worked with Marvel, publishing *Avengers Electric Rain* (2014) by Nasty Cat (aka KOH Young-hoon)—a story about Korean superhero White Fox. Daum has also worked with Lucasfilm, launching a licensed Korean-language version of the sci-fi series *Star Wars* (2015) by HONG Jacga, a story of the young Luke Skywalker. Within six months, an English-language version was released on Naver's Line Webtoon platform.

On the basis of the genre's remarkable successes and possible future configurations, webtoons deserve their description as a prime example of "collective innovation" (Cho 2016). We also borrow this term from an earlier study on innovations in the marketing industry by Kozinets, Hemetsberger, and Schau (2008), which conceptualizes how crowds, hives, mobs, and swarms of "innovation-oriented online consumer communities" are producing their own innovative content in the web 2.0 and uber-networked ICT era. Today we simply use the term *user-generated content* (UGC) to describe this everyday phenomenon in the webtoon ecosystem. Apart from the changes that webtoons have brought to the production, distribution, and consumption patterns of comics, the opportunities they have provided for creating a new visual aesthetics, developing and implementing new technology, and facilitating the creation and sharing of local content and international collaboration are truly revolutionary. It is precisely this holistic aspect of the webtoon industry that this book explores in previously unrecognized ways—especially as it connects to other major Korean Wave content such as films, television dramas, K-pop, e-sports, and webnovels.

THE K-POP CONNECTION

Capitalizing on Planet Hallyuwood's cinematic achievement, K-pop has propelled Korea's music industry well beyond the traditional production, distribution, and consumption channels dominated by the major international music labels such as Universal Music Group, Sony Music Entertainment, and Warner Music Group—the "big three" major international record labels. In particular, Korea's "big three" music giants—SM Entertainment, YG Entertainment, and JYP Entertainment—made YouTube, a free content-viewing platform on the Internet, one of their primary promotional platforms to showcase K-pop acts to the globe. As a result, viral exposure on YouTube and other social media entertainment platforms has enabled K-pop to become the most visible and far-reaching vehicle for promoting Korean popular culture across geographical and cultural borders, in ways that the analogue world could only dream of. Big Hit Entertainment, the management company for K-pop phenomenon BTS, is now at the forefront of this trend with its multiple webtoon initiatives, developments explored in chapter 8.

The presence of digital music on the Internet, and the subsequent revolution regarding distribution channels, has transformed traditional market structures and industry value chains (Bockstedt, Kauffman, and Riggins 2006, 7). By enabling individual users to watch and share videos, YouTube has effectively become an independent content-distribution channel for content creators and advertisers, as well as viewers (Oh, Baek, and Ahn 2013). This online marketing channel is now recognized and utilized by the industry as a revenue-generating platform, not just a viral promotional outlet. These new distribution and marketing channels have allowed K-pop, as well as webtoons featuring stories about K-pop groups like BTS, to sidestep more traditional global music-distribution routes and lengthy company and contractual approval procedures.

K-pop's new freedom has been complemented by the increasing power and voice of consumers (fans), who are also avid readers of webtoons. Both K-pop companies and consumers are tech-savvy and highly active in the online environment. YouTube and other SNS services such as Facebook and Twitter have become primary channels for disseminating K-pop music, videos, and fan news, as well as the promotion of related transmedia IP. In addition, the rapid advance of network technology and smart devices has encouraged these companies, particularly Big Hit Entertainment, to seek ever higher levels of innovation. SM Entertainment's strategic use of YouTube as its primary distribution channel and Big Hit Entertainment's more recent development of three BTS webtoons have expanded the K-pop industry's routes to global exposure, bypassing the abovementioned major international music labels.

As new media platforms, both YouTube and Naver Webtoon offer affordable and unlimited access to visual content that extends well beyond the promotional materials available to fans from K-pop company websites. As a result, revenue generated by Big Hit Entertainment's online and mobile operations has made a strong contribution to their total sales—received mainly from viral "branded entertainment," as well as overseas royalties derived from online downloading and streaming services. To date, K-pop video clips on YouTube have been viewed more than seven billion times in over 230 countries, and webtoon readership statistics are on the rise each day, too. Thus K-pop is a major engine driving the transformation of Korea's creative industries, earning the sobriquet "new Hallyu" (*shinhallyu* in Korean) and keeping Korea at the forefront of the global music industry.

Like K-pop, contemporary online and mobile webtoon series are attracting attention for the ways in which they exploit the cutting-edge affordances of the digital era, creating a new media ecosystem across all aspects of production, distribution, and consumption. The advance of the webtoon industry can be likened to the following epochs that mark the progress of the webtooniverse: first, attracting a significant base of practitioners and readers; second, encapsulating advanced aesthetic techniques and mainstream commercial growth; third, expanding genres and diverse narratives; and fourth and finally, featuring the relaunch and redesign of established characters, increasing licensed and commercial merchandizing, the maturing of assembly-line and team workflow practices, the rise of creator-celebrities, and the expansion of independent publishers. Considered as a whole, Korea's creative digital firms and practitioners have transformed the domestic and global media industries by attracting a strong and growing following among local and international audiences. Their efforts have produced universally accessible content with a Korean inflection, thus opening new spaces for cultural expression.

One such important epoch occurred in 2012. After a yearlong discussion and debate with industry representatives, MCST passed the Promotion of Cartoons Act (aka the Comics Support Law), signaling the government's explicit and newfound endorsement of comics as a platform for telling local stories and expressing cultural diversity. Until this pivotal moment—and speaking generally, of course—comics were considered to be a form of low culture that needed to be eliminated. Wanting to appear in tune with the times, President LEE Myung-bak's government (2008–2013) used this policy instrument to declare that comics were no longer considered "harmful to society." In turn, the promulgation of the Promotion of Cartoons Act brought a newfound confidence to comic artists whose livelihood as well as pride had been challenged for some time.

KOREAN WEBNOVELS AND A NEW GLOBAL READERSHIP

Similar to the diversity of webtoon genres, Korean webnovels display a diverse spectrum of formats, including Internet novels and fiction, visual novels, "infinite text adventures," and interactive fiction games. The distinctive interactive elements, story techniques, and aesthetics distinguish their production and consumption from their print predecessors and "closed" digital competitors, such as Kindle Direct Publishing. The spread of smart devices has enabled global cohorts of users to read webnovels and develop them themselves, anywhere, at any time, and at low cost. Practitioners and stakeholders across the globe are beginning to master and contribute to the unprecedented degree of openness available in this underexplored digital environment. As it happens, leading webtoon platform KakaoPage (discussed in chapter 5) is also a leader in this domain.

Webnovels differ from other media in that they are "open" in two important respects: First, similar to Korean-originated vertically scrolling webtoons (aka digital comics), YouTube, and other video- and image-sharing sites that generate profits from user clicks and ads, webnovel creators and practitioners can upload content to a number of webnovel apps and platforms for free. The aim is to attract positive reviews and an increasing readership that can be monetized via free or freemium content, micropayment systems, and the subsequent sale of transmedia adaptation rights. In turn, in order to secure their loyalty, platforms offer contracts to popular author-creators, generally sharing revenue on a 60 percent/40 percent basis, in favor of the creator. By comparison, traditional print publishers usually claim 90 percent of revenues for themselves. Second, webnovels are open to immediate feedback from registered readers, enabling content creators and platforms to codevelop or at least jointly shape future content in ways that are more responsive to reader preferences than print publishing scenarios. As a result, due to a quick production turnaround involving bite-sized chapters, authors and platforms can potentially transform original stories (and any embedded imagery) to suit different local and global tastes. This type of user-generated content originated in the webtoon ecosystem.

In early 2020, our cursory count of Asian and North American-based webnovels revealed forty-four different platforms and apps, featuring thousands of content creators. Most of these webnovel platforms are globally accessible and either free or low priced (for around 10 US cents), contrasting markedly with print publishing. Like their webtoon counterparts, webnovel platforms generally organize content creators into three distinctive groups: amateurs, intermediates, and stars, with the first two categories constituting about half of all practitioners.[12] On some platforms, such as KakaoPage, Munpia, and Joara, chapters are either free or available as a free sample for a limited time before fees are required. Similar to webtoon creator-owners, "star" practitioners on Korean webnovel platforms are progressively selling their remake rights to television and film producers, thus adding an incentive to develop and publish more titles. Thus Korean webnovels are at the cutting edge of media convergence, as well as the internationalization, localization, and coproduction of creator-centric digital content and social media entertainment. Similar to webtoons, webnovels are also at the forefront of IP transformation, particularly the array of transmedia adaptations that now form a significant proportion of entertainment-industry revenues. In these ways both webtoons and webnovels are having a substantial impact on both local and global screen-media technologies, practices, policy reform, and augmented digital content.

Major Korean digital players such as Naver and KakaoPage, China's Tencent (China Literature), and global giant Amazon (Kindle) are working to position webnovels as a significant contributor to the global creative economy (Brouillette 2014). Despite its "self-publishing" Kindle Direct Publishing platform, however, Kindle remains a closed publishing system in terms of cross-platform compatibility, open-source innovation, and transmedia storytelling (Ren 2019). It is as yet uncertain how both webtoons and webnovels and their accompanying "convergent culture" (Jenkins 2006) will become part of a "new screen ecology" and "new wave of media globalisation" (Cunningham 2015). The chapters that follow address these fundamental questions.

Korean-based webnovelists and titles are being produced in much larger numbers than those from other parts of the globe. Major firms in Korea are now producing, licensing, translating, and co-investing in webnovels as a major source of IP for adaptation as films, television series, webtoons, online and mobile games, and a range of other social entertainment media for global audiences and markets. These developments are driven by cutting-edge ICT innovations in Korea.

Nonetheless, despite the epochal shift marked by the swift evolution of this digital arena and the skyrocketing numbers of readers across all genres and formats, the scholarly attention paid to webnovels is lagging far behind canonical studies of global mobile media (Goggin 2011; Hjorth, Burgess, and Richardson 2012), conventional literature (Murray 2018; Hockx 2015), electronic literature (Wardrip-Fruin 2008; Taylor 2019), media-technology innovation in Asia (McNamara 2009; Hjorth and Khoo 2015; Keane 2016), and social media and online reading (Nakamura 2013; Martens 2016). The webnovel and webtoon eco-systems share many synergies and are both hosted on the same major platforms, such as KakaoPage and Naver Service. And like the webnovel, many aspects of the Webtooniverse remain unexplored. By focusing in this book on webtoons, one of the fastest-growing convergent sectors of social media entertainment, we propose a new approach to global media practice—one that is informed and shaped by the changing dynamics of the creative industries in Korea and the larger Asian region. In updating existing approaches to media "convergence" (Jenkins 2006); inter-Asian collaboration (Chua 2012; Keane, Yecies, and Flew 2018); and "top-down creator governance" (Cunningham and Craig 2019), we explore little-known aspects of the Webtooniverse in the following six chapters.

CHAPTER SUMMARIES

This book uses content analysis of webtoon series, industry interviews, and policy-document analysis to reveal how Korean webtoon series, artists, platforms, policymakers, and global readers are transforming Korea's larger media and creative-industries ecosystems. Each chapter offers readers new knowledge about the cross-media storytelling strategies and technological innovations that are driving the production and reception of online and mobile content for webtoons. While smart-phone apps and platforms have enjoyed increasing global penetration since the late 2000s, limited scholarly attention has been paid to the impact of webtoons on the media and entertainment industries and the mobile mediasphere. Through case studies of major issues, platforms, and series the book redresses this research deficit and explores the ways in which this new digital-screen media is taking its place as part of a "new wave of media globalisation" (Cunningham 2015). Its broad scope makes the book the first of its kind to investigate the complex impact and potential benefits of these transformations.

Chapters 2 and 3 build on the brief discussion of Korea's creative industries presented here by contextualizing the historical rise and fall of the print-comics industry and its rebirth as a new digital powerhouse in the form of webtoons. First, chapter 2 introduces a brief historical overview of Korean print comics, including some early notable work.

The general spectrum of print comics—which includes comic books mostly rented at *manhwabangs* (renting and reading comics rooms), comic magazines (and the magazines including several pages of comics) mostly sold at retail shops, and comic sections in daily sports newspapers—had been considered "harmful" to children since the 1960s with little to no relief or government support. Simply put, comics were too risky for the government to support. As a result, the print-comics industry suffered by being ignored—even after the liberalization of censorship that the film industry enjoyed after 1996. After 1997, with the passing of the Juvenile Protection Act , any comic book content deemed "harmful for school-age children"—often seemingly on a whim—was confiscated, and thus creators and publishers experienced limited freedom of expression. Without any hope for the future, print-comic artists disappeared, and the print-comic industry withered away to obliteration—or so it seemed. Second, chapter 2 also reveals how both the industry and the government struggled to control the industry's Janusheaded proclivity for pirating Japanese manga and also publishing stories that incited prejudices about the "negative influence" of comics on the nation's youth. *Manhwabang* and book publishers, as well as readers, played pivotal roles in these cultural debates, as did the content creators themselves—serving as unsanctioned cultural intermediaries who localized Japanese comics for the Korean market. Adding to the complexity of the comics scene was the Korean government's strict post–World War II ban on all Japanese popular culture products (magazines, books, television shows, and films) between 1945 and 1998.

Next, chapter 3 explores how the comics industry, including independent Internet comics websites, experienced a dramatic turn in the early 2000s as part of the wider advancement of the IT- and ICT-influenced creative industries. We show how a range of industry players collaboratively responded to a major threat to freedom of expression in 2012 after the Korea Communications Standards Commission—Korea's Internet censorship body—targeted a small number of webtoons. By addressing this cultural policy environment, we throw light on the webtoon industry's negotiations with the government through industry associations (i.e., the Korea Cartoonist Association, the Korean Comic Publishers Association, and the Cartoon and Animation Society) and self-regulation initiatives, such as the Cartoonists Emergency Committee Against the Korea Communications Standards Commission

(2012), as well as the Webtoon Self-Regulation Committee (2017). Chapter 3 addresses the ways in which these bodies assisted the industry's transformation, particularly as webtoons were becoming an important sector of Korea's creative industries.

Chapters 4 and 5 illustrate how a constellation of major domestic and transnational webtoon platforms—such as Daum, Naver, Kakao, and Lezhin—as well as individual "rookie," "intermediate," and "star" webtoonists, are contributing to this new and evolving media. We unwrap the intricacies of the term *webtooniverse* and discuss the range of webtoon firms and creator-owner practitioners operating in the new global digital economy. These platforms differ across a spectrum of monetization models, such as paid subscription or rental or purchase, loyalty and rewards, linkages to crowdfunding on Patreon or Kickstarter, and free; they also come with or without advertisements and product placement, freemium "free-if-you-wait," or some hybrid system. The in-app-purchase model, which requires users to make payments of between 100 and 300 KRW (between 9 and 27 US cents) per episode, has gradually become a significant revenue-generating strategy, particularly for online and mobile platforms that are aiming specific types of content at a narrow readership demographic. Against this background, these two chapters explore the initiatives of some of the most active Korean webtoon platforms, revealing how large, integrated corporations are contributing to the ongoing transformation of the transnational webtoon ecosystem and the energizing of transmedia "IP engines."

Chapter 6 sheds light on some previously unrecognized aspects of the history of the webtoon industry, as well as the strategic linkages between Korea's webtoon and ICT industries, and how they have contributed to the expansion of the webtooniverse. It investigates some of the major technological transformations and innovations that have shaped the modern webtoon industry and its ecosystem. To give the context for the rise of the webtoon industry, a brief explanation of various advanced experiments is offered in order to show the unique features of this digital format compared to conventional digital and web-based manga and other comics. Next we discuss the advanced interactive elements of particular webtoon types, such as the horror-toon, smart-toon, cut-toon, effect-toon, interactive-toon, and webtoon animation, to show how the industry (particularly Naver) has evolved. Smart-toons, for example, exploit the capabilities of smartphones and other "smart" digital devices, including 3D and augmented-reality applications, to maximize user experience. Smart-toons also use the touch screen to zoom in and out and to scroll up, down, left, and right, thus enhancing the reader's spatial perception. Chapter 6 reveals how the webtoon industry has been transformed at its core, as well as along the periphery, through major technological innovation led by major platforms and minor enterprises alike. We explore how these technological developments are contributing to a new wave of media globalization and enabling amateur artists to access a hierarchically structured commercial market with greater ease than is the case in other digital-media industries.

In chapters 7 and 8, the authors investigate the rise of a specific webtoon genre called *branded webtoons*, which has become a key source of soft power in the industry's ecosystem. First, an overview of webtoons as a nuanced form of narrative-based communication sets the context for this hybrid storytelling and advertising genre and viral promotional tool. Second, insights gleaned from a number of pioneering artists—such as PARK Jong-won, creator of the Wony Frame character and webtoon *Midnight Rhapsody* (2005–2008, 326 episodes); and JI Gang Min, creator of *Welcome to the Convenience Store* (2008–2014, 600 episodes)—shed light on how some of the longest-running and most notable webtoon characters are contributing to the industry through their IP value. We explore how these elements are extending virally beyond the core webtoon-platform environment into the larger advertising world. Third and finally, *We On: Be the Shield* (2014), *Hip Hop Monster* (2014), and *Save Me* (2019)—three webtoons featuring K-pop supergroup BTS—are analyzed to reveal previously unrecognized soft-power aspects of the webtoon industry and its transmedia storytelling strategies, merchandizing power, and crowd-sourced transportability. The investigation of these three unique branded webtoon campaigns underscores how webtoons have played a catalytic role in the formation of the BTS Universe—introduced in chapter 7—and the larger K-pop industry. In sum, both chapter 7 and chapter 8 reveal some of the wider synergies between the webtoon industry and its strategies for leveraging and profiting from transmedia IP, on the one hand, and the wider creative industries on the other.

Finally, in the conclusion the authors summarize how mobile webtoons are becoming deeply enmeshed within the global mediasphere and are pushing media convergence across the creative industries in new directions. Perhaps more than any other digital medium, webtoons exemplify the notion of "collective innovation" as well as a "digital-comics revolution" for their ability to circumvent the cultural, geographic, and economic barriers to entry (i.e., costs) associated with traditional media production and distribution channels. It is the ways in which the webtoon industry players investigated in this book are challenging the dominant companies across the global mediasphere that makes this story a timely and unique contribution to the field. It also deepens our understanding of Korea's rapidly transforming digital economy.

As a result of these ongoing innovations in the webtoon sector and their synergistic effects across the media and entertainment industries, the Korean Wave and, indeed, Korea's creative industries as a whole are taking on a new meaning. The spread of Korean cultural content is no longer a one-way street, and multidirectional cultural flows are developing through collaborations between Korea and other countries such as the United States and China. Some commentators speak of the emergence of an "Asian Wave," of which the Korean Wave has up until now been the driving force. Yet with the growing popularity of K-pop and webtoons in particular in regions as diverse as Asia, Europe, the United States, and South America, regional "tagging" of Korea's popular cultural products may no longer be necessary: what is important for both content creators and consumers in the twenty-first century is not where things are produced but how they are consumed. To us and to the many Korean and non-Korean practitioners with whom we have spent time while conducting research for this book this all typifies the substance of Korea's Webtooniverse and the digital-comic revolution underpinning it.

2

CONCEPTUALIZING THE IMPACT OF JAPANESE MANGA IN KOREA AND THE PREHISTORY OF WEBTOONS

Korea has a long and colorful history of comic book culture that underpins the creativity driving serialized webtoons that we see today. In 2009 the National Museum of Contemporary Art in Seoul held a comprehensive exhibition celebrating the centennial of *manhwa* (the Korean term for comics and printed cartoons), featuring over 1,500 pieces by 250 artists. Some of the first images to make an impression on readers were made using a centuries-old woodblock technique to print ink cartoons on paper. During their early commercial years, comics primarily appeared in newspapers, which flourished in the modernized newspaper industry established during the Japanese colonial period (1910–1945)—at least until 1937, that is, when Japan's total war effort subordinated all aspects of Korean society to Japan's military agenda. As the war economy escalated, leisure activities diminished significantly, raw materials including paper became scarce, and newspapers published cartoons (*manga* in Japanese) that primarily contained pro government propaganda.[1]

After Korea gained independence in August 1945, comics experienced a revival, especially political cartoons and children's educational comics. Evidently the very first Korean comic book published was *The Rabbit and the Monkey* (1946), a parable involving animal characters that cope with Korea's newfound independence and their survival of Japanese colonization (Young-hwan Kim 2012). Even during the Korean War (1950–1953) and the immediate postwar period, a small number of comic book titles—with a limited number of pages—continued to be published. This chapter briefly explores the comics industry with a view to understanding its beginnings as a cottage industry and how it struggled to remain viable (and even survive) in a hostile social and political environment.

To contextualize the rise of webtoons, this chapter sets out a brief history of Korea's print-comics industry, including its rise and fall before the year 2003, which heralded the birth of webtoons, a new digital force majeure. First, the authors investigate the impact of Japanese manga on Korea's comics industry—at a time when almost all Japanese popular-culture products were officially banned in Korea. Since Korea's liberation from Japanese occupation in 1945, the Korean government had maintained a strict ban on Japanese popular magazines, books, comic books, television shows, and films, a situation that lasted until 1998 when the policy was revoked. Despite the ban, both industry and government stakeholders struggled to control the flow of Japanese comics into Korea. This chapter sheds light on some of the complexities surrounding the illicit circulation of manga, as well as the Korean industry's proclivity for pirating Japanese manga for profit. As a result, domestic content creators effectively became unsanctioned cultural intermediaries, localizing Japanese comics for the Korean market, which in turn kept comic culture alive in terms of readership and artistic practices. Second, we present a historical overview of some early comic book and magazine artists and their works, along with the unique distribution and rental system operating in shops called *manhwabangs*—"comics reading rooms" in Korean. Third, we analyze some of the complications underpinning the conventional view of print comics as a form of "low culture" and thus harmful to youth, a perspective originating in the 1960s. We show how this prejudice, from both the general public and the government, hampered the growth of the comics industry as well as the morale of practitioners. The success of the contemporary webtoon industry, while perhaps appearing to have little to do with the history of print comics, has been built on a sustained readership base of Korean youth—a group that has maintained its interest in a comics culture that was at one time subjected to severe social and political censorship.

CAMOUFLAGING JAPANESE MANGA: THE IMPACT OF PRINT COMICS

Comic books were a major source of entertainment and companionship for children during the post–Korean War period. Radio and films were out of reach for most school-age children, and television did not arrive in Korea until the early 1960s. Targeting this youthful demographic, early comic books offered a variety of genres and narrative styles. Popular titles that stand out for their bold stories and experimental graphics include the sci-fi action *Lifi the Fighter of Justice* (1959–1962, KIM San-ho), the Western fantasy action *Sandyman* (1961, OH Myeongcheon), and the romance *Spring Song* (1961, PARK Mun-yun).

Lifi, comprising thirty-two books in four series and set in the 2100s, was Korea's first sci-fi superhero story, inspiring many young Koreans to overcome the hardships of the postwar era. KIM had founded and operated Sanho Studio, which employed a number of practitioners, going on to become one of the first Korean comics artists to work in the United States. KIM moved to the United States in 1966, where he continued to create horror and kung fu comics (often containing Korean stylistic elements) for Charlton Comics—a comic book publisher (1945–1986) known for its crime, sci-fi, Western, horror, war, superhero, and comical animal genre comics, and also known for paying its writers and artists lower rates than other publishers but granting them more creative freedom (Kruse 2017). To honor KIM's long-term contributions to comics, the 2012 Seoul Character and Animation Fair (SICAF) held a special exhibition of his work, which they titled The Artist Who Flies High and Dreams Freely. However, despite numerous small pockets of homegrown creativity, during this early period Korea's print comic writers and illustrators were best known for copying Japanese comics.

Comic rental and reading establishments (aka *manhwabangs*) began to appear in the late 1950s, serving as the primary distribution channel for comic books throughout the 1960s. In this way, *manhwabangs* served as a crucial circulation system for publishers and provided the chief catalyst in terms of customer demand. During the 1960s (and 1970s), the number of outlets publishing comics gradually increased, and many publishers began developing new monthly comics magazines for children, and later for adults. Such monthly magazines began to include a range of serialized comic content across different genres, including children's, sports, romance, and mature (adult) material to increase their appeal and find new readers. Select examples published for school-age boys and girls include *New Boy* (*Sae Sonyeon*, 1964–1989), *Boy Central* (*Sonyeon Jungang*, 1969–1994), and *Shoulder to Shoulder* (*Eokkae Dongmu*, 1967–1987). These youth-oriented titles contained educational articles along with serialized comics and also offered an additional comic booklet as a bonus. Alongside these journals a new type of weekly magazine targeting adult readers emerged; *Sunday Seoul* (1968–1991), *Weekly Kyunghyang* (1968–1995), and *Weekly Woman* (1969–?) were popular titles. With eye-catching headlines, sensationalist entertainment news snippets, and gossip columns, as well as low-key erotic imagery, these were all examples of "yellow journalism." Additionally, as discussed shortly, piracy also played a major part in these magazines. At this time publishers began increasing the size of the comics sections in their magazines in order to exploit comics' newfound popularity with adult readers. Newspaper publishers also began including comics in their editions. In 1969 Korea's first sports newspaper, *Daily Sports*, published by Hanguk Ilbo, featured serialized multipanel comics aimed at mature readers. Well-known comics artist KO Woo-young was recruited by Hanguk Ilbo and given up to half a page (approximately twenty-five panels) in *Daily Sports* to create appealing comics to increase the paper's readership.[2]

Yet despite the growing demand—or perhaps because of it—Korea's infant comics industry found itself unable to fully meet the needs of its readers. It could only just keep up with distributors' requirements in terms of quantity, and doing so entailed reducing the physical quality of the product and the aesthetic quality of the content. Thus, almost from its beginnings in the postwar period, the domestic comics industry was heavily influenced—in both positive and negative ways—by the styles and stories featured in Japanese manga. At the time, the Japanese comics industry was strong, especially in the youth market, with separate titles aimed at boys (*shōnen manga*) and girls (*shōjo manga*).

Throughout this period, and because of the Korean government's total ban on the import of Japanese cultural products, it was far easier and quicker to copy Japanese manga than to develop new material from scratch. Often manga was smuggled into Korea by individuals who had visited Japan. One of the earliest known successful pirated print comics is *Prince of the Jungle* (1952, SEO Bong-je), a faithful but "white-washed" version of *Kenya Boy*, a Tarzan-like story created by YAMA-KAWA Soji in 1951 that was set around British-controlled Nairobi (Kim 2014). Between the 1950s and 1970s, many other popular and profitable print comics were copies of Japanese comics drawn in the *shōjo* manga (girls' comics) style, including *The Glass Castle* (1969, WATA-NABE Masako), set in England and based on *The Prince and the Pauper* fairy tale, and IKEDA Riyoko's historical romances *The Window of Orpheus* (1975) and *The Rose of Versailles* (1973). According to Ito (2005), the *shōjo* manga style, which emerged in Japan during the 1960s, targeted a young female readership through stories about romance, girls' dreams, and fantasies.

Two distinctive methods were used to copy Japanese comics, which continued to influence Korean artists in terms of both narrative and visual style. First, Korean artists reinterpreted and then emulated the illustrations in the original material, requiring artists with advanced skills and well-practiced hand-eye coordination. Alternatively the existing illustrations were traced on a light box—a translucent surface with a light source underneath it. In this case, the artist needed less skill to trace the basic shapes and outlines of a scene or character in the original. Inconsistencies between the styles of the images within the same comic, particularly the character illustrations, were usually a clear indication that the comic had been copied (In-Ha Park 2009). Through these processes, Korean practitioners localized and molded popular Japanese content into popular Korean content, resulting in both job creation and market expansion. At the same time, this growth both attracted and expanded local readership, especially among school children and teenagers.

The outright plagiarism involved in these productions became an increasingly pervasive practice in the 1960s and 1970s, reflecting a general lack of awareness of copyright. Comics were simply disregarded as a source of creative content per se, and both artists and publishers prioritized quick profits. When interviewed in 2012, well-known Korean comics artist KIM Hyeong-bae explained how most people in the industry during this period had little choice about copying Japanese comics under orders from local publishers whose primary concern was to make money. For KIM, both the cartoonists and Korean society in general were victims of this plagiarism trend (Hong 2012b).

As one might expect, Korean practitioners were at pains to erase Japanese cultural references in these comics, thereby "localizing" the original texts for Korean readers. In so doing, artists and publishers rendered any form of "Japaneseness" or Japanese cultural presence invisible, removing their so-called "cultural odor" not only in order to mask their origins but also to increase their appeal to Korean readers.[3] In this period, a comic imbued with "Japanese color" could be considered to reflect "cultural features of [its] country of origin and images or ideas of its national, in most cases stereotyped, way of life" (Iwabuchi 2002, 27).

Given the ease with which Korean creators and publishers could replicate Japanese manga for a quick profit, little was done to encourage the development of stories and styles with a strong Korean "odor," despite Korean readers' general antipathy toward Japanese-inspired content. As other studies have noted, this trend reflected a "backdoor" pathway for manga and other Japanese products that flourished for several decades before Korea officially re-admitted Japanese popular culture products into the country (Choo 2010). "Camouflage" is also a term that we might use to describe what was happening to comics during this period. Whatever language we care to use, these practices—albeit in violation of basic copyright laws—nurtured new and advanced skills among some domestic practitioners.

Though he later decried the practice, KIM Hyeong-bae's work presents an interesting case of manga piracy. As far as we know, the supernatural *Babel II* (1971, YOKOYAMA Mitsuteru) was published in Korea in 1974 by Eomungak Publishing. Eomungak was the publisher of the children's magazine *New Boy* (*Sae Sonyeon*, 1964–1989), which contained localized versions of original Japanese manga such as *Babel II*. A number of the popular serialized comics, novels, and short stories in *New Boy* were later repackaged and republished in book form in Eomungak's Clover Book Collection series. The primary purpose of this strategy was to disguise the texts' Japanese origins. In the case of *Babel II*, the publisher deceitfully credited KIM Dong-myeong (the publisher's business manager) as the artist on the comic book's cover. This fake-name game quickly became an established practice, enabling publishers to hide the truth about the origins of their comics while allowing them to "pass" as local creations. KIM Dong-myeong and possibly many others with "pen names" built up large fan bases—followers who reacted badly upon discovering years later that publishers had deceived them. *Babel II* proved so popular that in 1980 Eomungak published an unlicensed sequel, *Babel III*, which was actually created from scratch in Korea. Although KIM Hyeong-bae was the real artist of this local creation, KIM Dong-myeong was still falsely credited as its artist (Kim 2007). Although unlicensed, *Babel III* was an original work, and thus it stands out as a highly unusual case of manga piracy, demonstrating how far publishers were willing to go to make a profit.

In the 1980s a new generation of artists emerged who were eager to develop styles of their own. Locally produced comics in the *shōjo* manga style, for example, experienced a rise in popularity in the 1980s following the launch of several new Korean-originated magazines including *Renaissance* (1989–1994) and *High Sense* (1989–1994), which targeted young female readers. The increasing readership for such magazines propelled to fame female writer-artists such as SHIN Il-suk, KANG Kyung-ok, and KIM Hye-rin, who attracted fans for their portrayal of strong female characters across a variety of fantasy, action, history, and sci-fi genre comics. In light of these developments, the Korean comics industry owes a debt of gratitude to its Japanese counterpart—not least for inspiring, or at least inconspicuously contributing to, the rise of local stories, styles, readers, and practitioners.

THE BLAME GAME

Throughout the 1960s, the number of *manhwabangs* continued to rise, making these local comics shops one of the key drivers of the increasing popularity of the medium. They remained one of the major channels for circulating comic books in Korea until the 1990s. Inside a *manhwabang*, readers could access a variety of popular comic book and magazine titles. These items could be borrowed relatively cheaply, and customers either read them for an hourly fee within the shop or rented them by the day to read at home. While the emergence of these comics shops was a response to the growing popularity of the genre, they also fueled the genre's growth and popularity. Younger customers were particularly drawn to these establishments as a way of entertaining themselves and also of escaping the cold, school, and other unpleasant realities. However, these places had a reputation for being dirty, smelly, and unhygienic—not ideal hangouts for school-age children, the primary demographic frequenting *manhwabangs*.

Comics were scapegoated as a "bad influence" on Korea's youth in the press. As revealed in a 1970 report in the newspaper *Kyunghyang Shinmun*, ordinary Koreans were blaming comics for encouraging aggressive, sarcastic, and troublemaking behavior in their young readers. Korea's abundant *manhwabangs* were singled out as a breeding ground for such tendencies, especially among teenagers (the report cited a runaway and/or a juvenile delinquent). Indeed some rental shops had reputations for overcrowding, uncleanliness, poor-quality snacks, stale food, and the pervasive stink of cigarettes, not to mention the constant blare of television (or radio) sets as an extra incentive for customers to linger (*Kyunghyang Shinmun* 1970). Complaints about comic books as well as the unsavory *manhwabangs* reached a peak annually around Children's Day (May 5), a national holiday in Korea. The perceived threats posed by these so-called "harbingers of muck" motivated civic and governmental organizations to aggressively lobby for their closure.

And according to a survey in *Dong-a Ilbo*, comics were blamed for teaching Korea's youth how to commit crimes, distracting them from study, and glorifying juvenile delinquency. The vulgarity and violence that allegedly marked comics' contents, as well as the "perverted" stories and images found in so-called "poor quality" comics (*bullyang manhwa* in Korean), were seen as a "plague" on society (Jo 1969). The Korean press was fast to pick up on these developments, especially comics' alleged antisocial influence. According to a report in the newspaper *Kyunghyang Shinmun*, of the thirty million comic books printed in Korea in 1976, the Korean Booksellers Association categorized 83 percent as "low quality." This expression was code for "harmful to children," referring to the comics' high content of Japanese color (*oesaek*), portrayals of violence, and coarse language (*Kyunghyang Shinmun* 1978). Unsurprisingly, similar concerns and debates about the "healthy development of youth" were also being aired in Japan at the time.[4] Public concern over the power of the mass media—and comics in particular—to influence the attitudes and perceptions of youth was commonplace in Korea (as well as in the United States, Japan, and elsewhere) at the time. Media commentators and policymakers regularly exploited such fears whenever a social problem or controversy involving youth came to public attention. Reproducing Japanese content was surely one of the factors behind the deep cultural malaise caused by comics.

Despite these public misgivings, competition among *manhwabangs* intensified, not only because the comics business was booming but also because each shop sought to be the first to acquire new releases. At this time, rental shops in both urban and rural areas were dependent on the personal networks that they had formed with regional distributors. Conversely, and through the expansion of a "rental" rather than a "buying" culture, Korea's comics industry had become dependent on *manhwabangs* as its primary channel for reaching readers. Hapdong Publishing, established in 1966, was one of a very few publishers dominating this part of the industry. It outstripped its competitors by creating a new publishing syndicate. In this way Hapdong became Korea's equivalent of today's Diamond Comic Distributors in the United States, which represents and delivers content from a range of publishers and suppliers (of all sizes) to both online and brick-and-mortar resellers.

Under founder LEE Young-rae, who had previously owned a small publishing company called Jinyeong, Hapdong introduced a monopoly distribution system in Korea by convincing seven publishers—including the top three comics publishers Bueongi, Jeil, and Clover—to merge under the Hapdong name. This mini-conglomerate then proceeded to contract a large proportion of the country's popular comic artists, effectively creating a monopoly. Hapdong first distributed a set number of print comics to *manhwabangs* in Seoul—a "first-run" strategy similar to the way feature film prints are distributed. Shortly after, these same copies were collected and distributed to other urban centers, and then finally to smaller towns and rural areas. Along the way, the tattered edges of the preread comic books were trimmed to give them a fresh look. As a result of this hierarchical distribution strategy, it could take about six months for regional and rural *manhwabangs* to acquire the same (used and deteriorating) copies of the print comics chosen for circulation. Given these items' poor condition, their rental at *manhwabangs* were often discounted.

As well as monopolizing distribution, Hapdong also dominated the printing and binding processes, thereby controlled the number of titles a particular comic artist could produce. Given the company's near total control of the industry, anyone speaking out against Hapdong or its practices would be undermining their own employment opportunities

(Jang 2012). There was certainly plenty of work for willing artists during this period. According to a 1970 report in the newspaper *Kyunghyang Shinmun*, Hapdong was publishing twenty new comic titles every day, each with a print run of more than two thousand copies. At least 120 registered members of the Korea Cartoonist Association were working for Hapdong, and on average each practitioner was creating one comic book every one or two days (*Kyunghyang Shinmun* 1970). Even the most experienced artists—working with a small team of assistants—struggled to keep up with this frenetic schedule. Little wonder that this was known as the era of the comic book production factory—a studio system in which large numbers of apprentices were put to work on an assembly line that mass-produced comic books in the shortest amount of time possible. For many years this kind of apprenticeship role was a prerequisite for anyone wanting to debut as a comics artist in their own right. In 1970 alone a total of 13,140,000 units was produced, representing an average print run of around 6,500 copies for each title; Hapdong was the only publishing and distribution company capable of handling this massive volume of printed materials (ibid.).

Looking back on this period when the comics trade was in the grip of an industrial monopoly, master comics artist HUH Young-man referred to Hapdong as a "giant evil monster" that prevented artists from earning a decent livelihood (Kim 1997). The company was also accused of unfair trade practices. For example, Hapdong allegedly reduced the price of some titles to serve its own purposes—for example, to oust new competitors. It seems that Gukje Books and independent comic publisher Ttaengi Books were both victims of this strategy in 1966 and 1975, respectively. The Hanguk Ilbo newspaper company was another potential competitor in the early 1970s—at least initially. Despite Hanguk Ilbo's financial strength, it eventually colluded with Hapdong by joining forces, thereby strengthening Hapdong's monopoly rather than challenging it.[5] Given these practices, competition in the industry was almost nonexistent, creativity was undervalued, and quantity and rapid turnover were prioritized over quality. In sum, Hapdong's dominance led to a prolonged period of decline for the industry in the 1970s.

Hapdong eventually folded in 1986, mainly due to the dwindling number of its primary distribution outlets—the much-derided *manhwabangs*. The company was also significantly impacted by Hanguk Ilbo's departure from the syndicate in 1982, which reduced the power of Hapdong's monopoly. New enterprises finally had room to step out from under Hapdong's shadow, making their own contributions to the development of the comics market through an increasing number of specialist magazines and comic books—for purchase at ordinary bookshops. Comic magazines such as *Treasure Island* (*Bomulseom*, 1982–1996) became known for their quality content as well as for their better treatment of artists seeking an alternative to Hapdong. The 1980s was the beginning of a new age for comics. In addition to *Treasure Island*, numerous other titles were launched to serve the industry's growing readership among the nation's youth, including *IQ Jump* (1988–2014) and *Boy Champ* (1991–present, currently known as *Comic Champ*) for school-age children and teenage boys and producing romance comics such as *Renaissance* (1989–1994), *High Sense* (1989–1994), *Daenggi* (1991–1996), and *Wink* (1993–present) for teenage girl readers. These publications formed a small part of the plethora of competing leisure and entertainment activities for teenagers that appeared at this time, including the launch of Korea's professional baseball league in 1982 and the rapid spread of color televisions and VCRs. Combined, these developments had a transformative effect not only on Hapdong but on the wider print comics industry as well.

COMICS OF DISTRACTION

Based on the assumption that comics had a detrimental effect on society, government officials launched numerous attempts to restrain the industry. The authoritarian governments of PARK Chung Hee (1961–1979) and later CHUN Doo-hwan (1980–1988) maintained the attitude that comics corrupted young minds and undermined official educational efforts. Government pressure was so relentless on print comics that as late as 2014 one commentator was arguing that the industry had sustained irreversible damage from the decades of government suppression (Baek 2014).

From the outset, the PARK Chung Hee government stepped in to control the comics industry, as it did with the country's major cultural industries, including the film industry. Under the government's direction, in 1961 the Korean Children's Comics Autonomy Group (Hanguk Adongmanhwa Jayulhoe) was created by a number of comic artists and publishers in order to prescreen comics prior to publication. As the group's name suggests, comics were at the time regarded as entertainment for children. However, the new organization was less effective than the government had expected. To show its allegiance to the government on this issue—and to improve their image—a group calling itself the Korean Rental Comic Shop Purification Association (Hanguk Daeboneop Jeonghwahyeophoe), comprised of owners of *manhwa-bangs*, held a number of comic book–burning ceremonies in Seoul in mid-1966 at which ten thousand "bad-quality" comic books were reportedly destroyed. Two years later, in May 1968, the group staged another public event at which they burned a further eight thousand comic books, creating the impression that such an "exorcism" would rid society of the menace.[6]

Contributing to the moral panic surrounding these events, or at least as a show of response to it, in September 1968 the Ministry of Public Information (today the Ministry of Culture, Sports and Tourism) established the Children's Comics Ethics Committee (Hangug Adongmanhwa Yulli Wiwonhoe), which replaced the Korean Children's Comics Autonomy Group. Korea now had an official censorship body to oversee children's comics prior to their publication in books, magazines, and newspapers. The committee enacted the Children's Comics Code and the Children's Comics Practice, regulating both the content (i.e., sexual references, violence, adult language, and procommunist messages) and the length of comic book series (Park 2012). The committee also issued a seal denoting censorship clearance, required by all comic books before they could be published. The exacting censorship standards required correct spelling and punctuation and proper grammar, accurate historical references and representations (e.g., avoiding illustrations of Vietnamese soldiers wearing Korean military uniforms), formal language (avoidance of slang), and avoidance of extreme violence (e.g., knifing someone) (*Kyunghyang Shinmun* 1968a). In 1970 the Children's Comics Ethics Committee merged with the newly established Korean Book and Magazine Ethics Committee, and the new body remained extremely busy. A total of 23,784 cases were processed over three and a half years (1968–1971), with almost 89 percent of these cases requiring either the modification or removal of content (14 percent of these required two censorship rounds); 9 percent passed without any changes, and 2 percent were confiscated and destroyed (*Kyun-

ghyang Shinmun 1971). Simply put, the Ministry of Public Information sought to consolidate its hold on the wider publishing industry, including comics.

Nevertheless, public ceremonies continued at which print comics were burned, as the perception of comics as harmful publications strengthened in the public's mind. In May 1970 the Seoul Police Department staged a public burning of over six thousand children's comic books deemed to be obscene (Ministry of Public Information 1970). At the time, comics were seen to magnetically draw in young readers, who had little chance of escaping the dangerous allure. It was feared that the raw power of these publications was invading the everyday life and culture of children, molding their social opinions, attitudes, and behaviors for ill. Again, *manhwabangs* received the lion's share of blame. According to a 1977 article in the newspaper *Maeil Kyungjae*, "bad-quality" comic books were believed to inspire children to copy the behaviors of the characters in them. Parents were encouraged to stop their children visiting *manhwabangs* or alternatively to read "uplifting" comic books at home together (*Maeil Kyungjae* 1977).

It was no coincidence that a similar moral panic over the comic book industry had broken out in the United States in the 1950s, threatening to undermine creative expression in the name of eradicating juvenile delinquency—a cultural phenomenon assumed to have been instigated by (horror and noir crime in particular) comics themselves. In response, the Comics Magazine Association of America implemented a number of self-censorship initiatives while also instigating the US Comics Code Authority.[7]

While the 1970s were marked by challenges stemming from public scrutiny, including censorship and moral panic, the comics industry largely broke free of its reputational constraints in the 1980s. For starters, the industry began exploring a wider mix of genres and creative expression than it had enjoyed in the previous decade. An expanding readership and increasing sales and profits followed. Until 1997, when the government enacted the Juvenile Protection Act , Korea's domestic comics industry enjoyed steady growth.

No one is better placed to offer a sharper perspective on the transformation of Korea's comics industry in the 1980s than master comics artist LEE Hyun-se, who has exercised a long-term influence on the industry. LEE's fifteen-volume series *A Dauntless Team* (1982) captivated readers with its tale of an unpromising baseball team that ends up winning Korea's professional league championship. Whether intentional or not, LEE's series aligned well with the CHUN Doo-hwan government's infamous "3S Policy" (sports, sex, and screen), which the regime had used as the guiding principle behind its cultural policy. Coming to power following a coup in December 1979, CHUN maintained ruthless control over all aspects of Korean society. His approach was crystalized in the national army's violent quashing of democratic protests on May 18, 1980, in the city of Gwangju, an event that has become known as the Gwangju Massacre. Another expression of CHUN's regime's control was the idea of using the entertainment media to distract citizens from their bleak existence.

The 3S policy—the so-called sexualizing and athleticizing of the nation—had the effect of drawing public attention away from the Gwangju Massacre and subsequent criticism of the government. At the time, commentators criticized CHUN's policy and the rationale behind it in terms of "stupefying," "hypnotizing," and "relieving the stress" felt by the public.[8] Perversely, as the 3S program was being rolled out across cultural industries, freedom of expression was being suppressed. For example, in 1980 a total of sixty-four newspapers and broadcasting companies were either forced to close or were merged into eighteen state-approved organizations, leaving 172 defunct periodicals and over one thousand journalists jobless. The number of publishers also shrunk.[9] Meanwhile, color television was launched nationwide in 1980. Professional baseball and soccer leagues were launched in 1982 and 1983 respectively.

Within the 3S policy framework, CHUN's government promoted the production of so-called "frivolous" content, including comics, which in turn became very popular. It was a peculiar boom time for many media enterprises, and they exploited as much permitted content as quickly as possible, including transmedia adaptations. LEE's *A Dauntless Team*, owing to its popularity as a comic book, was ripe for adaptation. LEE Jang-ho, one of Korea's best-known film directors in the 1970s and 1980s, adapted his story to make the feature film *Lee Jang-ho's Baseball Team* (1986). According to the Korean Movie Database (KMDb), the film attracted audiences of around 287,000 in Seoul alone, making it a blockbuster hit at the box office and the number one hit that year.[10]

The success of *Lee Jang-ho's Baseball Team* marks a notable moment when a print comic book transmedia adaptation gained national recognition. In addition, a lowly comics artist was applauded as a successful content creator. Around this time other well-known comics artists including HUH Young-man, GOH Haeng-seok, and PARK Bong-seong were also receiving credit for creating work that was sophisticated and intellectual—a far cry from copying Japanese manga. Their original stories provided rich sources for further transmedia adaptations. PARK's *Son of God* (1983), LEE's *Ring of Hell* (1985), and HEO's *The Chameleon's Poem* (1986)—all comics that dealt with boxers, a popular sport in the 1970s and 1980s—were adapted as feature films and released within two or three years of their comics' original publications. Although few comic book adaptations achieved the same level of success as *Lee Jang-ho's Baseball Team*, storytelling in comics had attained a new level of maturity and significance and exhibited a welcome diversity of content. [11]

THE PRICE OF FREEDOM OF EXPRESSION

While the comic book community was enjoying some unfamiliar positive attention, the Korean publishing industry was facing fundamental changes as a result of strengthened copyright laws. In mid-1987, some thirty-five years after it had been adopted by UNESCO, Korea finally joined the Universal Copyright Convention (adopted in 1952), signaling Korea's acknowledgment that protecting the IP rights of international cultural content was a government responsibility. (In 1996, Korea went on to adopt the Berne Convention, further extending its commitment to copyright protection.)

Korea's turn in this new direction coincided with the demise of CHUN Doo-hwan's military regime, reflecting the nation's newfound engagement with democratic reforms under president-elect ROH Tae-woo. Within a few months (in October 1987)—leading up to the 1988 Olympics in Seoul—the publishing industry was offered new opportunities after the ROH government allowed anyone to establish a registered publishing company. Suddenly the draconian restrictions that had hampered the industry were loosening; the number of publishers surged from 617 in mid-1980 to 1,115 new registered enterprises in

1988 alone (*Herald Economy* 2005). This intense competition in the industry shifted the balance of power away from a small group of dominant publishers, giving comics practitioners more choice and a little more leverage when seeking a distributor (or a producer) for their work.

However, a new source of competition from imported comics was to create a different set of industry challenges. One company that seized on this new opportunity in the post–CHUN Doo-hwan era was Seoul Media Group, formed in 1988. At the end of that year it launched a new comics magazine called *IQ Jump*, modeled on the weekly Japanese manga magazine *Shōnen Jump* then immensely popular in Japan. Teenage boys were the primary target readers for the Korean product, and instead of hiding the fact that the new publication had been inspired by a Japanese weekly magazine, *IQ Jump* flaunted this connection, releasing a licensed supplement called *Dragon Ball* in December 1989. Eager to exploit Korea's newfound alignment with international copyright laws, Seoul Media Group seemed to be in tune with the times. However, the ban on Japanese cultural products in Korea still created a legal headache for the company.

Unlike most of the other pirated materials circulating in Korea over the prior three decades, Seoul Media Group's publication of the martial arts–action adventure *Dragon Ball* was an officially licensed product legitimately obtained from Japanese entertainment-media company Shueisha. Almost unprecedented, the cover of *Dragon Ball* carried the name of Japanese author and creator TORIYAMA Akira, proclaiming the publication to be a licensed copy of the original Japanese manga. It proved a great success: Seoul Media Group sold 300,000 to 350,000 copies of the first edition of the *Dragon Ball* issue, reprinting up to six subsequent editions to keep up with demand (Yamanaka 2009). Oddly enough, it seems that the company received no legal challenges after publishing this Japanese manga in Korea, despite the practice being illegal under Korean law until the 1990s.

Seoul Media Group succeeded where so many others had failed because the Korean Publication Ethics Committee (the successor of the Korean Book and Magazine Ethics Committee) overlooked its illegal publication of Japanese manga. Such activities only became legal in 1991, when this committee introduced the Foreign Comic Screening System, allowing foreign comics with Korean translations to be included in its scrutiny of domestic publications. This measure aimed to strengthen the regulation of content and to manage the circulation of domestic comics. It also served to protect the domestic market from being flooded by foreign—primarily Japanese and American—comics. Nonetheless the Foreign Comic Screening System officially enabled pirated Japanese comics—which had been widely circulated through backdoor channels for three decades—to enter through the front door, as it were, and thus to be policed at an official level.

Thus, seven years before the ban on popular Japanese culture was lifted in 1998, the regulatory reform of the publication industry inadvertently legitimized the widespread practice of plagiarism, which publishers had tried hard to hide. As expected, industry reaction was swift; the Korea Cartoonist Association, for instance, immediately protested this move, as it would potentially open up a new market for imported Japanese comic books (Yonhap News Agency 1991). The industry was about to undergo a major shift.

In response to the introduction of the Foreign Comic Screening System, in December 1991 Daewon Media followed the lead of Seoul Media Group by publishing a weekly magazine, *Boy Champ*. To help launch the first issue, the company included a Korean-language edition of the noir romance–adventure fantasy Japanese manga *3 × 3 Eyes* (aka *Sazan Eyes*) by TAKADA Yuzo. Then, in February 1992 Daewon Media released the Japanese *Shōnen* sports manga *Slam Dunk* (by INOUE Takehiko) as a special supplement, ultimately inspiring a large fan following among teenagers throughout the 1990s. *Boy Champ* rose rapidly in popularity to become the second-best-selling comic magazine after *IQ Jump*.

Daewon Media—via its subsidiary Daewon Culture & Industry, established in 1991—along with partner company Haksan Publishing (formed in 1995) and competitor Seoul Media Group became the leading comic book and magazine publishers in Korea. Yet, as we discuss in chapter 3, they struggled to adapt their business models in the late 1990s when Internet service providers (ISPs) and search engines began leading the transition to the digital distribution and consumption of comics, and again after webtoons offered the mainstream comics (and publishing) industry a new path to profit.

Despite this new regulatory and industry turn from the early 1990s, the blatant piracy of Japanese manga continued. Alongside the "officially approved" translated versions of Japanese manga such as *Dragon Ball* and *Slam Dunk*, pirated copies of other manga were still found on the shelves of neighborhood *manhwabangs*. Only two other titles—including *Dr. Slump*, the light-hearted adventures of a young girl robot by TORIYAMA Akira (of *Dragon Ball* fame)—were published under authorized licensing contracts with Japanese publishers. At the time Yonhap News Agency estimated that around twenty million copies of comic books were in circulation between 1992 and 1993 and that at least one-third of these, drawing on around two hundred Japanese manga titles, were considered to be pirated. The combined total of Japanese-inspired comics, both illegal and legal, accounted for around 50 percent of the domestic market by the end of 1992 (Yonhap News Agency 1993).

KWON Young-sup, chairman of the Korea Cartoonist Association, suspected Japanese publishers of coordinating this "invasion" in order to cultivate Korean readers. In August 1992, in response to these suspicions, the Korea Cartoonist Association reached out to Japanese publishers (the original copyright holders), offering to work with them to sue any publishers involved in piracy; however, they failed to receive a response (Yonhap News Agency 1993). In accordance with international copyright law, the original copyright holder was expected to formally request that the offending party remove any suspected illicit content and, if this was not done, to promptly pursue legal action through the police. Yet in Korea's case the absence of complaints made by the original Japanese creators—at least according to KWON—offered no legal basis for curtailing, let alone regulating, these activities. And in reality there was simply too much contraband in circulation for the police to confiscate.

Korean comics fans were a fairly discerning bunch. Many readers could spot the difference between an original Japanese comic and a plagiarized one, in addition to an authentic Korean comic. In August 1993, Seoul YWCA conducted a survey of 569 primary and middle school students on their awareness and impression of Japanese manga. The survey showed that 61.2 percent of respondents were well aware that they were reading Korean-language versions of Japanese manga. A further 68.8 percent found Japanese manga to be entertaining, while 40.2 percent and 26.3 percent believed that they contained violent and sexual images and themes, respectively (Yonhap News Agency 1993). According to a 1997 report in the newspaper *The Hankyoreh*, Japanese manga promoted juvenile violence, homosexuality, and inappropriate relationships between young girls and adult males (*enjo-kōsai* in Japanese) (Jeong 1997). Above all, the rise in youth violence in the late 1990s, especially school bullying, caught the attention of the media, which in turn blamed Japanese comics (and their widespread appeal) for the situation.

Throughout the 1990s both officially licensed and (still) plagiarized Japanese manga were blamed for an increase in school-bullying incidents across the nation. MORITA Masanori's boxing-themed high school comic series *Rokudenashi Blues* (1988–1997), a story including high school delinquents and bullying, was singled out as one of the primary triggers for the behavior as well as for the rise of school gangs (Lee 1997). This series widely circulated in Korea among middle and high school students. In mid-1997 several school gangs emerged under the name Iljin Association (*Iljinhoe*), borrowed from the fictional gang in *Rokudenashi Blues*. These real-life gangs engaged in interschool fights, and many of their members were arrested by the police and charged with assault. If contemporary newspaper reports are to be believed, between January and June 1997 more than one hundred school gangs (and over nine hundred gang members) had robbed and abused their fellow students and over three hundred students arrested (Chou and Yi 1997). In Korea, manga-style comics had apparently become so influential that they were responsible for inciting a very specific kind of moral panic: *Iljinhoe* and *Iljin* became popular labels for school gang culture.

In early 1997, in an attempt to address this moral panic—and especially to placate worried parents—the KIM Young-sam government (1993–1998) established the Youth Protection Committee, which blacklisted over 1,700 Japanese and Korean comic book titles containing sexual or violent content (Gwon 1997). A few months later, in July 1997, the Ministry of Culture and Athletics introduced the Juvenile Protection Act, which gave further regulatory powers to the Youth Protection Committee, whose chief task was to control the publication and circulation of comics in order to protect students from being exposed to "harmful content" while also cracking down on the *Iljinhoe* school gangs. Even though the Constitutional Court of Korea had declared in 1996 that censorship of films was illegal, and despite the new life stirring in Korea's creative industries, print comics continued to face harsh treatment from the government. Under pressure from the government's newly reinforced Youth Protection Committee and the Juvenile Protection Act, comic rental shops continued to close and mainstream bookshops became unwilling to sell comic books and magazines. At the peak of their popularity in the late 1970s, *manhwabangs* had numbered around twenty thousand, and by the early 1990s they had already dwindled to less than five thousand (*Dong-a Ilbo* 1978; Im 1993). By the early 2000s less than three thousand *manhwabangs* were still operating in Korea (Kun-hyeong Park 2009).

Using the Juvenile Protection Act, authorities tightened their censorship grip over comic content, classifying certain comics as "harmful" to teenagers, pronouncing a death sentence for the titles in question. Thus the classification system established under the act simply replaced the by-now-defunct censorship laws. One of the high-profile cases involving the prejudiced and random attentions of the Juvenile Protection Act concerned the arrest of 1980s golden-age cartoonist LEE Hyun-se for creating the allegedly pornographic comic book series *Mythology of the Heavens* (1997). This charge, pressed soon after the act was passed, scuttled LEE's ambitious ten-year project aimed at creating one hundred epic fantasy comic series dealing with Korea's prehistory and its birth as a nation. *Mythology of the Heavens* ceased with the release of issue six after LEE was accused of depicting graphic violence and sexual activity in prehistoric society. In mid-1997 the prosecutor's office accused LEE of creating hardcore pornography, including bestiality and group sex, disregarding his creative approach to portraying primitive society (Ahn and Yi 1997). Despite a strong defense against these charges and pleas for freedom of expression, LEE was convicted in early 1998 and fined 3 million KRW ($3,363 USD).

This zealous and intimidating attack by the public prosecutor, with the press at his heels, strongly dissuaded LEE and his fellow comic artists, as well as publishers and rental shops, from persisting with comics. In fact, several months earlier, on November 3, 1996—now celebrated as Korea's Comics Day—LEE and numerous other comic artists had gathered in the Yeouido area of Seoul to protest harsh government treatment, calling for the same abolition of censorship of comics that the film industry was now enjoying (Seok-Hwan Park 2016).

This situation was all too familiar to practitioners who had been active in the 1970s, when for different reasons the industry had suffered under harsh production practices and low wages as the result of the dominant position of a few companies. LEE's conviction and the misuse of the Juvenile Protection Act was a major contributor to the demise of the print-comics industry in the late 1990s.

However, LEE's fight was not over. He refused to pay his fine in 1998, instead taking the case to court. His actions subsequently culminated in multiple trials—in 2000, 2001, and 2003. During his first trial, the Korea Cartoonist Association held a silent protest, at which its president, KIM Soo-Jung—creator of the immensely popular and commercially successful *Baby Dinosaur Dooly* cartoon and animated characters—and a few thousand professional and amateur artists, as well as students and fans, presented a united front in defense of LEE and the broader industry (Entertainment Team 2002). This mirrored similar attempts that had been made in the 1970s to protect freedom of expression led by Korean filmmakers (including YU Hyun-mok and LEE Man-hee).[12] Capitulating was not an option: LEE was seen as bearing the torch for all creators, especially junior artists seeking to develop careers in comics (Nam 2019), and yielding to this government witch hunt would harm the whole industry. Between 1997 and 2003, when he finally won his case before the Supreme Court, LEE fought a series of public legal battles to clear his name and to protect freedom of expression for the industry at large. In so doing, he became a role model for both junior and senior colleagues fighting for creative freedom and sheer survival. Had the KIM Young-sam government held a higher opinion of comics as a vehicle for telling diverse Korean stories and placed a higher value on freedom of expression, LEE and the comics industry in general may have enjoyed a larger share in the nation's creative industries—as webtoons do today.

In an unexpected turn of events, in 2017 newly appointed prosecutor general MOON Mu-il publicly apologized to LEE for the way in which he had been aggressively (and wrongfully) pursued by MOON's predecessors.[13] Due in major part to LEE's unwavering activism, industry conditions improved in the 2010s. Through his efforts, public officials and everyday citizens alike were reminded how comics were (and still are) an integral part of the nation's creative industries and thus, like their counterparts in the film, television, and music sectors, deserving of freedom of expression and creative diversity. For his dedication and persistence, LEE was elected president of the Korea Cartoonist Association (Hangunk Manhwaga Hyeopoe) in 2005 and appointed director of KOMACON in 2009. He received the prestigious Presidential Award at the Korean Popular Culture and Arts Awards in 2016 in a ceremony cohosted by the Ministry of Culture, Sports and Tourism and the Korea Creative Content Agency (KOCCA).

LEE, who has been a part of the webtoon industry since his launch of webtoon series on Naver in 2015, had succeeded in rallying support from within as well as outside the industry for improving workers' rights, increased training opportunities for aspiring creators, and facilitating networking among domestic and international enterprises.

EPILOGUE: BREAKING THROUGH THE CAMOUFLAGE VENEER

In their infancy, and while becoming increasingly popular following Korea's liberation in 1945, comic books and the comics publishing industry encountered prejudice over their contents, practices, and perceived negative influence on Korea's youth. Negative attitudes toward comic books and youth magazines in general were reinforced by the often poor quality of the printing materials used, not to mention the places where students and other young people were accessing comics— their unsavory neighborhood *manhwabangs*. Domestic comics "inspired" by Japanese manga were criticized for their alleged vulgarity and violence and for simply being "Japanese" (i.e., possessing an unwelcome "cultural odor") at a time when the Korean government had banned all Japanese popular culture. While the "menace to society" posed by comic books was being dealt with by the government, a loyal readership would not be discouraged.

During the 1980s, especially in terms of the sheer volumes of production and consumption, Korea experienced a brief "golden age" of comics. The industry produced an increasing number of comics that targeted both children and adult readers, and sports newspapers like *Daily Sports* featured long narrative serialized comics to feed an apparently insatiable demand for such material, thus contributing to the market's expansion outside the country's many comic book rental shops. However, the Juvenile Protection Act (1997) abruptly curtailed the growth of Korea's comics industry, stifling freedom of expression and creativity in this arena. The comics industry seemed to be heading in the opposite direction to the film industry, which had been liberated from censorship restrictions in 1996. The hounding and arrest of LEE Hyun-se exemplifies the difficulties experienced by the comic book industry during the 1990s.

After surviving this tumultuous episode, more than a decade later the comic industry decided that its best course was to publicly advocate for increased government support. In February 2011 WON Su-yeon, best known for her work *Full House* (1993) and cochair of the infant Manhwa Support Law Promotion Committee, addressed the National Assembly of Korea and advocated that changes to the industry be embodied in a Promotion of Cartoons Act.[14] As a spokesman for the industry, WON argued that, like the other cultural industries, comics had been an important creative vehicle for expressing national culture and practitioners across the comics industry deserved better conditions and remuneration. To lobby for the new law, a yearlong petition advocating for numerous bills was circulated online, with support from a number of industry leaders, including LEE Hyun-se. The campaign was successful, and the act was passed in December 2011 with unanimous support. For the first time in Korea's history, and although the act was imperfect, the comics industry was now acknowledged as a legitimate enterprise and regarded as part of the nation's larger creative industry cluster, worthy of protection and financial support.

In July 2015 Naver Webtoon—once seen as the comic book industry's nemesis—proclaimed the return of the legendary LEE Hyun-se to the webtoon arena (Naver Webtoon 2015b). Naver first released a free scanlation version of LEE's previously published and "banned" comic *Mythology of the Heavens*; due to its "mature" content, readers were required to log in to the platform and confirm their age. Naver Webtoon utilized this opportunity to introduce its readers to the original black-and-white *Mythology of the Heavens* series in 96 episodes (July 2015–December 2015). In December 2015, in further acknowledgment of this major collaboration, Naver Webtoon released a newly commissioned version of *Mythology of the Heavens*: a vibrantly colored, vertically scrolling webtoon in 98 episodes (concluding in November 2017) (Naver Webtoon 2015a). After a ten-year hiatus, Naver Webtoon and tens of thousands of readers welcomed the return of LEE and his magnum opus.

Despite the fact that webtoons were (and still are) a major disruptor of print publications, the shared lineage between webtoons and print comics must be acknowledged. A new breed of webtoon creators, including such well-known names as KIM Pung, Kian84, JU Homin, and Yaongy, who were nurtured on the work of LEE and WON, are now following in their footsteps. This new generation of practitioners has emerged as entertainers, celebrities, and industry advocates in their own right. [15] The work of these and other practitioners is evidence of the creativity that binds not only the print and digital comic worlds together but other sectors of the creative industries as well—in both conspicuous and hidden ways.

The Korean government's push for hyper ICT advancement in the late 1990s helped promote the digitalization of print comics as well as hasten the advent of webtoons. However, not all analog practitioners in Korea and elsewhere have embraced digital technologies. New enterprises in the digital arena—both those that have failed and others that have championed its rapid transformation—have expanded it, leading to the birth of webtoons in the early 2000s. Chapter 3 builds on this brief history of print comics in Korea to explore early developments in the webtoon industry.

3

POLICY INTERVENTION AND THE FORMATION OF THE WEBTOONIVERSE

This chapter builds on the history of print comics explored in chapter 2. It investigates some of the developments and stakeholder activities that facilitated the industry's transition to the digital distribution and consumption regimes that characterize the webtooniverse today. The authors show how a number of key enterprises, independent webcomics sites, and practitioners developed a radically new format—vertically scrolling webtoons—while responding to similar threats to freedom of expression that their print predecessors had experienced. By examining the cultural policy environment before and after the advent of webtoons, we offer an enhanced understanding of the webtoon industry's early negotiations with the Korean government and the self-regulation initiatives developed to meet the challenges of a new environment. Industry-support organizations—such as the Cartoonists Emergency Committee Against the Korean Communications Standards Commission and the Webtoon Self-Regulation Committee—established in 2012 and 2017, respectively—have empowered the webtoon industry and enabled it to become a progressively important arm of Korea's larger creative industries. In turn, as this book underscores, these developments signaled a dramatic shift in the early 2000s in the context of the general advancement and convergence of the IT, ICT, and creative industries.

Since the mid-1990s, and especially after 1996, when the Constitutional Court of Korea ruled that film censorship was illegal, Korea has witnessed the rise of a vigorous and diverse creative sector, buttressed by robust policy support from the government. The removal of censorship in 1996 saw the creation of new standards for freedom of speech as well as unprecedented press freedom. Yet, as chapter 2 demonstrates, print-comic enterprises and practitioners were unable to benefit from this newfound liberty in the same way as their filmmaker colleagues did. At this period in Korea's history President KIM Dae-jung's administration (1998–2003) was popularly understood to "support without intervention," a policy built on the radical changes initiated by two significant policy instruments promulgated in 2002: the Framework Act on the Promotion of Cultural Industries (superseded in 2011 by the Content Industry Promotion Act) and the Online Digital Content Industry Development Act. It is fair to say that the KIM government's unveiling of its Cyber Korea 21 vision in 1999 facilitated the dynamic linkages between Internet technology and cultural production, which allowed the Webtooniverse to assume the shape it takes today.

At the same time as it was guiding the nation to become one of the most Internet-equipped and ICT-savvy societies of the twenty-first century, the KIM government was also gradually increasing its financial support for creative industries. As part of this effort, it actively underwrote organizations such as the Korea Creative Content Agency (KOCCA), the Korean Film Council (KOFIC), and the Korea Manhwa Contents Agency (KOMACON). In turn, these key quasi-governmental agencies—under the umbrella of the Ministry of Culture, Sports and Tourism (MCST)—contributed to the accelerated domestic and global expansion, recognition, and economic prowess of Korea's creative industries. While it is difficult to quantify the contributions of these official bodies, it is clear that the Korean Wave, and indeed "Digital Korea," may not have reached as far, nor gotten there as fast as it did, were it not for the policy support provided by successive administrations. Over the years, KOCCA, KOFIC, and KOMACON, as well as MCST, have all made significant contributions, in both conspicuous and inconspicuous ways. Without drilling into the details of each policy, many of their efforts—in particular those making a direct impact on the shape, size, and direction of the webtooniverse—are discussed in this chapter.

THE ICT TURN AND THE PRE–DIGITAL COMICS REVOLUTION

While 2003 marks the birth year of webtoons, individual comic panels had been distributed online at this point by enthusiasts and a few companies in Korea for some time. The government's promotion of advanced computerization and the development of a national network infrastructure underpinning cutting-edge ICT since the 1980s had laid the foundation for the nationwide high-speed broadband network for which Korea is known today.[1] Thus, even before the Cyber Korea 21 initiative and the 2003 announcement of the Broadband IT Korea 2007 Vision, the government had committed to a comprehensive "national informatization" strategy that paved the way for market competition— accompanied by regulated Internet usage fees—and ultimately the advent of a Digital Korea.

Internet outlets known as *PC bangs* emerged in the mid-1990s and began to mushroom across the nation, taking advantage of Korea's expanding high-speed broadband infrastructure, effectively replacing the *manhwabangs* discussed in the previous chapter. Similar to the Internet cafés found across the world, Korea's *PC bangs* provided individual computer workstations for everyday Internet services as well as optimal conditions for playing PC-based and online games. Similar to their *manhwabang* predecessors, *PC bangs* attracted Koreans (mostly male) in their teens and twenties. For only 1,000 to 1,500 WON per hour (less than $1.50 USD), customers could stay for hours on end. They also had access to real-time and massive multiplayer online role-playing games (MMORPG) such as the war fantasy game *Warcraft* and military sci-fi *StarCraft* strategy games—both developed by United States–based Blizzard Entertainment. It is no coincidence that Korea's reputation as a highly competitive (and successful) e-sports hub began to take shape around this time.

A minor player in this IT revolution, the comics industry, also benefitted from advancements in Korea's IT infrastructure, which opened the door for a range of publishers, Internet service providers (ISPs), entrepreneurial individuals, and artists to experiment with new digital comic content and formats.

Throughout the 1990s Koreans had few—but slowly increasing— opportunities to read comics online. Unauthorized reproduction or "scanlation"—a process in which whole comic books are digitized and then distributed via a bulletin board system (BBS) or website—soon became widespread. While brick-and-mortar comic rental shops were gradually disappearing from neighborhoods across Korea, digitized comics were becoming readily accessible. Many commercial ISPs began including scanned comics among their main services. For example, in 1995 Korean computer and telecommunications companies Nowcom and Chollian—similar to Prodigy, CompuServe, and AOL in the United States—began offering *manhwa* (comics) as a regular feature on their BBS along with news, games, travel advice, weather, and discussion forums. Nowcom carried the Nownuri *"PC manhwabang,"* enabling users to download *manhwa* files for roughly one-third of the usual purchase price of a printed comic book. For its part, Chollian launched its Anytime service, offering comics, music, and animation online. In 1996 Interpia ISP entered the field by launching a new online *manhwa* service featuring the ten-book series *Eighteen Histories in Brief* (1994), created by well-known comic artist KO Woo-young. In 1999 another ISP, Shinbiro, introduced a "day pass" that enabled users to access nine hundred digitized comic books for 1,000 WON (about $1.00 USD). In 2000 Chollian trumped its rivals by offering a new online comic book service (www.cyberland.chollian.net) at the significantly reduced price of 1,000 WON per month. By canvassing these various schemes, Korea's ISPs were experimenting with different methods of drawing and sustaining traffic to their platforms (Jeon 1995; Yu 1999; *Hanguk Kyungje* 2000).

Not to be outdone, traditional comic book publishers also entered the online comics arena by launching their own cyber-*manhwabang* (aka Internet *manhwabang*). In early 2000 (five years after its founding), Haksan Publishing—close partner to Daewon Media—began distributing digital versions of existing as well as new comics via multiple webzines available on its website (www.D3C.com). Differentiating itself from other publishers as well as Internet enterprises, Haksan created the webzine *Hacking Comics* specifically to feature a range of original content by newly hired artists. In 2001 Seoul Media Group and Daewon Media (via its subsidiary Daewon Culture & Industry) also began contributing to this online community, launching their own sites, www.imcomix.com and www.candy33.co.kr, respectively. These cyber *manhwabang* had a number of advantages over visiting a physical comics rental shop: they were cheaper, safer to access in the confines of one's home, and convenient.

Looking back at these three sites via the Internet Archive's Wayback Machine,[2] it is apparent that Haksan, Seoul Media Group, and Daewon Culture & Industry—all of which required a user ID and password to log in—were almost as advanced as most digital comics sites are today. Yet they had less content. However, piracy (in this case, illegal sharing) of these fee-based scanned versions of print comics was rampant, and there were no effective methods to prevent it. This probably explains why the digital comic initiatives launched by Haksan, Seoul Media Group, and Daewon Media/Daewon Culture & Industry all eventually folded, failing to match the levels of success that Daum Webtoon and Naver Webtoon achieved when they started up a few years later (H. S. Kim 2000). In their time, however, these online *manhwabangs* offered a new monetization model for the declining print comic market, leaving the practitioners of the future to worry about solving the piracy issue and warding off its serious economic threat to the print and digital comics industry.

A number of independent webcomics sites—notably N4 (www.n4.co.kr) and Comics Today (www.comicstoday.co.kr), which were established in 2000—differentiated themselves from these other enterprises in five exceptional ways. As we have learned from discussions with industry representatives such as LEE Jae-sik, Comics Today chief editor and current CEO of the C&C Revolution webtoon agency, these initiatives were inaugurated by entrepreneurial professionals from the traditional printing industry who sought radical new pathways for the comics industry. In sum, they exceeded the limitations of simple scanlation technology. First, N4 offered a new type of free digital comics with embedded sound effects and flash animation techniques. It also established seven different webzines, featuring 120 star cartoonists, including YOON Tae-Ho, KIM Jin, and SHIN Il-Sook (currently president of the Korea Cartoonist Association) among them. In spite of these innovations, N4 soon failed, partly because its investors prematurely attempted to take the company public and sell it (Jeon 2000).

Second, around the same time, Comics Today launched with 90 percent of its comics titles in color, created by popular artists including LEE Hyun-se, HWANG Mina, and YANG Young-soon. Third, unlike most other platforms at the time, its titles were uploaded regularly every fortnight. Fourth, thinking globally from the outset, the site also offered comics in Korean and Japanese, with Chinese- and English-language versions in the offing. Fifth, Comics Today (and also N4) shocked its competitors by operating as a free site—at least initially—aiming to build a strong customer base that would garner healthy revenues in the future.

About a year after its launch, Comics Today began charging users, not just to remain afloat but also to expand its business model. To assist with this aim, it published a newly commissioned digitized volume of LEE Hyun-se's *Mythology of the Heavens*—but only after LEE had been acquitted following his appeal trial in mid-2001 (see chapter 2). LEE was a celebrity in creative-industry circles and thus a hot commodity. Thanks to LEE's name value, and the quality storytelling in his *Mythology of the Heavens* series, Comics Today had already attracted around eight hundred thousand registered members—with a small percentage of them paying to read daily content (*Maeil Kyungjae* 2001). If Haksan, Seoul Media Group, and Daewon Media/Daewon Culture & Industry had primed the market for digital comics, then Comics Today and N4 had primed Korea for paid serialized content created by star artists.

However, despite Comics Today's lofty ambitions, it eventually succumbed to financial difficulties and the subsequent negative publicity—problems from which it would never recover. In late 2001 its artists began complaining of withheld payments and of copyright violations resulting from the company's exploitation of their work. To press their case, some artists went on strike, casting the enterprise in a poor light. Once again, paying customers complained about the absence of newly updated content, and the website was plagued by technical glitches. Clearly the site was struggling to handle the traffic generated by all of its registered members and other casual visitors. Although the company issued a public apology, it was unable to recover from the technical problems, accumulated debt, and damage its brand name had sustained (*Cine21* 2002). In January 2004 Comics Today was acquired by one of its online competitors, Comic Plus (www.comicplus.com). Established in 2000 by major print publishing company Sigongsa, Comic Plus experimented with an early type of online "moving comics," utilizing multimedia elements including sound effects, background music, and rudimentary motion for its characters. In spite of the company's relatively early timing and innovations, a lack of user traffic and interest seems to have prevented Comic Plus from becoming a serious competitor to the webtoon platforms that succeeded it.

The monetization and technological trials of these early independent webcomics enterprises and cyber *manhwabangs* illustrate how they were precursors of webtoons—despite the fact that webtoon enterprises were all new companies formed outside of the printing industry.[3] Nonetheless, within a relatively short period around the turn of the millennium, a new audience for digital and online comics made an appearance.

Augmenting the efforts of the print publishers and the independent webcomics enterprises discussed above, domestic Internet search engines soon began entering the comics market. They too helped pave the way for the birth of webtoons. In early 2000 Internet search company Daum Communications introduced a comics service on its portal (comic.daum.net), and within only eight weeks it became the fourth most frequently used service after Daum's e-mail, search, and online community (Café) services. Two months later (in mid-2000), the one-year old Lycos Korea—a localized version of the US–originated Lycos search engine—joined the trend after launching its own comics service (comics.lycos.co.kr). Within about two months, Comics-Lycos Korea was also attracting large numbers of visitors: five hundred thousand users per day, with fifteen million page views within two months (G. H. Kim 2000). Yahoo! Korea, a localized version of the US–originated Yahoo! search engine, created its own comics service in 2002, joined by Naver in the same year (discussed in detail in chapter 4). As discussed later in this chapter, Yahoo! Korea began featuring webtoons in 2008 on its online Cartoon World service but ceased in 2012, ironically after webtoons had become firmly established as a revolutionary digital comic.

Thus the comics industry took a major turn toward digital after these domestic and localized search engines began including comics as part of their services. However, the conventional page-turning scanlation style used by all these enterprises would soon be eclipsed by something new. Daum Communications eventually rose above the pack by trialing a new type of digital comic in early 2003 on its Comic World service, innovating the vertically scrolling images that became known as webtoons.

THE SPARK THAT CREATED THE WEBTOONIVERSE

In the Korean context, the term *webtoon* was probably used for the first time in April 2000 in a newspaper article headed, "The Webtoon, A New Genre Unfolds" (*Chosun Ilbo* 2000). Here the term was used to describe a new mixed-media format containing both comics and animated effects created with Flash animation software. A few months later, in August 2000, the ISP Chollian released a new comics website that it called *Webtoon* (webtoon.chollian.net), containing aggregated links to various online *manhwabangs* and other comic webzines, as well as relevant industry news items and links to the homepages of individual authors. For 1,000 WON per day, users had unlimited access to scanned versions (scanlations) of print comic books on Chollian's metasite. Considering that Chollian had been operating a similar website and service since 1995, the only innovation was the use of the term *webtoon* in its branding; the site contained none of the technological or aesthetic features associated with contemporary webtoons. Around the same time, SK Telecom had also used the term *webtoon* when referring to the digitized black-and-white comics it had augmented with color and sound using object-oriented Java programming and Flash software on its portal site.[4] Thus, when Daum Communications launched its new webtoon section called Comic World in 2003, both the term and concept referred to something different from these other offerings; Daum's webtoon service unveiled the media format and industry standards with which we are familiar today.

Self-published short-form webcomics distributed between the mid-to-late 1990s and 2003—when webtoons as we know them were released on the Daum Communications search engine—are too numerous to mention. One early representative example is *Snowcat*, created by amateur comic enthusiast KWON Yun-ju, who in 1998 began posting images of an appealing feline and its amusing ponderings on daily life on her website (http://www.snowcat.kr/). *Snowcat* contained only a couple of cuts in each post, and they were arranged vertically rather than in the conventional horizontal layout. JEONG Cheol-yeon's *Marine Blues* (2001–2007)—no longer available at www.marineblues.net—is a slice-of-life comic story in color presented through the eyes of different undersea characters. Similar to the now-well-established webtoon slice-of-life genre, *Marine Blues*'s portrayal of the author's lonely life gained strong empathy from readers. In 2003 *Marine Blues*, which comprised several panels organized in a vertical layout, received the grand prize Korean Manhwa Award from MCST. Both the self-published *Snowcat* and *Marine Blues* were precursors to webtoons.

Finally, the bizarre slice-of-life vignette comics *X-file* and *Everyday Life Common Things*—which included references to poo and vomit—were created by KANG Full and shared on his website (www.kangfull.com). KANG's site was very popular; when the authors revisited it on December 1, 2002 (via the Wayback Machine), it had accumulated a grand total of 1,005,259 visits, with 10,629 visitors in the prior twenty-four-hour period. The sheer volume of comic and film reviews on the site, not to mention KANG's own uploaded comics, is impressive even by today's standards. As a result of KANG's growing following and reputation, he was soon recruited by Daum as a critic for its lighthearted *Let's Play with Movies* review service. Playing to his artistic strengths, KANG wrote film reviews containing a combination of text and illustrations. Thus, when Daum's search engine was ready to launch a fresh online comic service, KANG was one of the names at the top of their list. In 2003, to assist with the launch, KANG created *Love Story* (October 2003–April 2004)—one of the earliest, if not the first, serialized webtoons of the contemporary era. Thus the webtoon as we know it was born.

KANG's forty-two-episode *Love Story* series differed from previous webcomics, especially in terms of its format and narrative structure.[5] The series explores a pair of awkward and intertwined taboo relationships. First, Yeon-woo, a timid thirty-year-old civil servant, and his eighteen-year-old high school student neighbor Soo-young unexpectedly fall in love. Then Yeon-woo's twenty-two-year-old coworker Kang Sook (who has yet to complete his obligatory military service) falls head over heels for a moody twenty-nine-year-old photographer named Ha-kyung, whose boyfriend has recently died.

Love Story offered over twenty colorful comic images in each episode—all vertically arranged to form a story that was relatively lengthy at the time. Most previously published webcomics had been short and episodic and had included only a few images. *Love Story* was so well received that the series locked in the conventional webtoon format of today—a serialized, vertically scrolling color comic with a complete story arc broken into single weekly episodes. When his contract for writing film reviews ended with Daum, KANG was asked to create a new webcomic for Daum's Comic World service, which was accessible via the Daum search engine (Lee 2008). Comic World also published various short comics, essay-toons, and omnibus episodic cartoons, as well as single-cut political cartoons republished from newspapers. Recognizing that he was introducing something revolutionary to the site, KANG used *Love Story*'s epilogue to explain how he approached this challenge: "I've always wanted to draw a long-form narrative comic instead of the short omnibus style of Internet comics that I used to draw . . . Before doing any drawing for this long-form narrative comic, I spent a month creating the completed story. Drawing *Love Story* only began after the entire story was completed." KANG gave other practitioners the confidence to follow in his footsteps by explaining his novel development process, creating the story first and then illustrating it in stages—now standard practice.

Between October 2003 and April 2004, average daily page views of *Love Story* reached two million. KANG's popularity also skyrocketed, and his personal website crashed, unable to cope with the increased traffic resulting from his newfound fame (Lee 2004). During the release of *Love Story*, it became clear to Daum Communications that individual artists such as KANG had significant potential to cultivate a large following of readers. Clearly there was huge potential for capitalizing on of the booming interest in online content. Despite KANG's successful introduction of this new type of webcomic service, his work was hardly electrifying by today's standards; although *Love Story*'s narrative is well structured, the strip has a different look from today's vertical style. It has more dialogue, smaller images of characters, and shorter episodes. Nevertheless, *Love Story* set the tone for something radically different in the comics world; the series was so successful that it provided the impetus for Daum Communications to fast-track the development of other webtoons in the mold KANG had created.

Due to its immense popularity, *Love Story* was ripe for transmedia adaptation. It was published as a print comic in May 2004 and then adapted as a theatrical play in 2005; its transmedia journey continued with the feature film adaptation *Hello Schoolgirl* in 2008. Along the way both KANG and Daum Communications profited from selling the licensing rights. A wave of webtoonists soon followed this new pathway, creating a long list of serialized webtoons in the hopes of expanding their IP across various transmedia adaptations.

The success of *Love Story* created a ripple effect across the Internet in Korea. A new generation of digital comic artists emerged, utilizing their personal websites as well as webzines and community forums available on various search engines; these included Daum (2003–present), Naver (2005–present), Paran (2004–2012), Empas (1998–2009), Yahoo! Korea (2008–2012), and Nate (2009–2019). These portals all jockeyed for position in the domestic search-engine business. Following on the heels of Daum, in 2004 Paran launched its own Ntamin (ntamin.paran.com) webtoon service, and Empas launched its Manhwa Engine (comics.compas.com). To draw new customers, Paran and Empas featured webtoons by YANG Young-soon and KANG Doha, respectively—both of whom were well-known for their traditional comics artwork. YANG had made his debut in 1995 with the mature-content series *Noodle Nude* featured in the adult comic magazine *Mr. Blue*. KANG had debuted in 1987 with *Run, Ppasagari*, featured in the children's comic magazine *Treasure Island*. These two artists' first webtoons—YANG's *1001* (2004–2005), which was inspired by the folk tale *One Thousand and One Nights* (aka *Arabian Nights*), and KANG Doha's romance drama *The Great Catsby* (2004)—gathered impressive followings of their own. KANG's *Great Catsby* was adapted as a television series and a musical in 2007 under the same name, which only added to his reputation.

KANG Full, YANG Young-soon, and KANG Doha were all webtoon pioneers, innovating a long-narrative format very different from the single- and multicut webcomics that were being created and circulated at the time. The portals and platforms, which supported their work regardless of their individual longevity, were key players in expanding audiences for webtoons in the industry's early days.

In chapter 4 the authors build on these early foundations by detailing the rise of webtoon giants Daum Webtoon and Naver Webtoon. Their history and impact on the shape, direction, and velocity of the Webtooniverse covers the period from 2003 up to the present day. Their story includes several major challenges and conflicts that industry stakeholders have faced and overcome—in particular, some major battles fought to uphold freedom of expression. In what follows we discuss major policy instruments introduced by successive Korean administrations as well as some of the key conflicts shaping the transformation of the webtooniverse. Shedding light on some of the high-profile and headline-grabbing controversies over government policy—before circling back in the next two chapters to the continued rise of the webtoon industry in the mid- to late 2000s—we show how policymakers intervened in the webtooniverse, often contributing to the industry's growing pains rather than alleviating them.

PLANNING A FUTURE FOR THE INDUSTRY AND AN OFFICIAL BACKLASH

Beginning in 2003 and continuing almost every five years since then Korea's MCST—with input from KOCCA and the Bucheon City–based KOMACON—has sought to nurture first the print comics industry and then the webtoon sector through a series of Five-Year Development Plans for the Comics Industry (2003–2007; 2008–2012; 2014–2018; 2019–2023) (KOCCA 2019). Each of these policy blueprints outlines ideas and frameworks for the structured development of the comics industry. Reviewing these plans in 2020, it is clear how the government's priorities for the comics industry gradually shifted from the print to the digital and web domains.[6]

As we saw in chapter 2, at the turn of the millennium comics still had a reputation as a bad influence on Korea's youth. Thus it came as no surprise that the inaugural Five-Year Development Plan for the Comics Industry (2003–2007) outlined strategies for improving the public image of comics, as well as for reforming distribution structures, establishing production infrastructure, and facilitating exports (Ministry of Culture and Tourism 2003). The measures proposed in these framework documents were designed to enhance public awareness and appreciation of Korean *manhwa* at home but especially overseas. At the same time they stressed the importance of devising strategies for developing transmedia IP—or one-source-multi-use (OSMU) content, as it was known at the time. The second Development Plan (2009–2013) sought to assist the webtoon sector's expansion trajectory while also encouraging the print comic industry's transition to the digital arena. Specifically the plan aimed to strengthen digital-infrastructure support for webtoons and other digital comics and to advance the development of transmedia IP content and licensing business models (Korea Creative Content Agency 2009).

Despite the best intentions of government, very few of the Korean industry players we interviewed for this project had ever heard of these five-year policy blueprints. Nevertheless, MCST, KOCCA, and KOMA-CON have been responsible for a plethora of high-profile award initiatives, educational programs, and domestic and international industry events—a direct result of the federal and municipal funding that reflected the recommendations made in the five-year plans. Representative ongoing industry awards supported by MCST and these two quasi-governmental bodies include the Our Comic of the Day Award (enacted in 1999), the Bucheon City Manhwa Grand Prize (since 2004), and the Korean Content Award (since 2009). Other quintessential competitions and events include the Korean Creative Cartoon Contest (since 2003), the Naver Webtoon Best Comic Competition (since 2012), and Daum World's Best Webtoon Competition (since 2013, initially with CJ ENM). Essentially, winners of these competitions receive cash prizes and an opportunity to publish their webtoons on Naver Webtoon and Daum Webtoon (and KakaoPage), respectively.

In terms of facilitating international promotion and networking, KOCCA has been supporting webtoon industry delegations to attend high-profile events such as the Frankfurt Bookfair (since 2003) and the Beijing Bookfair (since 2014). More broadly, since its creation in 2001, KOCCA has supported the globalization of Korea's creative industries through a "go out and sell" strategy, innovating domestic and global development strategies across the webtoon, gaming, animation, character licensing, music, fashion, and radio and television broadcasting sectors. As of 2020 KOCCA operated seven global outposts, in China (Beijing, since 2001; Shenzhen, since 2017), Japan (Tokyo, since 2001), the United States (Los Angeles, since 2004), the United Kingdom (London, since 2004), Indonesia (Jakarta, since 2016), and the United Arab Emirates (Abu Dhabi, opened in 2016). Based on the conspicuous consumption of Korean popular culture, including webtoons, Asia is still KOCCA's primary target market, with the United States and United Kingdom collectively as a close second.

Taken together, these various awards, competitions, and initiatives have greatly assisted the domestic development of the webtoon industry, as well as its "going global," underwriting the ongoing evolution of the webtooniverse.

Despite the support offered by this plethora of official agencies, nothing has impacted the development of Korea's digital comics revolution more than the rapid spread of smartphones and tablets—especially in the period spanning 2011 and 2012. During this time, and outside of any government policy instrument, the webtoon industry experienced rapid growth in terms of quality as well as quantity of content through the activities of the major platforms discussed in this book. This unexpected progress raised alarm bells for some who felt threatened by the rapid evolution of the sector, and they soon began devising ways to halt the growth. Their efforts to challenge the rising strength and complexity of the webtooniverse represented a clear threat to freedom of expression.

One of the webtoon industry's most significant battles to retain freedom of expression was fought in early 2012 after the Korea Communications Standards Commission—South Korea's Internet censorship body (hereafter KCSC)—singled out twenty-three webtoon titles and criticized them for containing content deemed harmful to adolescents (portrayals of violence, murder, bullying, and mayhem) (Kyung-hun Kim 2012). By this time, and as chapter 4 shows, webtoons were firmly established as an expanding sector of Korea's creative industries. It was no coincidence that the timing of this witch hunt coincided with the promulgation of the Promotion of Cartoons Act, which aimed to "to invigorate the creation of cartoons, promote the development of the cartoon industry, and contribute to the improvement of citizens' cultural lifestyle and the development of the national economy by providing for matters necessary to promote the creation of cartoons and the cartoon industry" (Korea Law Translation Center 2012b). Among the KCSC's list of violators, which we call the "naughty twenty-three," were *The Five* (2011), *Legendary Fist* (2010–2011), *Murderer's DIEary* (2010–2011), and *Oksu Station Ghost* (2011).

This controversial episode began with an article in the major right-wing newspaper *Chonsun Ilbo*. On January 7, 2012, its front-page headlines asked, *"Furious Elementary School Students*—DO YOU KNOW THIS VIO-LENT WEBTOON?" (Seong-min Kim 2012). Sparked by a school bullying case that had led to a middle schooler's suicide in December 2011, comics (*manhwa*) and gaming were blamed for the escalating violence involving school students (Seo 2012). Responding to the *Chonsun Ilbo* article, KCSC announced that it would be tightening its monitoring process. This attack was reminiscent of the draconian treatment experienced by the print comics industry under the 1997 Juvenile Protection Act (discussed in chapter 2).

The webtoon *Furious Elementary School Students* (2008–2012) that had drawn *Chosun Ilbo*'s ire was featured on Yahoo! Korea and was created by writer-artist KIM Sung-hwan (aka Gwigwi). KIM's story and illustrations resembled Mike Judge's adult cartoon Beavis and Butt-Head, chronicling the exploits of a pair of vulgar and obstreperous high school students. *Chosun Ilbo* condemned *Furious Elementary School Students* for the light-hearted way it portrayed school bullying and for its frequent depictions of violence and use of coarse language. Although no one at Yahoo! Korea had thought to identify it otherwise, the offending webtoon represented a youth subculture known as *Byeongmat*, a popular webtoon genre at the time. Meaning something absurd, abnormal, and plucked out of context, *Byeongmat* had become popular since the late 2000s—especially in television dramas, live entertainment, and music, attracting an increasing fan base in their teens and twenties. *Furious Elementary School Students* was a black comedy portraying Korea's dog-eat-dog society set against the backdrop of a primary school. Crude drawings depicting characters committing senseless acts of violence were a vehicle for the dark satire that Gwigwi aimed to communicate. The term *Byeongmat* (or *Byeongmat* code), which referred to unconventional and antiestablishment online content, was widely known on popular Internet community sites such as DC Inside (https://www.dcinside.com/), one of Korea's largest Internet forum websites in operation (since 1999) (Hun and Yu 2017; Park 2010).

In addition to Gwigwi, other webtoonists including KIM Pung, MindC, LEE Mal-nyeon, and Mega Shocking also pushed the envelope of avant-garde creativity and antiestablishment sentiment by utilizing a "*Byeongmat* code" in their webtoons, portraying crude, inconsiderate, sexist, or self-destructive characters doing or saying dumb things for a laugh. In the late 2000s, *Byeongmat* had become an unmistakable part of Korea's youth culture: *Byeongmat* webtoons and other user-generated content paraded a motley crew of fools, losers, social outcasts, and failures, utilizing a language and style relatable to Korea's youth—broadly, the "880,000 Won generation," referring to the average monthly salary (equivalent to a little less than $900 USD) of a typical casual worker in their twenties. The term first appeared in 2007 in the title of a book by economist WOO Seok-hoon and journalist PARK Gwon-il, *The 880,000 Won Generation* (*Palsippalman-won Se-dae*), in which the authors describe a youth demographic at the mercy of unstable and limited employment opportunities. For many readers in this larger group, the *Byeongmat* webtoons that flourished online between the late 2000s and the early 2010s offered a brief opportunity to escape the financial and social stresses of everyday life. Their dark humor and satirical critique of Korean society held a strong appeal for creators, readers, policy stakeholders, and ordinary readers alike.

Within two days of *Chosun Ilbo*'s scathing report (published on January 7, 2012) and KCSC's promise to launch an investigation, a spooked Yahoo! Korea dropped Gwigwi's webtoon from its site. However, Gwigwi continued to upload the series to his personal blog. Yahoo! Korea's decision was surprising, given that it had a reputation for being a "liberal" search engine in terms of the subject matter that it featured on its site. As a latecomer to the webtoon market in 2008, Yahoo! Korea had recruited a number of nonmainstream artists including LEE Mal-nyeon, MindC, Gwigwi, and Kian84, giving them unfettered freedom to create imaginative strips that would enable the company to differentiate its site from its rivals (Lee 2015). For instance, MindC's *2 Dimensional Gag* comprised only two cuts with condensed humorous dialogue while other webtoon platforms preferred longer, vertically scrolling episodes. The levels of creativity and autonomy embraced by the company's stable of webtoonists bucked the trend. On the other hand, because Yahoo! Korea was experiencing some financial difficulties at the time (it ceased business at the end of 2012), this localized search engine may have been either too preoccupied to self-censor its *Byeongmat*-style content, or, conversely, it was making a final attempt to resuscitate its site by hosting titillating material. Whatever the case, *Furious Elementary School Students* caused enough controversy for Yahoo! Korea to cave to the KCSC's assault on its wayward webtoon (Shin 2012). Unlike Yahoo's operations in Japan and Taiwan, Yahoo! Korea lacked the human resources, capital, and traffic to compete against local heavyweights Daum and Naver, which dominated search and Internet traffic in Korea.

The furor over *Furious Elementary School Students* and the parts of the webtoon industry that embraced *Byeongmat* culture was a timely reminder of the need for a self-rating system of some kind. Had the industry adopted a suitable classification system from the outset, then the "naughty twenty-three" would have been categorized as mature or adult content and presumably the KCSC would have looked elsewhere to exercise its powers. At the very least, a "parents advisory" or some such label for *Furious Elementary School Students* and similar titles might have drawn less negative attention to both the artist and the platform(s) hosting such content. As we discuss below, while the industry gradually moved toward a self-regulation system, there was still an important battle to be won.

In a swift response of its own, the Korea Cartoonist Association made a public statement on January 10, 2010, the same day Yahoo! Korea removed Gwigwi's offending webtoon, asking "If manhwa disappears, does the school bully disappear too?" (Kyung-hun Kim 2012). When the KCSC released its list of "harmful" webtoons in February 2012, practitioners and other industry players realized that the past was creeping back into the present. It was as if Korean society had suddenly been transported back to 1997, when LEE Hyun-se had been arrested for allegedly depicting pornographic content in his epic *Mythology of the Heavens* print comic series. The situation was both serious and scary, especially for those practitioners (and readers) who had become used to enjoying freedom of expression in the wider creative industry.

As in 1997, some commentators now considered this moral panic patently absurd, as a number of the webtoons on KCSC's list had been recognized by the LEE Myung-bak government for their artistic achievement. In particular, JEONG Yeon-sik's fifty-four-episode thriller-horror series *The 5ive Hearts* (2011) and Kkomabi's forty-nine-episode murder mystery *Murderer's DIEary* (2010–2011) had both been granted the 2011 Korean Contents Award from KOCCA (and MCST) (Seo 2012). In addition, artist Horang's horror-toon *Oksu Station Ghost* (2011) (discussed in detail in chapter 6) had garnered international fame for its innovative use of 3D-style Flash animation techniques. All three of these critically acclaimed webtoons were recognized as having expanded the spectrum of creativity and diversity across the industry.

To add to this sense of irony, fifteen out of the twenty-three proscribed webtoons had already been categorized as 19+ by the webtoon platforms (and artists) themselves, meaning they were accessible only after passing the required log-in stage with adult identification (Choi 2012). As these examples show, KCSC's brief to oversee the regulation of Internet content (and broadcast programs) was subjective and haphazard, and its logic (if there was one) was lost on most commentators and industry personnel following the issue.

Within five weeks of the publication of the *Chosun Ilbo* piece, and out of sheer frustration with KCSC, a group calling itself the Cartoonists Emergency Committee Against KCSC (hereafter CECA-KCSC) was formed in mid-February 2012. Uniting the major industry bodies behind a single cause, the organization included representatives from the Korea Cartoonist Association, the Cartoon and Animation Society, and the Korean Comic Writers Association. Reminiscent of the joint initiative that had led to the formation of the Comic Copyright Council of Korea in 2002 (involving the Korea Cartoonist Association, the Korean Comic Publishers Association, and the Cartoon and Animation Society), the new coalition launched a "No Cut" campaign to protest the KCSC's actions. Over the next few weeks, many prominent webtoon artists, including YOON Tae-ho (known for *Moss*, *Misaeng*, and *The Insiders*), JU Homin (*With God*), and KANG Full (*Love Story*, *Apartment*, *26 Years*, and *Lamp Shop*), picketed KCSC headquarters in Seoul. They stood in solidarity with the accused practitioners, many of whom were major industry names.

As president of the CECA-KCSC, YOON criticized KCSC for its perpetuation of outdated views of webtoons and comics more generally and also for its scapegoating the industry for problems associated with Korea's youth. Unwilling to remain quiet on the issue, industry representatives were vocal in their demands for artistic freedom of expression and the elimination of censorship (Cartoonists Emergency Committee Against KCSC 2012). When the authors interviewed YOON in 2018 and 2019, he still showed some bewilderment over these events, which initially had caught him and others off-guard.

Never in a strong moral position, KCSC's witch hunt eventually backfired, making the organization look rather foolish. In April 2012—only two months after passing the Promotion of Cartoons Act and four months before the act's ratification by presidential decree—KCSC and the Korea Cartoonist Association mended fences and agreed to establish a formal self-regulation system for the industry.[7] They also agreed to consult with each other whenever complaints were made against webtoons. In theory, complaints were first to be lodged with KCSC and forwarded to the Korea Cartoonist Association, which would then consult its members. Next, the association would seek an appropriate response from the platform hosting the allegedly offensive content—either dismissing the complaint or agreeing to take some action. In some cases the platform in question was asked to block minors from accessing objectionable content. Essentially all parties committed themselves to promoting a "sound Internet culture" for school-age children through webtoons (and other comics). As a result of these negotiations, and to prevent KCSC from blocking a website or a particular webtoon without consultation, all webtoon platforms were encouraged—not compelled—to identify material as either suitable for "all ages" or "19+."

Thus one positive outcome of this dispute was the opening of a channel for discussion between government and industry on the need for a self-rating system and how to implement it. With the industry about to swell up in 2013—with the launch of the paid webtoon platforms KakaoPage and Lezhin and the introduction of an advanced monetization system (discussed in chapter 5)—this was a timely and necessary discussion that would have implications for the industry for years to come.

STANDING UP FOR *BASTARD* AND THE MOVE TO SELF-REGULATION

These abovementioned events of 2012 mark a pivotal and unprecedented moment when the comics industry split from its past, unifying into a cohesive voice, and demanding respect from the government (which it received). The Korea Cartoonist Association also began serving as a willing partner in the industry's move toward self-regulation. From this time, the webtoon industry has became an influential cultural sector in its own right, driven by an officially recognized commercial imperative based on an expanding readership not only among teens but also among people in their twenties and thirties.

Comics were no longer to be used as a scapegoat for youth problems in Korean society. Or so it seemed, as similar problems were to emerge only a few years later, raising new questions about the industry's autonomy and capacity for self-regulation. One such scandal erupted in 2015 when KCSC blundered by blocking the fee-based, mature-content platform operated by Lezhin Comics (see chapter 5). KCSC's poorly judged decision was overturned after just one day, revealing the highly subjective nature of the censorship process. This is further illustrated in what follows as we investigate the development of the industry's self-rating system and, in particular, the *Bastard* case of 2016.

In June 2016 the thriller series *Bastard* (2014–2016) inspired an overzealous parent to sue Naver Webtoon, KCSC, the Korea Cartoonist Association, and the series creators, writer KIM Carnby and artist HWANG Young-chan. At the crux of the case was Naver's alleged violation of the 1997 Juvenile Protection Act. A sophisticated psychological thriller, *Bastard* focuses on a boy raised by his serial killer father and trained to be his accomplice. Evocative of the popular US television series *Dexter* (2006–2013), *Bastard* is laden with brutality and graphic murders and broaches serious issues such as illegal organ trafficking and kidnapping—all of which apparently upset the plaintiff. Initially Naver Webtoon had assigned a G rating (general viewing) to *Bastard* because its "coming-of-age" story had been considered appropriate for all ages. However, after the company was sued, its content managers changed the series' rating to 19+ in consultation with the artists (Jeong 2016). A police investigation ensued amid a heated public debate, with people questioning whether the government had gotten the balance right between regulating webtoons and upholding freedom of expression. The legitimacy and effectiveness of the industry's self-rating system was at stake.

In October 2016, after a four-month police investigation, Naver Webtoon and the creators of *Bastard* were cleared of all charges. The lessons to be learned were complicated. One the one hand, the litigation had been baseless, given the series' coming-of-age message: a confused boy ultimately finds the inner strength to escape his father's control. The controversy might have been resolved through measured discussion between the complainant and the platform rather than require formal legal action. On the other hand, had the case been allowed to escalate and the plaintiff won, a dangerous precedent would have been established, reversing the positive gains made through the industry's self-regulation scheme and the Promotion of Cartoons Act. The incident was a poignant reminder for Naver and the broader industry that any agreement between KCSC and the Korea Cartoonist Association would inevitably have its limitations and that all platforms would benefit from bolstered efforts to self-regulate.

The negative attention directed at Naver Webtoon and the subsequent controversy over *Bastard* exposed divergent views on implementing the self-regulation agreement as well as on individual platforms' approaches to ratings. It exposed the difficulties involved in achieving a solid consensus over webtoon ratings and the different approaches to identifying "mature content." The case also revealed that as a result of their agreement both KCSC and the Korea Cartoonist Association had been approaching problems reactively rather than proactively—a response proving inadequate for the sheer diversity and volume of content that the industry had amassed by the mid-2010s.

In the enlarging and complex webtoon ecosystem, by now involving around sixty different platforms, a more sophisticated system of regulating content was required. The time was ripe for a self-regulating system similar to that adopted in the United States. Hence, on November 3, 2016—Korea's Comics Day, which honors a major comic artists' protest against the government in 1996—industry representatives signed an agreement to form a new sector group to be called the Webtoon Self-Regulation Committee. Its membership comprised the Korea Cartoonist Association, KCSC, and the Ministry of Gender Equality and Family, as well as eleven of Korea's largest platforms, including Naver Webtoon, Daum Webtoon, KakaoPage, Comica, K-toon, Lezhin, Mr. Blue, and Bomtoon. The committee's goal was to manage complaints against webtoons in a more aggressive and proactive manner than the Korea Cartoonist Association had achieved in the past.

In August 2017 the Webtoon Self-Regulation Committee was formally launched; members were determined to reduce negative publicity as well as any fallout arising from complaints against the industry. Subsidized by monthly membership fees and voluntary contributions, and eager to conduct its own research surveys, this collaborative initiative aimed to raise the public image of webtoons (and comics), repairing the damage that their reputation had sustained in recent years. One of the first major reports the committee commissioned and released in

October 2018 was a study of age-rating standards for webtoons, laying the foundation for a more robust self-regulation system (Park, Hong, and Jeon 2018).

The 2018 study recommended four ratings categories: All Ages, 12+, 15+, and 18+. In addition, eight core elements were to be considered when a rating was given: theme, violence, sexuality, language, drug use, gambling, risk of imitation, and discrimination. Under this new system—which promoted creativity, diversity, and freedom of expression, with little government involvement—practitioners rated their own work voluntarily, enabling readers (and parents) to choose age-appropriate content. This fresh approach, which was formally enacted in May 2019, mirrored previous rating standards used for printed comics (and enforced by the Korean Publication Ethics Committee) and also resembled the self-regulation categories for comics in the United States.

Surprisingly it had taken over fifteen years for the webtoon industry to adopt the type of unified rating system that had been utilized in the film industry in Korea since 1999 under the Media Rating Board—and in the United States through the 1968 Motion Picture Association of America (MPAA) film rating system. In addition to protecting practitioners, this new robust ratings system confirmed the rising status of the webtoon (and comics) industry as a powerful, commercially viable, and significant sector of Korea's creative industries.

CONCLUSION

The legacy comics publishers, small independent enterprises, and ISPs that made forays into the comics market—primarily by exploiting scanlation to circulate comics online—were pioneers in the history and evolution of the digital comics revolution in Korea and deserve credit for contributing to the development of the webtooniverse. However, the direct forerunners of the webtoon industry comprised a few individual practitioners who experimented with and initially self-published digital comics in a variety of genres and styles through their own blogs, websites, and webzines. In time, search engines began hosting this content, and some charged readers for accessing it. The Daum Communications search engine took a significant risk by hosting such content for free. Kang Full's *Love Story* (2003) on Daum transformed the medium by presenting webcomics in a new, vertically scrolling format—hence to be known as webtoons. As we learn in chapter 4, this free content became a major driver of traffic to both the Daum and Naver search sites and could be monetized in a number of ways. At the turn of the millennium, Korea offered the ideal environment for introducing these serialized webcomics, especially given its advanced Internet infrastructure and maturing netizen culture. The state had an important role to play here: the early success of the webtoon industry was partly built on the KIM Dae-jung government's 1999 Cyber Korea 21 plan.

In this chapter the authors have also considered the various social, industry, quasi-governmental, and governmental pressures that the webtooniverse faced while maturing into a more complex ecosystem. A careful balance of self-regulation and activism were required to counter the suppression of creativity and threats to freedom of expression posed by quasi-governmental bodies—such as the Korean Publication Ethics Committee and the Korea Communications Standards Commission—under the guise of concern for the moral well-being of Korea's youth. The 2012 industry agreement on a voluntary ratings system, and its subsequent rollout, was paramount in achieving the right balance between creativity and freedom of expression, on the one hand, and meeting the public's expectations for appropriate moral and ethical standards, on the other.

The 2012 self-regulation agreement was similar to the self-rating conventions adopted in the United States in recent years, with platforms such as Marvel Unlimited, DC Comics, and ComiXology adopting multiple age categories. These include All Ages, Teen 9+ (for content containing some humorous misbehavior and mild violence), Teen 12/13+ (some bad language and/or suggestive themes), Teen 15+ Parental Advisory (moderate violence, mild profanity, and graphic imagery), and, finally, Mature 17+ or Adult 18+ (for content containing intense violence, extensive profanity, nudity, explicit sexual themes, and gore). In the United States these age categories superseded the Comics Code administered by the Comics Code Authority (hereafter CCA, 1954–2011). The CCA was the US print industry's primary self-regulatory body, enabling publishers to adopt a voluntary "seal of approval" under the Comics Code. Commercial advertisers and retailers, as well as some readers, were reassured by the seal, which appeared on the front covers of comic books until the code was gradually abandoned in the 2000s (Adkinson 2008; Nyberg 1998). Today publishers in the United States have adopted their own system for categorizing the age-appropriateness of comics. Although later than expected, Korea too has moved in a similar direction.

From a policy perspective, the Promotion of Cartoons Act (2012) underlined the government's view that the creative industries were one of Korea's greatest assets and thus worthy of protection and encouragement. On paper the act addressed the needs, development, and opportunities of the modern digital comics industry, which stood on the threshold of a revolution of sorts. In reality, the Promotion of Cartoons Act simply acknowledged the remarkable rise of webtoons as a dominant format and platform and their outstripping of print comics in terms of market share and local and global reach. At the same time, it became apparent that the two primary governmental bodies responsible for webtoons—that is, the Ministry of Science and ICT (overseeing the Internet distribution of webtoons and other digital content) and the MCST (responsible for nurturing and promoting webtoons)—would remain challenged to adopt a unified approach. Nevertheless, with the rollout of this 2012 legislation, Korea's comics and webtoon industry became an integral part of the digital economy.

It would be fair to say that the historical examples and cases canvassed in this chapter have been cherry-picked from a much larger array of events, enterprises, policies, and practices that constitute the Korean webtooniverse. Public policy is still struggling to keep up with the technical, fiscal, and cultural advances and issues driving the shape and direction of the print and webtoon industries. At the same time, both policymakers and other public stakeholders, as well as the artists themselves, continue to face challenges to protecting freedom of expression. As the webtoon industry has advanced, policymaking and policing bodies such as the Korea Communications Standards Commission, the MCST, and the Ministry of Science and ICT have struggled to identify effective strategies for supporting the broader comics industry. Five-year plans had limited ability to effect radical change on their own. Nonetheless, eventually these and other quasi-governmental agencies, including KOCCA and KOMACON, devised strategies to develop and promote key aspects of the industry, including diversifying genres, developing an efficient monetization infrastructure, introducing appropriate ratings guidelines, and enhancing global outreach. As it happens, as of mid-2020 the government (i.e., the Ministry of Land, Infrastructure and Transport and MCST) has broken ground on a new Webtoon Convergence Center in Bucheon City (near KOMACON), promising over eight hundred apartments and offices exclusively for artists, which is likely to expand the webtooniverse in new directions (Seo 2019).

The legislation and five-year plans passed by successive governments have certainly been well intentioned. Indeed, the cultural policy mantra of "support without intervention" introduced by the KIM Dae-jung government remains an important stimulus for the Webtooniverse. In reality, however, as the next two chapters show, the main driver is the ideas and strategies devised by a wide variety of platforms and practitioners for sustaining the webtoon industry and pushing it to ever greater levels of achievement.

4

DAUM AND NAVER: THE SEARCH PORTALS UNDERPINNING KOREA'S TRANSNATIONAL WEBTOON IP ENGINES

In this chapter we investigate how large integrated IT corporations such as Daum Communications (now part of the Kakao family) and Naver are contributing to the expanding transnational webtoon ecosystem. Specifically we explore how these two major platforms, as well as a range of their internal small-to-medium enterprises, are energizing "IP engines" designed for transmedia adaptation. We focus on the major early adopters, such as Daum Webtoon and Naver Webtoon, that are fueling the creative industries, especially in terms of creator-owned transmedia IP.

When Korea's two giant Internet portal sites Daum and Naver first launched webtoon services, this digital Korean-language content was accessible for free. Free webtoons—all owned by their creators—served as a significant lure for increasing traffic to these portals, which hosted a range of other media and consumer products (or "services"). In other words, webtoons served (at least initially) as a kind of loss leader—that is, a money-losing service utilized to drive traffic toward their other paid content and commerce services. Naver, in particular, became known for its success with this strategy, while Daum became known as a leading contributor to both monetizing webtoons and facilitating the transmedia adaptation trend for which the industry is known today. Since 2006 Daum Webtoon has forged new layers to the webtooniverse via its aggressive transmedia-IP activities, thus offering its artists certain opportunities unavailable via other webtoon enterprises.

In the same year Naver Webtoon launched its Challenge league, inviting amateur artists to post their work, including series with short episodes. This strategy has helped Naver boost the numbers of web-toonists connected to its site (and thus the wider industry) while also attracting more readers in their teens. Naver's Challenge league has become an incubator for a plethora of creators that eventually began populating many other domestic platforms, thereby crowning Naver as a primary germinator for the webtooniverse.

One of Naver's other major achievements is its mid-2014 launch of a global webtoon platform called Line Webtoon (www.webtoons.com), which features a Challenge league–like system called Canvas, as well as almost ninety creator-owned series accessible across multiple markets and in multiple languages. As a result of Line Webtoon (renamed sim-ply "Webtoon" in September 2019, and redirecting to https://www.webtoons.com/en/) and these other aforementioned developments, Naver's global footprint has surpassed Daum's. Hence, when it comes to size—excluding the webtoon and webcomics portal Bufftoon and its parent online and mobile gaming company NCSoft—Naver operates the largest webtoon operation by far, with the biggest archive of exclu-sive webtoon series titles, enabling its parent Internet search-engine company to maintain its position as the world's leading webtoon plat-form.

By 2012, thanks to the rapid proliferation of mobile apps and de-vices, the consumption of webtoons had surpassed that of print comics (KOCCA 2013, 13). Daum Webtoon and Naver Webtoon combined were now attracting over fourteen million monthly visitors to their on-line sites and mobile apps, respectively, representing one-third of all Korean Internet users (Hong 2012a). Investigating some of the wa-tershed moments of both Daum Webtoon and Naver Webtoon (and their parent companies) helps us to understand the transformations undergone by the larger industry, which have determined its character today. Not least, webtoons have acted as midwife to the rebirth of Korea's comics industry, which had all but vanished in its former print-based format.

Between them, both Daum Webtoon and Naver Webtoon have marked off their digital content from the other entertainment products and services represented by their parent companies while also maximizing user experiences through their now-conventional vertically scrolling format and weekly upload systems. Although Daum was the first to experiment with a regimented weekly uploading model, both companies regularized it by recruiting talented artists covering a wide range of genre stories, striving to satisfy the entertainment needs of a global audience. Still, although both Naver and Daum overhauled the webtooniverse in the late 2000s and early 2010s, Daum was the first major company to release webtoons in the marketplace. Since then, the gap between the two companies has become ever larger, as we explain below.

DAUM WEBTOON: THE EARLY WEBTOON INNOVATOR

Since its launch in 1997 Daum Communications has attempted to exploit its market position as one of Korea's first ICT/Internet search companies. The company—predating Naver, which debuted in 1999—used its lead to grow a loyal base of Daum e-mail (Hanmail account) users. As discussed in chapter 3, the main Daum website began featuring an online comics (scanlation) service in May 2000. Then, innovating something new in 2003, Daum released KANG Full's vertically scrolling *Love Story* series, which predated similar content on Naver by about two years. KANG Full's webtoon series *Apartment* (2004) was adapted into a feature film in 2006, becoming the very first instance of transmedia IP. Daum Webtoon has also been a pioneer, establishing the industry's standard weekly update system and monetization practices, as well as leading the way for negotiating transmedia adaptations of webtoons published on its platform (see table 4.1). Building on its early start, Daum Webtoon has maintained a loyal following among audiences in their twenties and thirties who enjoy the platform's strong genre features, mature themes, and character-driven stories.

Increasingly since the late 2000s Daum Webtoon has expanded its recruitment efforts and nurtured new talent through a single creator-centric space for amateur comic artists called *I Am a Comic Artist*. In 2011, due to the increasing number of titles uploaded to its site, this UGC space was modified into a two-tier "league system" separating novice and established creators. In mid-2011 Daum gradually intro-

Table 4.1.   Select Transmedia Adaptations of Daum Webtoons

Webtoon title	Genre(s)	Transmedia IP title	Transmedia type (distributor)
Love Story (2003)	Romance	Hello Schoolgirl (2008)	feature film (CJ Entertainment)
Apartment (2004)	Horror	Apt. (2006)	feature film
26 Years (2006)	Action, drama	26 Years (2012)	feature film
Moss (2007–2008)	Thriller	Moss (2010)	feature film (CJ Entertainment)
I Love You (2007)	Drama	Late Blossom (2010)	feature film
Covertness (2010–2011)	Action, comedy, drama	Secretly, Greatly (2013)	feature film
Fist of Legend (2010–2011)	Action, drama	Fist of Legend (2012)	feature film (CJ Entertainment)
The 5ive Hearts (2011)	Thriller, action	The Five (2013)	feature film (CJ Entertainment)
Steel Rain (2011–2012)	Action, drama	Steel Rain (2017)	feature film
Won't Hurt You (2011–2012)	Comedy, drama	Secret Zoo (2020)	feature film
Misaeng (2012–2013, aka Incomplete Life)	Drama	Misaeng (tvN–CJ ENM subsidiary, 2014); Hope (Japan TV, 2016); Ordinary Glory (China TV, 2018)	TV series
Buamdong Revenge Social Club (2014–2016)	Drama	Avengers Social Club (2017)	TV series on tvN (CJ ENM)
Start-Up (2014–2016)	Comedy, drama	Start-Up (2019)	feature film
Love Alarm (2014–present)	Romance	Love Alarm (Netflix, 2019)	TV series
July Found by Chance (2018–2019)	Romance, fantasy	Extraordinary You (2019)	TV series
Itaewon Class (2020)	Drama	Itaewon Class (Korean TV, 2020)	TV series (Netflix)

Source: Webtoonguide: Webtoon Analysis Service, https://was.webtoonguide.com/dashboard (accessed 1 May 2020), and via authors' own research.

duced a new monetization model that would become a standard for the industry. Continuing in 2013 Daum Webtoon implemented further recruitment strategies—for example, through the hosting of a Daum-branded Online Manhwa Competition in collaboration with KOMA-CON and KOCCA. Not only did this event increase awareness of Daum Webtoons among the next generation of aspiring webtoonists, but it also strengthened links between the webtoon industry and the Korean government.

As for its expanding archive of transmedia IP (see table 4.1), Daum Webtoon has an impressive portfolio of successful adaptations—created by artists such as KANG Full, YOON Tae-Ho, and HUN—who are all now among the best-known, wealthiest, most prolific and original writer-artists to have benefitted from transmedia adaptations of their work. Daum has collaborated actively with CJ ENM, the family-run entertainment conglomerate (aka *chaebol* in Korean). Together, Daum and CJ ENM (previously known as CJ Entertainment) have launched the Daum Webtoon Competition (discussed in chapter 3) and also regularized the sale of coveted adaptation rights to numerous Daum Webtoon series (i.e., webtoon IP). In turn, CJ ENM has produced and/or distributed these transmedia remakes as television series (on its OCN network and tvN channel) and as feature films.

One of the first "proper" weekly serialized webtoons to be published on a corporate platform is the romance-drama *Love Story* (2003–2004). Today most of the episodes of *Love Story* can be read for 100 KRW each ($0.09 USD). Created by the now-well-known KANG Full (the pen name of writer-creator KANG Do-young), this titillating series was released nearly two years ahead of Naver's introduction of vertically scrolling webcomics on Daum's extensive search website. As the previous chapter mentions, the series became a hit, giving birth to the Korean and international webtoon industry that we know today. Thus Daum Webtoon deserves credit on two counts: for being the first platform to launch a webtoon service in Korea and for backing *Love Story*, which went on to become one of the earliest examples of webtoon transmedia IP. *Love Story*'s rich IP history includes a print comic (2004), a theatrical play (2005), and a feature film called *Hello Schoolgirl* (2008).

In fact, many of KANG Full's webtoons, which are widely appreciated for their well-structured story lines, have been adapted into feature films, including horror story *Apartment* (2004, released as *Apartment* in

2006), drama *Fool* (2004, released as *BaBo* in 2008), action drama *26 Years* (2006, released as *26 Years* in 2012), romance *I Love You* (2007, released as *Late Blossom* in 2010), horror thriller *The Neighbor* (2008, released as *The Neighbors* in 2012), and supernatural thriller *Timing* (2005, released as the animated *Timing* in 2015). KANG's other webtoon series, under contract but yet to be adapted at the time of writing, are *Again* (2009, a sequel to *Timing*), zombie horror-drama *Every Moment of Your Life* (2010), horror-thriller *Lamp Shop* (2011), occult romance *Witch* (2013), and superhero action *Moving* (2015).

One of the first examples of transmedia IP, in this case a webtoon adapted into a feature film, KANG's horror webtoon *Apartment* (2004) opened up a new pathway for utilizing webtoon IP. Although it was a relative failure at the box office, *Apartment* was adapted by writer-director, producer, and all-around horror master AHN Byeong-ki—then known as writer-director of well-received horror movies *Nightmare* (2000), *Phone* (2002), and *Bunshinsaba* (2004). *Apartment* centers on a female character who makes the disconcerting observation that the lights of many apartments in her complex are snuffed out in rapid succession at precisely 9:56 PM every night. The next morning she catches glimpses of a corpse being whisked away from her apartment block. These mysterious and unsettling events inspire her to launch her own investigation. Despite the popularity of the webtoon series, the film adaptation was poorly received due to its disjointed story line and its use of too many horror film clichés. One critic panned AHN for failing to exploit the creative sense of mystery and suspenseful plot of the original webtoon, as well as its well-developed characters (Djuna 2006). Another critic used the film's weaknesses to highlight the challenges of transmedia adaptation (Kim 2006). The film's critical reception aside, the failure of *Apartment* confirmed the risks and challenges associated with transmedia adaptations of webtoons.

Commenting on the film adaptations of *Apartment*, *Hello Schoolgirl*, and *BaBo*, KANG himself admitted in an interview that the adaptation and conversion process was like a "double-edged sword" for screenwriters: audiences familiar with the original webtoon were especially unforgiving about any perceived shortcomings in the remake, pressuring the filmmakers to be faithful to the original and skeptical that success could be achieved at all (Hong 2008). Nonetheless, industry doubts about the potential for transmedia were beginning to wane in 2010 after the film adaptation of master webtoonist YOON Tae-ho's thriller *Moss* (2007–2008) became a box office hit.

Directed by seasoned filmmaker KANG Woo-seok and released in 2010, *Moss* is generally regarded as the first successful webtoon transmedia adaptation; it attracted 3.4 million viewers in Korea and nearly $22 million USD at the box office worldwide.[1] This suspenseful mystery-thriller explores themes of corruption, patriarchy, misogyny, and historical trauma, providing an acerbic critique of the psychological darkness lurking beneath the bright exterior of contemporary Korean society. The audience is transported to the fringes of urban society as seen through the eyes of Ryu, whose obsessive-compulsive behavior forces his estrangement from his wife and child. Ryu attends his father's funeral in a remote village where the latter had lived since returning from the Vietnam War. In this rural backwater, Ryu meets a sinister group of elderly men dominated by a corrupt retired police officer. Ryu befriends a young woman—the sole female villager (a male character in the webtoon)—and gradually discovers the sordid truth about his father's death and the villagers' involvement in it. YOON's creative use of color in the original webtoon illustrations—especially the dominant blacks, browns, and grays—is re-created faithfully in the live-action adaptation. Most of the story occurs at night or in dimly lit underground spaces, creating atmospheric, noir-like shadow effects. Both the webtoon and the film adaptation present an allegory of the abuse of power that affected everyday life during Korea's decades of military dictatorship (1961–1988) while confronting contemporary issues of class and gender inequalities, as well as the wealth gap between urban and rural communities.

Released three years after *Moss*, the next successful transmedia adaptation made for the big screen was the action comedy-drama *Secretly, Greatly* (2013), which told the story of three young North Korean spies who infiltrate a small neighborhood in Seoul. The film attracted 6.9 million viewers in domestic cinemas, becoming the fifth-ranked film at the box office in 2013 and the biggest hit film based on a webtoon to that time (Suh-young Yun 2013). These successful adaptations, as well as the television drama series *Misaeng* (2014)—which was so successful that it caused subsequent licensing and royalty fees for future remake deals to spike—reassured both webtoonists and filmmakers about the value of transitioning between media formats.

THE SEARCH FOR A VIABLE MONETIZATION APPARATUS

As we have seen, Daum beat Naver in the race to become the first search company to introduce a monetization model. In mid-2011 Daum Webtoon began charging readers to unlock episodes of a select number of popular completed series. Around this time both Daum and Naver's parent companies dominated the domestic market, forcing their competitors, including the fourth- and fifth-ranked webtoon service providers Yahoo! (2008–2012) and Paran (2004–2011), to cease or reduce their operations. Ignoring potential resistance from readers who had become accustomed to reading webtoons for free, writer-creator KANG Full adopted this new model in mid-2012, charging a nominal fee to access all episodes of his collected series. This development added a new dimension to the nascent webtooniverse, generating an additional revenue stream for creators and rewarding them with up to 90 percent of the fees collected from reader payments. The sole exception was KANG's action thriller *26 Years*, inspired by the 1980 Gwangju Massacre and the attempted assassination of President CHUN Doo-hwan—a profoundly topical story that KANG wanted to be read as widely as possible. However, the decision to monetize content in this way—as opposed to employing a loyalty or rewards model that incentivizes readers by encouraging them to fulfill certain tasks (such as watching videos, registering for third-party services, or installing sponsor apps)—was a risky experiment that could have turned off KANG's readers in droves. The decision to monetize KANG's webtoon series was warmly welcomed by readers as well as industry groups—including the Korea Cartoonist Association, the Korean Comic Publishing Association, the Korean Manhwa and Animation Academy, and the Korean Manhwa Storywriters Association—which now saw a new opportunity for their members (i.e., practitioners) to earn a living from the platform ecosystem.

Daum Webtoon's longtime CEO PARK Jeong-seo (who had joined the company in 2006 as a content producer and editor and was a friend of Naver Webtoon visionary KIM Junkoo) justified the new model as a necessary step toward the systemization of the webtoon industry. Daum Webtoon's wage system, which had been in place since the platform's genesis in 2003, only covered an artist's production costs, leaving very little for living expenses. Thus monetization was seen as an effective strategy for making webtoon creation viable as a career. While it would not be easy to overcome readers' habituation to accessing free content, fears of a user backlash quickly faded only one month later when readers were queuing up to pay for Daum's webtoon service (Yoon 2014). The company has never had cause to regret this commercialization strategy. Within a year Naver Webtoon joined Daum by charging readers a small fee to access a range of new and popular titles, and starting in 2013 a number of new webtoon platforms, including KakaoPage and Lezhin Comics, began entering the market with a fully monetized model designed to generate sales from their titles.

As we have seen, the major industry groups were very supportive of Daum Webtoon's move to this new payment structure. Previously, in mid-2009—following the release of its iOS app—Naver Webtoon had declined to introduce a paid mobile webtoon model, even though the industry groups believed it was an opportune time to do so. At this pivotal juncture, coinciding with the proliferation of smartphones, industry representatives lambasted Naver Webtoon for prioritizing the flow of free webtoon content as a way of driving traffic toward its other commercialized services rather than using webtoons as a vehicle for generating income for their creators.[2] Thus, at least initially, Daum succeeded where Naver had failed—in terms of finding a workable mechanism that would secure its artists a viable income. Maturing into an industry in its own right, particularly in terms of infrastructure, numbers of creators, and quantity of content and readership—that is, an enlarging ecosystem—the webtoon industry was undergoing its biggest transformation since its birth in 2003. With new possibilities for generating sales and profits, 2013 saw the release of Daum Webtoon mobile apps for Android (June) and iOS (December), as well as the construction of many new webtoon platforms (the largest of which, KakaoPage and Lezhin Comics, are discussed in chapter 5). The webtoon industry was now entering a new major era of development.

Looking back, Daum Webtoon was a major disruptor for radically challenging the traditional free webtoon model, which it had implemented from the outset. The move to a payment system not only increased the potential income of webtoonists whose titles could attract paying readers but also increased the labor rights (at least in theory) and economic solvency of content creators. In terms of government policy,

Daum Webtoon's seemingly long-overdue move to monetization pre-dated the Promotion of Cartoons Act that the Ministry of Culture, Sports and Tourism had introduced in February 2012. This initiative was the first of its kind to include *manhwa* (both print comics and webtoons) under Korea's legal intellectual-property system, formally recognizing the *manhwa* industry as a legitimate creative-industries sector. This newly developed policy framework, discussed in chapter 2, responded to the need to promote and protect both the webtoon and comics industries, especially the facilitation of diverse content, additional distribution channels, IP protection, and support for internationalization and export activities. In turn, webtoons became formally recognized as a new Hallyu genre and format.

DAUM'S INTERNATIONALIZATION PUSH

In addition to being one of the first digital entertainment enterprises of its kind to implement a monetization strategy, Daum Webtoon was also an early initiator of a new globalization strategy. In 2014 it partnered with global content providers including Marvel and Disney, featuring promotional tie-in (aka "branded") webtoon series such as *Avengers: Electric Rain* (2014) and *Star Wars: The Force Awakens* (2015). Daum Webtoon was also the first to export webtoons outside of Korea via a business-to-business (B2B) arrangement. In September 2014 Daum Webtoon released the world's first Korean-born Marvel webtoon—predating Line Webtoon's coventure with US comics industry heavyweight Marc Silvestri's Top Cow Productions (a partner studio of Image Comics) to create a webtoon version of the story *Cyberforce* (August 2015–October 2016, aka *Cyber Force*). Daum Webtoon collaborated with Marvel Entertainment and Disney Korea to create a licensed original Korean webtoon series called *Avengers: Electric Rain* (September 2014–April 2015). Outside of Korea it was promoted as Marvel's first official webtoon series, introducing a brand-new character to its stable.

Previously known for creating the popular superhero webtoon series *Trace* (2007–present), and a big Marvel fan himself, KOH Young-hoon (aka Nasty Cat) was handpicked by C. B. Cebulski (senior vice president for Creator & Content Development at Marvel Entertainment) and other Marvel editors for his dynamic style and understanding of

American aesthetics and storytelling modes.[3] KOH wrote and illustrated *Avengers: Electric Rain*, setting the story in Korea and introducing a female superspy character called White Fox. Inspired by Korea's mythical nine-tailed fox (aka *gumiho*), White Fox has now appeared in over twenty comic book issues featuring characters from the Marvel Universe. These include *Contest of Champions* #1–3 and 6–10 (2015); *Civil War II: Choosing Sides* #6 (2016); *Deadpool*, vol. 4 #1 (2016); *Totally Awesome Hulk* #1 (2016); *Domino: Hotshots* #1–5 (2019); *Marvel Comics Presents* #8 (2019); *War of the Realms: New Agents of Atlas* #1–4 (2019); and her very own *Future Fight Firsts: White Fox* (2019). As far as we know, no other Korean webtoon character—from either Daum or Naver—has traveled as far or as widely as KOH's White Fox.

In early 2014—about six months before Naver's launch of Line Webtoon in the United States (under Head of Content Tom Akel, with whom the authors spoke in July 2018 at Comic-Con International: San Diego)—Daum Webtoon began partnering with California-based start-up Tapas Media and its English-language platform Tapastic (now known as Tapas), thus officially becoming a B2B exporter of Korean webtoons and enabling them to be translated via their partners for the North American market. (Individual and/or one-off export deals may have occurred earlier; however, such deals are untraceable today.) Tapastic, established by Korean-American entrepreneur Chang KIM in 2012, focused chiefly on introducing Daum's popular Korean webtoon series to a new market of English-language readers. As of 2020 the partnership had been relatively successful, at least according to its online footprint. The platform's website as well as other indexes such as Crunchbase promote Tapas as "bite-sized stories on the go," "daily story snacks," the "YouTube of Comics," and "Candy Crush for Books."[4] The company boasts a community of almost fifty thousand content creators responsible for 1.2 million episodes and over seventy thousand stories. Webnovels (discussed briefly in this book's introduction) were added to the site in 2016 through a partnership with KakaoPage. In addition, over eleven thousand (nearly a quarter of the total) creators have been paid to date, stimulating the growth of a thriving community of practitioners who can publish their work for free—a community that this privately held company and Daum Webtoon have developed together.[5]

For Daum Webtoon and its parent company, Daum Communications, 2014 was a year of transformative change. In May 2014 Daum

Communications merged with Kakao—a company formed in 2010 by KIM Beom-soo, former CEO of Naver. Kakao is well known for developing KakaoTalk, Korea's most popular social media messaging app. The merger created a mega ICT enterprise called Daum-Kakao (later renamed Kakao), reportedly worth almost ten trillion KRW ($9.45 billion USD) at the time (Shu 2014; Tay 2014). As chapter 5 explains in greater detail, initially Daum Webtoon was placed under the subsidiary Podotree (eventually becoming KakaoPage)—a content-provider platform launched in 2013—operating along with parent company Kakao's other mobile apps, including KakaoTalk, KakaoStory, KakaoTaxi, KakaoMap, KakaoDriver, KakaoMusic, KakaoPlace, KakaoAlbum, and KakaoStyle.

To anyone watching these developments, Daum's obvious next move was to create synergy between all of these content platforms and their overlapping user bases. In September 2016 Daum Webtoon was formally upgraded to the status of a company in company (CIC). This allowed Daum Webtoon to operate separately from the parent company, with a large degree of autonomy—for instance, to recruit new employees and modify its operational budget, thereby loosening some of the restrictions on its decision-making abilities.[6] With this move, Daum Webtoon maintained its original brand name and status as the oldest webtoon platform in Korea. At the time, PARK Jeong-seo, longtime CEO of Daum Webtoon, stated that, following the internal restructuring, as well as its aggressive pursuit of transmedia IP adaptations, the company would benefit from its newfound independence and reduced levels of bureaucratic interference in its day-to-day operations (Sungwon Yoon 2016). In 2019 PARK reaffirmed these points in conversation with the authors when they met at the Daum Webtoon headquarters in Pangyo Techno Valley, near Seoul, known as the Silicon Valley of Korea. (Be that as it may, and in the name of synergy, numerous online and mobile Daum Webtoon titles can also be found on KakaoPage's mobile platform.)

By early 2020 Daum Webtoon had published around nine hundred completed series, as well as a further 160 ongoing titles—many of which are available under the fast-pass model. As mentioned above, a few sample episodes of older popular series—including KANG Full's *I Love You* (2007, 29 episodes), YOON Tae-Ho's *Moss* (2008–2009, 80 episodes), HUN's *Covertness* (2010–2011, 67 episodes), and CHON

Kye-young's *Love Alarm* (2014–present, 168 episodes)—are accessible for free, while most of their remaining episodes are unlockable for 200 KRW (approximately 15 US cents). These four series, regarded as representative contents on Daum Webtoon, have all been adapted into either feature films or television dramas. Under the partnership of Kakao subsidiary Kakao M—a vertically integrated music production and publishing company and talent agency, as well as a media production studio—and in direct competition with Naver's StudioN, additional IP managed by Daum Webtoon is being lined up for adaptation into new films and TV dramas. Possibly as a result of the challenges that accompany such rapid growth, as of mid-2020 web traffic to Daum Webtoon has been declining steadily, providing new opportunities for other paid platforms, such as Lezhin Comics, to poach some of Daum's readers. Such shifts are to be expected as the webtooniverse continues to evolve.

NAVER AND THE RISE OF THE WEBTOON INCUBATOR

Naver is Korea's largest search engine and one of the largest portals in the world in terms of online and mobile-user traffic. From its humble beginnings in 1999 as an Internet search engine, and especially after it merged in 2000 with online game company Hangame Communications, Naver has expanded into a comprehensive, transnational "super-portal," or a "netizen playground" (Chae and Lee 2005). The parent platform now features a number of services, including *Knowledge iN* (2002), the Naver Café online community and the Naver Blog platform (both since 2003), Naver Webtoon (2005), the Band social-networking service (2012), webnovels (2013), V Live video streaming (2015), and the Papago multilanguage translation tool (2017).[7]

While Daum has so far dominated the discussion (and although it preceded Naver as Korea's first major Internet search engine), another remarkable development of the webtoon industry and its global rise can be traced back to 2002. This is precisely when Naver launched a pioneering online question-and-answer UGC (user-generated content) service called Knowledge iN—and when it began to outstrip Daum. With Hangame's powerful gaming engine behind it, and as a collective intelligence tool that effortlessly enables users to exchange information, Knowledge iN formed the infrastructure driving Naver's general search engine and its ability to offer users a customized and consistent experience, encouraging ongoing and repeat traffic. Within two years the Naver brand name was being equated with Korea's leading web portal site, commanding over 70 percent of the market. Still operating in 2020, Knowledge iN predated the better-known Yahoo! Answers and Quora services, which were launched in 2005 and 2010, respectively. Knowledge iN is just one example of a long line of innovations illustrating Naver's constant experimentation with and investment in cutting-edge technology. Unlike Daum, which failed to innovate in this way, Naver and its influence has continued to grow.

The year 2002 is also when Naver's online site began hosting paid scanned versions of print comics (*manhwa* in Korean). However, in 2004 Naver upsized its contributions to the digital comic revolution by experimenting with (or "beta-testing") a new "webtoon section" featuring a new type of free content on its website. Since these early days (and still today) Naver's comics and webtoon activities have been orchestrated by KIM Junkoo, founder and current CEO of Naver Webtoon. KIM is largely responsible for championing the vertical layout of webtoons, which differentiated them from other types of scanned comics. In late 2005 Naver formally launched a webtoon section separate from the *manhwa* section. In exchange for free access to this webtoon content, Naver attracted increased traffic to its general website, and the modern webtoon as we know it today was born. Yet this new digital media did not become fully mature until 2010, when smartphones began to proliferate in the domestic market. During several interviews in 2018 and 2019 with longtime webtoonist (on Naver) JI Gang Min, creator of the popular *Welcome to the Convenience Store* series (2008–2014), JI explicitly linked the popularity of his and other webtoons with the rapid take-up of smartphones in Korea between 2009 and 2010.

Over the years webtoons have gradually achieved the status of flagship content for the Naver portal. Under KIM's direction, slice-of-life series such as *Midnight Rhapsody*, *The Sound of Your Heart*, and *Jungle High School* and the fantasy series *Noblesse* blossomed. As one of the earliest webtoon series to contribute to Naver's enlarging reputation, *Midnight Rhapsody* (2005–2018, 327 episodes) offered fresh perspectives on the traditional comics format, and its short length made it the first hit title on Naver Webtoon. *Midnight Rhapsody*, which reflects a cynical view of society seen through the eyes of the main character, Wony the wolf, gained a large following for its satirical humor. Written by PARK Jong-won (nicknamed Wony) and illustrated by SIM Yoon-soo, *Midnight Rhapsody* uses a vertically scrolling format, for which Naver and the webtoon industry at large is well known today, and was officially launched in late 2005. Two other series that KIM Junkoo had recruited also utilized this same format: the dramas *Banana Girl* (2005–2007, 82 episodes) and *Love-in* (2005–2007, 39 episodes).

Although as of 2020 Naver Webtoon was the leading webtoon platform in Korea, back in 2005 it lagged behind Daum, which showcased the first big star webtoonist, KANG Full, and his romance drama series *Love Story* (2003). Shortly after, another competing platform called Paran, which is now defunct, featured another celebrity webtoonist, YANG Young-soon, and his fantasy series *1001* (2004–2005). In order to differentiate itself from rival platforms, Naver Webtoon sought series with stylish looks and an emphasis on the twin themes of comedy and empathy, targeting readers in their teens and twenties. Meanwhile, Daum Webtoon concentrated on working with experienced artists who produced webtoons with long and sophisticated plots that attracted large numbers of female and mature readers in their twenties and thirties. In so doing, KIM recruited writer-creators who offered fresh narratives and arresting styles, including CHO Seok, known for his comedy/slice-of-life webtoon *The Sound of Your Heart* (2006–2020); KIM Kyu-sam, with his black comedy/high school drama *Jungle High School* (2006–2011); and writer SON Jeho and illustrator LEE Kwangsu, for their high school drama/sci-fi/action series *Noblesse* (2007–2019). Such webtoons helped boost usage of the Naver search engine in terms of the quantity and quality of popular digital content. During its first four years, the number of new webtoon series published on Naver more than doubled each year, growing from three titles in 2005 to fifty-eight titles in 2008. The number of new webtoon series doubled once again from eighty-three titles in 2009 to 168 in 2012. By comparison, Daum Webtoon (http://webtoon.daum.net/) uploaded only fifty-eight titles in 2009. Naver reached a peak of 368 titles in 2019, and the number of original series continues to climb.

On Naver, webtoons are organized according to a three-tier structure: (1) "Featured," which showcases professional webtoon artists who are paid a monthly wage, (2) "Best Challenge," which curates amateur owner-creator series, and (3) "Challenge," which also features amateur content, but with little curation. Introduced in 2006, the two UGC sections have become an incubator for aspiring amateur webtoon artists. Both sections present user-led opportunities, as any artist can upload their work autonomously. After a particular series in the Challenge section becomes popular—indicated by likes and readership statistics, and/or noticed for its story and artwork—Naver staff bump it to Best Challenge. A similar screening process applies in the Best Challenge section in order to promote "featured artists"—such as *Cheese in the Trap*'s Soonkki—who have generated a fan following and who ultimately serve as paid ambassadors for the site. *Cheese in the Trap* was first shown on Naver's Best Challenge middle-tier section in early 2010, shortly afterward earning a coveted spot in the Featured webtoon section—elevated by high ratings. In advancing certain titles, such as *Cheese in the Trap*, Naver Webtoon staff seek to achieve an even spread of content and story types across different genre categories (*10Asia* 2012). In this way, content curation is an important aspect of the ecosystem—at least on Naver Webtoon (https://comic.naver.com/index.nhn).

MINING NEW SOURCES OF VALUE

Between 2004 and 2014, the decade prior to KIM's launch of the globally facing Line Webtoon platform, KIM ran the Korean-language webtoon service on Naver as a start-up enterprise within the parent company. A number of milestones gave momentum to the burgeoning enterprise. In mid-2009 the company released its Naver Webtoon iOS app, and in late 2010 its Android app was released. In 2013, following in the footsteps of Daum Webtoon—which had instituted a partial monetization system in 2011—Naver Webtoon released a new monetization model called PPS (page profit share). Explained in detail below, PPS tracked revenues generated by reader micropayments, advertisements, and product placements. Particularly, the micropayment model was applied to a select few popular series. JU Homin's fantasy-drama webtoon *With God* (2010–2012, 213 episodes)—the inspiration for the Pan-Asian box office hit and transmedia adaptations *Along with the Gods: The Two Worlds* (2017) and its sequel *Along with the Gods: The Last 49*

Days (2018)—was one of the first series for which readers were charged a small fee to access archived episodes. JU's original webtoon satirizes the fate of humanity through the eyes of common people and traditional Korean gods. *Along with the Gods* producer WON Dong Yeon explained to the authors in an interview in 2018 that the original story's underlying melodramatic elements were extended in the adaptation in order to increase its purchase among non-Korean audiences in overseas markets. The main idea was to focus on shared values and traditions such as family loyalty and Buddhist beliefs. Clearly JU (and Naver) had highly valuable transmedia IP that was leveraged in *Along with the Gods*, the most successful example of a transmedia-IP in the webtooniverse to date.

As a part of PPS, Naver sold eager readers a "fast-pass" in 2013 to access selected new series, unlocking episodes of "Featured" series immediately upon release. By systematizing PPS, KIM and his team also inserted advertisements at the end of various episodes, as well as embedded product placements (hereafter PPLs) within an episode—but only in Featured series. Outside the online and mobile Naver Webtoon platform, webtoon character merchandise was licensed and sold (also tracked via PPS) on the parent Naver portal as well as in retail stores. More importantly, "sharing" here meant passing some of the now-identified profits to Featured artists.

A pivotal development for the infrastructure and analytical capabilities of the wider webtoon industry occurred in 2013, after Naver Webtoon innovated its PPS system. Long-awaited, this mechanism offered artists an effective and potentially transparent model for assessing the value or cost per click of content on its web and mobile platforms. PPS enabled the webtoon ecosystem to catch up with the pay-per-click Internet advertising model that major search engines such as Google, Yahoo!, Baidu (in China), Microsoft, and Naver had already been using to determine the costs to advertisers based on the number of times one of their advertisements is clicked. For webtoon creators, this feature included a method of quantifying and also maximizing the reach and impact of all types of webtoons—based on viewing behavior. Moreover, this innovation (theoretically—unless a platform agreed to share the data) enabled stakeholders, especially artist-creators, to access accurate data about the reception of their webtoons. In turn, the page-profit-sharing tool became a critical device for setting advertising rates and also for assessing the real and potential profits generated by advertisements and product placements.

In order to exploit the mostly free content on Naver Webtoon, some webtoon series were also monetized through various strategies, including free-to-play mobile role-playing games. In 2016 an adaption of *The Sound of Your Heart* was released by Neowiz Games on Google Play Store, and it was also adapted as a web series the same year on Naver TV Cast, as well as the Chinese streaming platform Sohu TV. Finally, Netflix hosted a television sitcom series based on *The Sound of Your Heart*. Chapter 7 explores numerous other examples of webtoon merchandizing and product tie-ins—transmedia IP originating from original webtoon content. Previously the gradual monetization of webtoons had offered Naver's Featured artists new opportunities for earning an income in addition to their regular monthly wage. During discussions with the authors, industry representatives from *WebtoonInsight* (LEE Jae Min) and *WebtoonGuide* (TJ KANG) both confirmed that profits generated through the sale of fast-passes and accessing archived series—that is, PPS—usually were split between artists (70 percent) and Naver Webtoon (30 percent). In addition, artists received more than half of the profits derived from embedded advertisements and PPL in their episodes. Thus Naver became the first and the largest enterprise to embrace the monetization trend, backing a successful profit-sharing model that benefitted both the platform and its artists. In this way both Naver and its loyal bevvy of webtoon creators collaboratively innovated a new wave of media globalization that continues to expand in both quantity and quality.

Naver's monetization and cross-licensing efforts were so successful in terms of revenue generation that in 2014 KIM's start-up venture was accelerated to become its own internal subsidiary company. Over that company's lifespan, KIM has been closely associated with its various transformations, and since its formal incorporation in 2014 he has been Naver Webtoon's CEO. In turn, the entry of these new players motivated Naver to continue innovating—an approach best demonstrated by the launch of its globally facing transnational webtoon platform, Line Webtoon, in July 2014. As a result, Naver achieved a level of global expansion that the webtoon industry at large had yet to experience. Almost overnight the international spotlight was shone on a large number of Korean (and a much smaller number of English-language) webtoons as they appeared on Line Webtoon and on its five official multi-language sister sites in Simplified Chinese (https://www.dongmanmanhua.cn/), Traditional Chinese (https://www.webtoons.com/zh-hant), Japanese (https://manga.line.me/, which is now only accessible within Japan), Thai (https://www.webtoons.com/th), and Indonesian (https://www.webtoons.com/id).[8] In late 2019 Webtoon (previously known as Line Webtoon) launched sister sites Spanish (https://www.webtoons.com/es) and French (https://www.webtoons.com/fr) that link to its now truly global platform.

Outside of Korea the launch of the Line Webtoon platform has helped KIM become recognized for his entrepreneurial acumen and technological savvy. In 2014 *Forbes* magazine selected him as one of the year's most notable next-generation innovators.[9] Between mid-2017 and mid-2018, largely due to the platform's expansion of its staff and digital content, KIM began transforming the in-house enterprise into an independent corporation after receiving 150 billion KRW (approximately $135 million USD) from the parent company (Kim 2018).

Elsewhere the authors have explored how these multilanguage Line Webtoon sites, and especially the translators working on thirty-two different languages between them, have contributed to the globalization of Naver and the webtoon industry more generally (see Yecies, Shim, and Yang 2019; and Yecies et al. 2020). Suffice it to say, these advances have enabled Naver's Korean and multilanguage webtoon platforms to become the leading digital comic platform in Asia while also gaining an increasing proportion of the digital comics market in North America and other parts of the globe.

It is perhaps surprising to learn that Naver's webtoon side of their business is a loss leader in terms of overall operations. As a Web 2.0 enterprise, Naver Webtoon continues to attract vast numbers of users—hundreds of millions of readers worldwide—while at the same time generating an annual total comprehensive income loss. In 2018, for example, this was $58.1 million USD (Naver Corporation 2019a, 128). However, this "loss" is regarded as a relatively small price to pay to realize the company's primary aim of exposing its brand and driving traffic to its main portal site. This strategy has paid off handsomely, contributing directly to the parent company's nearly $5 billion USD in annual sales in 2018. Two-thirds of this figure was derived from Naver's primary business activities in both online and mobile environments—its business platform (Search and Search Shopping), advertising (display advertising and video advertising), IT platforms (Naver Pay, Cloud, and Line Works), and content service (Webtoon, V Live, Naver Music, and Naver Series), while one-third was generated from LINE and other apps and platforms, such as its multimedia-sharing app SNOW (Naver Corporation 2019a, 107).

By September 2019 Naver's four international webtoon platforms (Naver Webtoon, Webtoon, Line Manga, and Dongman Manhua) were attracting over sixty million unique readers per month, split almost evenly between domestic and international readers. Accumulated webtoon app downloads reached 150 million, daily visits totaled thirty-two million, users spent an average daily reading time of twenty-seven minutes, and monthly page views reached 10.5 billion. The statistics for the creative side are equally impressive. To date a total of 1,600 professional writer-creators across the globe have developed 3,300 serialized titles. And even more impressive are the 580,000 amateur creators who have published 1.3 million webtoons. At home, in late 2019 a total of 359 "Featured" Korean artists actively uploading weekly content were earning an average income of 310 million KRW (around $275,000 USD). Among this industrious cohort, about 60 percent (221) were earning about 1 billion KRW per year (approximately $888,000 USD). Superstar webtoonists—the top twenty creators—earned 1.75 billion KRW per year (approximately $1.55 million USD).[10]

In all, Naver Webtoon has sustained its leadership position in the industry in terms of the number of content creators, diversity of content, domestic and international readership, and sales and advertising revenue. These are all key elements required to nurture and exploit IP for transmedia adaptations—especially of the kind discussed throughout this book. As a result of this sustained growth, Naver Webtoon Corp. has achieved unprecedented economies of scale and scope, enabling it to innovate research and development from within its company and specialize in different aspects of the production and distribution of webtoons. Its parent company, Naver Corp.—which has been cementing its common ownership of different media sectors (e.g., social media and information-communication apps, character licensing, online and mobile games, film and television production, web and mobile payment, HR, and music)—has also been a strong ally in its expanding business operations. As of September 2018 Naver's growing list of sub-

sidiaries includes the mobile content–aggregation platform Naver Series, which hosts a growing collection of e-books, webtoons, webnovels,
and films.

At the time of writing, Naver is becoming an even more integrated
and diverse enterprise through the establishment of its own film production company, StudioN. Formed in August 2018, and probably in-
centivized by the huge success of the *Along with the Gods* adaptations,
this initiative aims to foster an "IP-bridging" company that will create
transmedia adaptations of the platform's abundant stockpile of creator-
owned stories and characters. These are exemplary materials for extending into live action and animated feature films and into television,
web, and streaming series, as well as into advertisements and other
promotional and marketing tie-ins. According to its website, StudioN
has been busy adapting original webtoons and a select few webnovels
into a slate of new television series and feature films. Television adaptations include thriller *Strangers from Hell* (2019, OCN), comedy *Pegasus
Market* (2019, tvN), thriller-creature-sci-fi *Sweet Home* (to be aired on
Netflix), romantic-comedy *True Beauty* (2020–2021, tvN), drama *Gold
Spoon*, fantasy *Tomorrow*, romantic-comedy *A Good Day to Be a Dog*,
and drama *What She Wants*, as well as original webnovel adaptation
romance *The Romantic, Fake Marriage*. Feature films in various stages
of development include action-thriller *Vigilante*, thriller *Three*, growing-up drama *Your Letter* (animation), action-thriller *Blood for Blood*,
thriller *Ghostwriter*, comedy *The Sound of Your Heart*, comedy-fantasy
Genie of Love, action-drama *Brave Citizen* (published on Comico), and
thriller *Money Game*.

Although the term "dream" does not figure on the StudioN website
(https://studioncorp.com/en), the company's launch is intended as a catalyst for converting webtoon IP into a range of transmedia adaptations—transformations that fill the dreams of many active and aspiring
writer-creators. Naver Webtoon's move in this direction—albeit later
than the authors expected—is one of the most obvious ways of exploiting the enormous cache of IP that the company manages.

CONCLUSION

Comparing Daum Webtoon and Naver Webtoon together is not easy as they are very different enterprises with divergent platform strategies and featured webtoon genres. However, from the beginning, webtoon transmedia-IP pioneers PARK Jeong-seo (CEO and early content producer–editor at Daum Webtoon) and his rival KIM Junkoo (founder and current CEO of Naver Webtoon Corp.)—both well known for their love of comics—helped the giant Daum and Naver search engines establish new streams of traffic and also a new, youthful, identity based on webtoons (Lee 2015). Many of their webtoon series—only a smattering of which are discussed in this book—have become important vehicles for telling stories that not only are interesting to look at and easy to read but also are platforms for critiquing society. The range of genres and visual styles developed across the major webtoon platforms constitutes a significant development in itself. In these and other ways both PARK and KIM, as well as the platforms that they operate, offer us a privileged window through which to view and understanding the rise and development of the webtooniverse—the webtoon industry and the ecosystem it has created. In these ways both companies have established complementary strategies for leveraging untrodden territories and new talent.

The trailblazing contributions made by Naver (and Daum in the first instance) to the monetization of webtoons no doubt inspired other enterprises such as Lezhin Comics (2013) and KakaoPage (2013), which both employed a pay-per-view model from the outset, charging users a small fee to read their webtoons.[11] In turn, the increasing success of these new competitors from 2013—particularly in terms of diversifying and expanding user numbers and generating sales—inspired the rise of a further wave of competitors, including Toptoon and Mr. Blue in 2014 and Toomics, Bomtoon, and Comica in 2015.

Having said that, Naver Webtoon may continue to outpace Daum Webtoon and its other competitors as a result of the strategies discussed in this chapter, especially in terms of the number of listed webtoons and page views. In addition, with the research and support of its parent company, Naver Webtoon has utilized big data to understand the nuanced behavior of its diverse readership and thus maintain a leading position in the industry, especially over its major rival. In particular the launch of its globally facing multilanguage Webtoon site and its mobile apps has enabled Naver to maintain a leading position in Korea and across most of the globe. Taken together, these moves reflect a more aggressive business strategy than that deployed by Daum and most other competitors. Clearly Naver's huge operating budget has been key to the success of Naver Webtoon and its ability to extend its reach far beyond Korea's geographic borders.

This chapter has shed light on the activities initiated by the two oldest enterprises in the vanguard stages of webtoons and the so-called digital comics revolution in Korea. Despite the medium's rapid evolution, 2003 and 2005, as well as 2013, remain watershed years in terms of the emergence and transformation of webtoon enterprises and the industry as a whole—pivotal moments that radically altered how, where, and when readers accessed Korean digital comics. The platforms discussed in this chapter have both contributed to and benefited from new webtoon trends, which continue apace—particularly given the level of governmental as well as private support for more diverse platforms and genres and the exploration of new international markets. These developments have made possible new phases of webtoons in Korea and their spread across the globe. Each new turn in the industry has caught observers off guard: the webtooniverse continues to surprise many who believe that the industry has reached a saturation point. However, as both this book's introduction and conclusion show, newly formed linkages between the gaming and webnovel industries are pushing webtoons into a whole new stratosphere in terms of the diversity of content, creators, platforms, readers, and markets.

5

ASIA'S NEW TITANS OF PAID CONTENT: SECOND-GENERATION WEBTOON PLATFORMS KAKAOPAGE AND LEZHIN COMICS

The industry history and analysis in this chapter builds on the representative cases of Daum Webtoon and Naver Webtoon in chapter 4 by investigating the rise of two of their biggest rivals: KakaoPage and Lezhin Comics. At the same time, we explain some of the strategies and features that make these competing platforms unique among webtoon enterprises.

From the start, both KakaoPage and Lezhin Comics were launched as paid content platforms, especially targeting smartphone users, as opposed to users accessing their websites on a PC. In April 2013 KakaoPage released its iOS mobile and tablet app, and two months later Lezhin Comics joined the field. KakaoPage's service primarily provides content via mobile apps (iOS and Android) and a limited online service via its website for PC users. In fact, the KakaoPage website (https://page.kakao.com/main) offers users a mere taste of its archive of digital content of webtoons and webnovels, as well as a range of other digital contents. It instructs visitors to download the app in order to access the full catalog. As a consequence of the revenue generated via their monetization strategies—that is, by charging readers a fee to access all episodes of their stories—both platforms have avoided becoming dependent on commercial advertisements. In this way—and especially compared to Daum Webtoon and Naver Webtoon, as well as KT's

Ktoon, and NCSoft's Bufftoon—KakaoPage and Lezhin Comics have been able to present themselves as premium services. Yet KakaoPage, like its competitors, has adopted an infrastructure that enables user comment and posting functions, which in turn has facilitated interactivity between consumers and content creators. For its part, Lezhin Entertainment chose a different pathway, eschewing the then-conventional practice of enabling readers to post comments at the end of an episode.

Outside of Daum Webtoon and Naver Webtoon, the KakaoPage and Lezhin platforms are leaders among a growing field of enterprises populating the webtooniverse, including Toptoon, Ktoon, Toomics, Battle Comics, Justoon, Comica, and Comico.

KAKAOPAGE: OFFSPRING OF A DOMINANT PARENT IN THE MOBILESPHERE

This story highlights the beginnings of one of Korea's most successful ICT and mobile services firms: Kakao. As a subsidiary of Kakao, which owed its market dominance in the social media app arena to KakaoTalk (launched in 2010), KakaoPage was designed to be a social media entertainment content aggregator.[1] It procures digital content from other parts of the parent company as well as nonexclusive webtoons from external enterprises and individual providers. From the outset this strategy differentiated KakaoPage from Daum, Naver, and Lezhin Entertainment (hereafter Lezhin), which all focused chiefly on developing and featuring original content produced and/or recruited from within their organizations. KakaoPage was also unique in the sense that it distributed multiple types of mobile content, including vertically scrolling webtoons and page-turning digital comics (i.e., scanlation), as well as a spectrum of short and long-form videos and webnovels, plus music and songs. Actually, KakaoPage only began releasing original content (under the brand of Kakao Original) in 2019.

Podotree, the initial operator of KakaoPage, was established in mid-2010 as a start-up developer of multilingual education applications. Working with Kakao CEO KIM Beom-soo (one of the original founders of NHN), Podotree CEO LEE Jin-soo expanded the company with umbrella control of both KakaoPage and later Daum Webtoon. This created a new hierarchy and branding opportunity—although, as discussed in chapter 4, Daum Webtoon continues to maintain its own identity. Between 2010 and 2015 Podotree maintained a high degree of control over the recruitment of new employees and the direction of its operations budget, thereby maintaining the traditional restrictions on the organization's decision-making processes. In 2015 Podotree was officially merged with Kakao as a content business subsidiary, and in 2018 it was rebranded under the name KakaoPage (the same name as its platform).[2]

As a subsidiary of Kakao, KakaoPage undertook to provide a paid webtoon service as well as a larger quantity of other paid content than was offered by its primary competitors, Naver Webtoon and Daum Webtoon (which ceased to be a rival after the merger between Daum Communications and Kakao in May 2014). Given that the Yahoo! Korea and Paran search engines ceased operation in 2012, the introduction of KakaoPage was a welcomed addition to the webtoon industry. As a new enterprise, KakaoPage brought the promise of increased stability and financial strength as well as a new distribution channel to the sector, all backed by a giant ICT and mobile-services firms. It also implemented a robust monetization model from its beginnings, serving the interests of content creators in a way that distinguished it from all other webtoon platforms. By concentrating on mobile transactions, KakaoPage adapted the conventional profit-sharing model associated with in-app purchases, dividing sales profits between Google Play/App store (30 percent), KakaoPage (20 percent), and webtoon content creators and IP owners (50 percent) (Wee 2013). In theory, once proven successful in terms of sustained content and the mobilization of readers willing to pay for each episode, the new KakaoPage digital market space would generate an amount equal to or in excess of an average monthly salary.

Following its launch, KakaoPage was reportedly hosting eight thousand separate items created by over five hundred amateur and professional practitioners as well as corporate publishers. The high-profile media stars whose names were used to promote the launch of the new KakaoPage mobile platform included singer-songwriter and music producer YOON Jong-shin, K-pop boy band 2AM (2008–2014), and master cartoonist HUH Young-man, who has released over fifty print comic book titles since the late 1970s. Celebrity hairstylist CHA Hong and well-known novelist JUNG Ihyun also joined this initial lineup of content creators. YOON and 2AM's music, HUH's webtoon, CHA's hairstyling video clips, and JUNG's webnovel represent only a fraction of the top-flight paid social media content that KakaoPage hosted to lure new customers. A constant and regularized feed of this type of serialized content was expected to attract a new generation of mobile media natives, thus drawing users away from other platforms.

In particular, comic master HUH, who debuted in the mid-1970s, used this new mobile platform to steer his career in a new direction by creating a digital sequel to his popular print comic *Sikgaek* (2002–2010, twenty-seven books), which had originally appeared in serial form in daily newspapers. HUH aimed to attract his comic book fans to his new webtoon and to KakaoPage and at the same time to introduce his work to a new generation of comic readers who had grown up with the webtoon format. *Sikgaek* is a drama in which the eponymous protagonist pits his culinary skills against rival chefs. He travels the country looking for outstanding Korean foods and dishes, seeking opportunities to share his knowledge and challenge others with his cooking skills. With its classic recipes and ingredients, and attention paid to the historical and cultural background of particular dishes and the stories of the people that make them, *Sikgaek* has become Korea's outstanding food comic. It has been adapted into a number of films and television shows, including *Le Grand Chef* (2007), *Le Grand Chef 2: Kimchi War* (2009), and television series *Gourmet* (2008).

It seemed the right time to add a webtoon adaptation to the existing transmedia portfolio of HUH's work. Each episode in the series was priced at 500 KRW (just over 40 US cents)—more than twice as much as readers pay to see a webtoon episode on Daum Webtoon created by master webtoonists KANG Full or YOON Tae-ho. In adopting this revenue model, KakaoPage challenged the conventional notion of webtoons as a source of free content. Moving to revenue-sharing from in-app purchases was a paradigm shift welcomed by content creators and others across the industry.

Cartoonist HUH expressed high hopes for the new monetization system established by KakaoPage and its promise of remunerating practitioners exclusively via reader payments, rather than directly by the platforms themselves. Prior to creating his *Sikgaek* webtoon series for KakaoPage, HUH had contacted multiple publishing companies, food enterprises, and government bodies, but no one had been willing to cover the costs involved in reenvisioning his series in print format. Thus a digital comics version, or webtoon, became the most viable option for him. In taking this route, and as an ambassador for KakaoPage, HUH was advocating for a major change in attitudes and beliefs about the economic value of webtoons (and comics in general) and the people who make them. In HUH's own words, the challenge he faced to transition from print to digital was a matter of desperation rather than anything else.[3] At the same time, it presented an opportunity to blaze a new pathway for the next generation of cartoonists by engaging with a company willing to offer financially stable working conditions to experienced as well as amateur creators.

Nevertheless, and despite the best efforts by ambassadors YOON, 2AM, HUH, CHA, and JUNG, it did take longer and prove to be more difficult for KakaoPage to reverse well-entrenched perceptions about webtoons as a free service. The rising wave of paying readers envisaged at first seemed like a mirage. Only three months after its launch, KakaoPage was being spoken of by its practitioners as a failure. In July 2013 some frustrated content creators staged a boycott of KakaoPage, refusing to upload any new content; they were extremely disappointed in the new platform's failure to secure a base of subscribers (or registered users) and thus a reliable income stream. Creator expectations were so high that in June 2013 HUH publicly expressed regret for the time he had spent developing and uploading his new series *Sikgaek* 2 on KakaoPage, given the minimal sales it had generated. Participating companies also ceased to upload their webtoon series and other digital contents on KakaoPage, in view of the poor sales figures (Jung 2013). As the authors have learned from numerous conversations with company executives and practitioners, pessimism about the monetization of mobile webtoon content led industry players and content creators alike to direct their attention back to Naver Webtoon and Daum Webtoon, which were thriving on the old pay-per-click models that they had established over the past decade.

In order to survive this crisis, KakaoPage required a radical change in its platform infrastructure, the numbers of loyal users on its iOS and Android apps, and the ways that the platform was integrated with the popular KakaoTalk social media app. They found that the mobile payment system was complicated, making it difficult for readers to purchase content, that and users had difficulty accessing the company's content across multiple devices. KakaoPage had yet to offer users a seamless experience when switching between smartphones, tablets, and PCs. Furthermore, the built-in recommendation function—absolutely necessary for KakaoTalk friends to signpost and share likes and ratings—would require a more user-friendly design to be truly successful. Although KakaoPage had been eager to leverage the millions of users and their social networks swarming around the KakaoTalk app, this was far from happening (Ahn 2013). In other words, it would take more than Kakao's brand name alone to make KakaoPage viable on all the desired levels. Hence over the next few years KakaoPage did its research and then worked to continuously update its platform infrastructure; this effort enhanced user experience while establishing a revised monetization model featuring a combination of free and paid content.

In late 2013, as an alternative to shutting down the whole operation, KakaoPage totally revamped its platform infrastructure, including the payment service and business structure, as well as the type of content featured. The new and improved KakaoPage focused on aggregating webtoons and webnovels, significantly reducing other social media entertainment, including music, short videos, and feature films. This new emphasis on webtoons and webnovels with arresting stories across a variety of genres proved key to expanding the platform's user base. Numbers of new users began increasing gradually, especially after KakaoPage began hosting bite-sized chapters of the popular novel *The Legendary Moonlight Sculptor* (2007–2019), written by NAM Heesung (his fifth novel) in October 2013. The company seemed to be turning the corner.

Looking back, hosting *The Legendary Moonlight Sculptor* was an important move for KakaoPage, as it almost singlehandedly resuscitated the struggling platform. To modify this series for its platform, KakaoPage recast the original fifty-eight-volume novel into a webnovel series divided into 1,450 bite-sized chapters. Each chapter was (and still is) offered for 100 KRW (around 9 US cents)—a significant reduction from its initial price of 500 KRW for content. Based on the rapid uptake of viewings, readers couldn't read the webnovel in its new episodic format fast enough. Munpia, a Korean webnovel platform launched in 2012 (and now owned in part by Tencent's China Literature and Korea's giant NCSoft video game firm), had employed a similar pay-per-chapter monetization model, and KakaoPage was likely inspired by this precedent.

The Legendary Moonlight Sculptor follows protagonist LEE Hyeon as he journeys through a massive multiplayer online role-playing game (MMORPG) called *Royal Road*. In the novel, *Royal Road* is an extremely popular VR game world created by gaming company Unicorn. To make a living, LEE decides to become a gamer and enters *Royal Road* under the character name Weed. Weed undertakes a job as a sculptor and becomes known as the "legendary moonlight sculptor" after successfully leveling up by completing a series of quests. Similar to the setup in the novel (and film) *Ready Player One* (2011), Weed must compete in a gaming world that is accessible only by wearing VR gear and playing in a VR capsule. However, any rewards gained in this cyber world can be used in the real world—hence its appeal to LEE, who is obsessed with getting his grandmother and sister (and himself) out their life of poverty and debt. Lee's rise as a skillful and powerful player in *Royal Road* leads him to acquire wealth and fame in the real world.

In its guise as a literary role-playing game (aka LitRPG) novel combining the conventions of role-playing games with fantasy novels, *The Legendary Moonlight Sculptor* had already achieved bestseller status following its original release in 2007, selling over six hundred thousand copies before being adapted as a webnovel by KakaoPage in October 2013. Supported by its already large literary fan base, *The Legendary Moonlight Sculptor* was an ideal candidate for transmedia adaptation. Since the release of this webnovel, it has been further adapted as a serialized Korean-language webtoon published in early 2015 under the same name on KakaoPage and later in English on KakaoPage's North American partner platform, Tapastic, in October 2016. This title was KakaoPage's first attempt to adapt a popular webnovel to the webtoon format, a process that KakaoPage now calls its integrated "novel comics" business model. Adapted by LEE Do-Kyung and illustrated by KIM Tae-Hyung, the same-titled webtoon consists of 131 episodes (as of November 2019).

The Legendary Moonlight Sculptor was KakaoPage's earliest and most sustained megahit IP. Initially in 2013 it attracted 7.8 million returning paying readers across its webnovel and webtoon series, and by January 2020 this adapted IP had clocked up 370 million cumulative views (Ahn 2020). In October 2019 Kakao Games also released a mobile MMORPG game of the same name based on the fictitious *Royal Road* game, and the webtoon's original score "I Will Give You All" (sung by popular vocalist LEE Seung Chul) and a music video (starring Korean Wave heartthrob PARK Bo-gum) were released by Kakao's music subsidiary Kakao M (formerly LOEN Entertainment) in January 2020.

To supplement its new content strategy, KakaoPage eventually decided on a hybrid payment method featuring a "free-if-you-wait" strategy, which differed from the free and paid models on Naver Webtoon and Daum Webtoon, respectively. This alternative and more flexible monetization model, inspired by one used in popular gaming apps, offered a few episodes of a particular series for free, as bait to hook a reader's interest in a particular webtoon (and webnovel) series. With some titles available under this plan, additional and archived episodes were released for free after a certain period, and at various times. This hybrid system enabled the platform to publicize both known and fresh webtoons with special monthly promotions, adding a sense of excitement and buzz to the site. Fast-passes were available to those who craved early access to the newest episodes. Ultimately this mixed approach to revenue gathering, supplemented with giveaways and cash rewards, encouraged readers to keep returning to the site. Users never knew what they might find for free on KakaoPage on any given day.

Perhaps most importantly in this area, KakaoPage has benefitted immensely from the highly successful mobile payment app, Kakao Pay, that the parent company launched in 2014. No other webtoon enterprise (apart from Naver and its Naver Pay—launched in mid-2015, roughly nine months after the introduction of Kakao Pay) has its own proprietary payment infrastructure and app. This makes it difficult for KakaoPage's competitors to integrate with their operations, while third-party systems such as PayPal or Apple Pay are expensive. Due to the exclusivity of this pay app, it is impossible for outsiders to track KakaoPage's (and Naver's) revenue rankings from the Android Playstore. In turn, utilizing a mobile payment system has enabled KakaoPage to achieve (and process) a level of sales that few other platforms have matched thus far.

According to KakaoPage's celebrated list of 110 "million-page" webtoon titles (the total as of February 2020)—defined as a series that has generated either a million users or a million dollars in profit—the company's leading titles (with their registered user numbers in millions in brackets) include the romantic comedy *What's Wrong with Secretary Kim?* (615), fantasy-romances *Bride of Habaek* (577) and *They Say I Am Born as a King's Daughter* (289), romances *Emperor's Only Daughter* (392) and *Imitation* (364), boys' love's (BL) *Hot Blood* (382), vampire romance *Honey Blood* (273), zombie-action *Dreamside* (181), LitRPG fantasies *The Legendary Moonlight Sculptor* (241) and *Solo Leveling* (211), and fantasy–medical drama *Doctor Choi Tae Soo* (220). An increasing number of titles are appearing as both a webtoon and webnovel adaptation, including *What's Wrong with Secretary Kim?*, which is available in the site's Novel Comics area. This title is also available for streaming on KakaoPage as a live-action web drama, divided into 112 segments of ten minutes each—derived from the original sixteen-episode television series on tvN (2018). Extending the transmedia IP of its content—that is, producing multiple adaptations from a single source—is now one of KakaoPage's key strategies, and one that most rival webtoon enterprises aspire to emulate. It is no wonder that industry people often call this transmedia content a "Super-IP."

While KakaoPage was expanding within Korea, Kakao, its parent company, was busy expanding in Asia through a particular international collaboration strategy, revealing yet another dimension of the webtooniverse. Although Kakao's expansion overseas occurred later than Naver's international activities, its trajectory offers an equally interesting story—and one that involves "blending in."

GLOCAL LIKE A CHAMELEON...

In April 2016 Kakao Japan, Kakao's Japanese subsidiary, launched a new digital comic service called Piccoma, utilizing KakaoPage's free-if-you-wait monetization model, which had by then become an industry convention. In addition to offering a large number of Japanese manga titles—representing around 120 Japanese writers and publishing firms—Piccoma also offered a few popular Korean titles (roughly 2 percent of the platform's total titles at first, and slowly rising since then) (Park 2020). Among these exemplary Korean titles introduced to Japanese readers in their own language were YOON Tae-ho's *Misaeng*, CHON Kye-young's *Love Alarm*, and MEEN/BAEK Seung-hoon's

Tong series. In addition to being translated, these and other Korean webtoons were subtly localized—for instance, by giving Korean characters Japanese names, changing Korean signage to Japanese, and also translating some familiar exclamations into Japanese. This attention to detail, or what we might consider "adding cultural odor" to the text, demonstrated Kakao's interest in maintaining a strong relationship with the established Japanese publishing and digital media industries while positioning Piccoma as a platform for mostly Japanese content.

But because Piccoma was presented as a Japanese platform, it created an opportunity to introduce Korean content to a Japanese audience that had been fiercely loyal to its diet of manga and anime content—the products of an industry that had long shut out foreigners due to an inflexible production and publication system that is still rigorously maintained by Japanese industry leaders (Oh and Koo 2018). However, Piccoma was able to successfully challenge these hidebound traditions—precisely because of the large percentage of Japanese content that it featured. As a result, Kakao succeeded in creating new revenue streams for both the parent Korean firm as well as its partner Japanese publishers and local content creators—all by blending in like a chameleon.

Resembling a local app is one of the most effective strategies for success adopted by Korean app developers in Japan. Naver's LINE social-messaging app, for instance, is one of the most widely used communication apps in Japan—and, as far as we know, Japanese users believe that it is a Japanese-originated platform. According to a report released by Statista in February 2020, between 2013 and 2019 the number of monthly active users on LINE in Japan reached a peak of eighty-three million at the end of 2019 (Statista Research Department 2020). To further maximize appeal to Japanese readers and Japan's well-established manga market, Piccoma featured most of its content in a traditional horizontal page-turning format, the most common format outside of Korea. It also broke its various series up into small bite-size chapters—a feature that matched the chapter system of traditional manga.

Since mid-2016 Piccoma has gradually expanded its offerings and the size of its operation in Japan. In 2018 it became the most downloaded manga app in both the Google Play Store and App Store in Japan. Between April 2018 and April 2019, the amount of manga content available on Piccoma rose from 2,205 to 6,727 items, feeding the daily readership appetites of over 2.2 million Japanese readers (Lee, Park, and Kim 2019). Throughout 2019 Piccoma was the second-highest-grossing manga (comics) app in Japan, following Naver's LINE Manga app in top position.[4] Today Piccoma features a wide variety of genre titles and styles, including sci-fi and alternative worlds, reincarnation fantasy, drama, adult comics, romance, infidelity/adultery, light novel, BL, manga magazines, horror-mystery, action, sports, and slice-of-life. Other transmedia content on their platform includes digital comics adapted from popular television shows, such as *Prison Break*.

In early 2019, in a move designed to boost mobile traffic and sales, which were both slow to take off, platform content managers borrowed KakaoPage's strategy of recruiting famous practitioners and celebrities to both contribute to and promote the site. Piccoma recruited MATSU-MOTO Leiji—now in his early eighties—well known for directing science-fiction anime space-opera series *Space Battleship Yamato* (1974) and also for writing and illustrating manga series *Galaxy Express 999* (1977–1981).

MATSUMOTO was given the challenge of working with coauthor WACHI Masaki and artist Anajiro to create an exclusive new manga series, *Dokuganryū Masamune: Sengoku no Arcadia Gaiden*, based on MATSUMOTO's well-known manga character Captain Harlock.[5] As of early 2020 the series contained 31 episodes—all presented in a vertically scrolling format—with the first three episodes free to view. Remaining episodes can be unlocked (also for free for a limited time) after readers register for an account. Within four months this Japanese series was celebrated as a triumph in Korea, justifying Kakao's aggressive leap into the Japanese market (via Piccoma) and its "big bet" on luring Japanese fans away from manga and toward webtoons (Lee, Park, and Kim 2019).

Of course the jury is still out regarding Kakao and Piccoma's long-term success in this area. However, Kakao's foray into the supposedly impregnable Japanese market is based on both the Korean technology underpinning the Piccoma platform and on content that is, to borrow the language of a study of Japanese games, "so blatantly rooted in Japan that it becomes the opposite of *mukokuseki* [nonnationality]—ultra-*kokuseki* [ultranationality]" (Hutchinson 2019, 25). A truly transnational move on Kakao's part, albeit involving collaboration with Japanese companies, Piccoma's initiative has now firmly "put Japan's print manga on notice" (Osaki 2019).

Back home—and like its major rival, Naver—Kakao has sustained efforts to exploit a vast collective archive of IP represented by its webtoons and webnovels published on KakaoPage and Daum Webtoons. The primary aim is to collect materials for an "IP engine" that transforms and adapts them into live-action and animated feature films, television dramas, and online and mobile games. Rather than restrict itself to selling or licensing the remake rights from its IP catalog, or work with a third-party producer, Kakao has assumed the role of a transmedia producer and is thus expanding its operations through vertical and horizontal integration.

Kakao further expanded its closely integrated services in early 2016 after it acquired LOEN Entertainment, a combined record label, music publisher, talent agency, and event-management company. Seemingly overnight the new organization (which was rebranded as Kakao M in early 2018) diversified into a mobile video–production company, Krispy Studio. Then, in mid-2017 it acquired the television production company Mega Monster, forming a new joint venture with CJ ENM and its subsidiary Studio Dragon. Kakao M's new coventure with CJ ENM predated Naver's StudioN by more than a year. One of the first projects that Mega Monster coproduced was the romantic-comedy television series *Touch Your Heart* (2019), based on the webnovel of the same name published in 2016 by KakaoPage (which in early 2020 had an approval rating of 9.9/10 and 403,000 active readers). *Touch Your Heart* was also adapted into a fifty-six-episode webtoon in 2019. Studio Dragon and Mega Monster jointly produced the adapted television drama, which was aired on CJ ENM's tvN and its original soundtrack released by Kakao M.

In recent times Kakao M has been vocal about the company's aspirations to produce a slate of original content, and even to put Netflix on notice (Baek 2019). However, after Studio Dragon signed a three-year partnership deal with Netflix in late 2019 for exclusive content distributorship, Kakao M has found itself in bed with Netflix rather than competing directly with the streaming giant. Kakao M's production momentum and industry integration was strengthened further after it acquired three new entertainment-management agencies (BH Entertainment, J Wide, and SOOP) as well as the Ready Entertainment talent agency in September 2019 with a view to leveraging a growing pool of talent. A further step toward achieving this aim was reached in September 2019 when Kakao M acquired a large share in two film production companies, Moonlight Film and Sanai Pictures, both of which had a reputation for producing genre hit films. Moonlight Film, for instance, had produced the historical action movie *Kundo: Age of the Rampant* (2014), which had racked up one of the highest opening-day box-office totals for either a foreign or domestic film released in Korea, and the crime-action drama *A Violent Prosecutor* (2016), which had become the second-highest-grossing Korean film of 2016. Sanai Pictures was already known for the gangster noir *New World* (2013) and crime-action film *Asura: The City of Madness* (2016)—both of which are critically acclaimed.

The Kakao story is unlikely to end here. In 2020 exploiting the vast range of webtoon (and webnovel) titles in the archives of Daum Webtoon and KakaoPage is the primary focus of all of Kakao's subsidiaries, including Kakao M. In 2019 a television adaptation of *Love Alarm* by CHON Kye-young was the first Korean webtoon to be adapted and distributed as a Netflix original (excluding the historical horror-thriller zombie series *Kingdom* (2019–2020), which is based on the *Kingdom of the Gods* comic book). A slate of new film adaptations is in the works, building on the recent coming-of-age drama *Start-Up* (2019, based on the 2014–2016 webtoon of the same name) and comedy-drama *Secret Zoo* (2020, based on the 2011–2012 webtoon *Won't Hurt You*). Other adaptations for television series include thriller mysteries *Memorist* (2016–2018) and *Dead Man's Letter* (2019–2020), teenage romantic drama *July Found by Chance* (2018–2019), and start-up drama *Itaewon Class* (2016–2018). *July Found by Chance*, which aired in October 2019 (under the new title *Extraordinary You*), is the story of several cartoon characters in high school who are on an existential journey to break free from their cartoon world. By early 2020 *Itaewon Class*, starring Korean Wave celebrity PARK Seo-joon, had gone to air; this K-drama follows an ex-convict who rebuilds his life by creating a successful food company with his friends while seeking revenge on his father's killers.

Transmedia adaptation looks set to be the future for this super mobile and social media entertainment company, and it is aiming to penetrate global markets through its own efforts as a producer as well as its numerous deals with Netflix.

UNICORN AMONG THE PACK: LEZHIN ENTERTAINMENT

Emerging in 2013, Lezhin Entertainment has weathered many of the webtoon industry's growing pains—some of which the company has brought on itself. The enterprise was hatched in early 2012 by programmer KWON Jeong-hyuk and power blogger HAN Hee Sung (whose online nickname was "Lezhin"). Aiming at creating something more like KakaoPage than Naver Webtoon and Daum Webtoon, the pair worked to establish a mobile-friendly and fully monetized webtoon platform they called Lezhin Comics.

Between May 2012 and mid-2013 KWON (CTO) and HAN (CEO) received funding through both an angel investor and several Korean government channels, resulting in the successful launch of the first paid specialized webtoon platform. Lezhin received 30 million KRW (about $27,000 USD) in angel seed funding from the Korean Big Bang Angels Accelerator (established in 2012). Korean Big Bang Angels Accelerator aimed to nurture "unicorn" start-ups that focused on developing innovative industrial ecosystems into various companies worth over $1 billion USD.

Unlike most of its peers, which have relied heavily on revenues generated by user traffic and e-commerce, Lezhin Comics initially had received financial and in-kind support from the Korean government. Both the Ministry of Culture, Sports and Tourism (MCST) and the Ministry of Science, ICT and Future Planning (MSIT) played a key role in the enterprise's early days, especially in terms of financial backing, business matching, and networking support (see table 5.1.) This cross-ministry support enabled Lezhin and a select number of other emerging digital-media enterprises in the webtoon and other industry sectors to develop both content and technical infrastructure for their businesses. From a policy perspective (covered in greater detail in chapter 3), MCST was seeking to diversify distribution channels, a move seen as necessary to the further development of the then-nascent webtoon industry.

As a new start-up initiative, Lezhin Entertainment won support from MSIT after presenting a detailed globalization plan for its new webtoon platform (*Korea's Policy Briefing* 2013; Jo 2014). At the time, the PARK Geun-hye government (2013–2017) was seeking ways to boost Korea's creative economy, and Lezhin found itself in the right

Table 5.1. Government Funding and Other Support Received by Lezhin Entertainment in 2013

Funding title	Funding body	Details
2013 New Talents Recruit Management (Small-to-Medium Media) Support	KOCCA & MCST	100,000,000 KRW (approx. $94,500 USD)
2013 Comics Production Support for Global Comics (Short/Medium Length and Long Narrative Series)	KOCCA & MCST	50,000,000 KRW (approx. $47,250 USD)
Global Operational Foundation Support	KOCCA & MCST	Overseas smart-content platform-service infrastructure support
2013 One Man Business Center Support	KOCCA & MCST	Workspace support
Global K-Start-Up Program	Korea Internet & Security Agency (under MSIT)	3 million KRW/month, for 5 months (approx. $2,800 USD), plus other cash rewards
2013 Global New Business Consulting Support	Global Start-Up Center (under MSIT)	Consulting support for overseas expansion

Source: Korea.net 2013

place at the right time to benefit from government support. In turn, according to James KIM (former Lezhin Entertainment president and head of US Business Development and Marketing)—with whom the authors spoke in Seoul in January 2018, this government aid gave Lezhin Comics newfound credibility, assisting the company in its recruitment of creators to its then-little-known platform while also making it easier to attract private funding sources.

In April 2014 Lezhin received 5 billion KRW (approximately $4.8 million USD) in venture capital (Series A) investment from major Korean gaming company NCSoft, which had launched its own Bufftoon webtoon platform in 2013. This cash injection enabled Lezhin to develop the necessary infrastructure and translation services to enter the Japanese and then the US markets. It also signaled gaming giant NCSoft's continuing interest in the webtoon industry and its potential as an incubator for transmedia IP spin-offs and adaptations. This government support, NCSoft's backing, and an increasing customer base of 1.3 million subscribers in its first year of operation all positioned Lezhin Comics as a competitive webtoon platform (Song 2014). Following Naver and Daum, Lezhin was now the third-ranking company in Korea's webtoon market, earning it the reputation as the most successful startup of 2013. Against all odds—why would readers pay for webtoons when they had been accessible for free over the past decade?—Lezhin blazed a new trail for other paid webtoon enterprises in a market dominated by Naver and Daum.

Lezhin Comics' aspirations and expectations for the enterprise were very high from the start, and this injection of government funding was seen as way of introducing competition into the webtoon industry, as alternatives to Daum and Naver.

The strategy adopted by the two entrepreneurs and their investor-mentors was to position the Lezhin Comics start-up as an alternative enterprise, targeting a notable gap in the webtoon industry: fee-based mature and adult content for Korean and international readers. Lezhin Comics launched its Android webtoon app in Korea with forty series in June 2013, followed by an iOS app two months later, and then a website in September 2013 (https://www.lezhin.com/ko). All three elements of the platform utilized a cohesive monetization model that required readers to pay a small fee to access all content. The profits resulting from this revenue stream, at least initially, were shared with creators on a 90/10 split in favor of the creators (reduced to a 70/30 split in early 2015). As we have seen in relation to KakaoPage's model, this fee-based system (and the large share of the profits enjoyed by creators) was a radical departure from the practice followed by Daum Webtoon and Naver Webtoon, which had been offering free webtoons for around a decade. Despite the general expectation that webtoons should be viewed for free, however, Lezhin successfully launched a pay-to-view model. Today this payment system has shifted to a hybrid model, involving a mixture of pay-to-view plus free-if-you-wait content (the model adopted by KakaoPage).

To jump-start a new community of digital comic readers, Lezhin targeted HAN's existing online blog followers, which he had amassed through his outspoken and humorous commentary on films, sports, and sex. At the same time, Lezhin began recruiting writer-creators attempting to make a name for themselves—for example, in Naver Webtoon's Best Challenge section. Established in 2006 (see chapter 4), the Best Challenge section on the Naver Webtoon platform was essentially an incubator for semi-professional webtoonists. There was intense competition among this ever-increasing cohort of aspiring practitioners—a pool of talent that Lezhin Comics identified and was eager to harness.

Lezhin was able to offer both established and aspiring creators working in the mature- and adult-content area new opportunities to display their serialized work and also to earn an income. As anticipated, many practitioners from Naver Webtoon's Best Challenge section began migrating to Lezhin Comics, bringing their ideas and realized webtoon series with them. CTO KWON, who grew up reading comics in his mother's comic book shop, designed and managed Lezhin's UX (user experience) section, enabling Lezhin Comics to become new webtoon service with a unique place among the small number of existing platforms in Korea. There is no doubt that Lezhin Comics benefited from CTO KWON's range of skills as an IT developer and from his experience with mobile navigation-mapping software and cloud infrastructure. Under KWON's direction, and as a result of his charismatic technoevangelism, Lezhin innovated a simple-payment system using virtual coins that could be purchased through a variety of payment methods including in-app purchases (Android and iOS), local and international credit cards, and special vouchers issued by Lezhin and a range of participating merchant partners. In these ways, unlike KakaoPage, Lezhin succeeded in gaining rapid user acceptance of paid webtoons on its sites, as well as pioneering a new concept for the broader industry.

Not only did users have to pay for content, but Lezhin also initiated a no-advertisement and no-comments policy on their mobile apps and website, further distinguishing the platform from its competitors. Commenting capabilities had been an established feature of Web 2.0 and a long-standing tradition that Daum and Naver had inaugurated a decade earlier. Lezhin's decision to exclude these features differentiated it from its larger rivals and underscored its aim (and promise) to deliver a "premium," advertising-free viewing experience to readers who had been regularly exposed to comments—including negative material—at the end of an episode on other platforms. For their part, creators were intrigued by this radical departure from tradition and the new degree of freedom it offered them to experiment with mature and adult genres without being trolled by readers. Lezhin also welcomed work across all genres.

Ease of accessibility between its mobile app and online site, a simple payment process, and high-quality paid content were the primary sell-

ing points of Lezhin Comics and its UX, which was designed to habitu-
ate readers, encourage purchases, and attract continuous traffic to its
platform (Kim 2015). While KakaoPage had the same goals, Lezhin
succeeded at the start—whereas its competitor had almost failed—with
a relatively fast and reliable mobile-service and -payment system. Likely
due to its smaller size and insulation from the type of bureaucracy
endemic to large corporations such as Kakao, Lezhin readily overcame
related technical challenges. In its first month of operations, Lezhin
reportedly exceeded a turnover of 100 million KRW (approximately
$90,000 USD), maintaining a steady growth rate of 20 percent over the
next six months (Han 2013). As KWON and HAN had predicted, Koreans were ready and able to purchase quality content, providing it was
easy to access.

The launch of Lezhin Comics offered food for thought to both webtoon readers and established and new practitioners, who had mixed
feelings about the missing user-comment feature that was a staple on
other platforms at the time. On the one hand—according to our conversations with well-known creators YOON Tae-ho and LEE Jong-beom,
as well as published responses by webtoonists such as HA Il-kwon and
Neon B—positive reader comments posted at the end of an episode
were welcome; reader feedback and reviews (both good and bad) were
seen as "precious hidden treasure."[6] Conventionally, the commenting
feature had facilitated an immediate and intimate bond between creators and their fans—a two-way connection difficult to generate and
maintain with other, especially nonconvergent, media. On the other
hand, reader comments had often caused stress and consternation for
many practitioners. Not only had creators felt pressured to respond to
hundreds of thousands of fans and their posted comments, reflections,
and suggestions for improvement, but negative (often offensive) comments on webtoon platforms had been hard to monitor. Malicious comments containing personal attacks on the webtoon creators, which had
nothing to do with the webtoon itself, had disrupted the platform's
demanding daily and weekly deadlines, as well as the mental health of
the creators.

In the end, Lezhin's radical no-comments policy was welcomed by
creators, especially those working at the more controversial end of the
webtoon-genre spectrum, including BL and girls' love (GL)—portraying homoerotic relationships between same-sex characters, gore, and

mystery, as well as semi-erotic romance fantasy and adult-thriller series. Still, many creators on Lezhin Comics and other platforms were happy to utilize Twitter, Facebook, and Chinese social media app Weibo, as well as their own personal websites and blogs, to maintain active communication with their fans.

As a result of the cyberbullying, which Lezhin's action was designed to remove, some webtoon readers have made a bad name for themselves and other fans over the years. In 2015, after a short break following his father's death, KANG Full received so many malicious and offensive comments. He collected a number of them and filed suit against the people who had posted them in response to his series *Moving* (Min-ji Jin 2015). LEE Jong-beom and his family also suffered personally as a result of negative comments posted during his work on season 3 of *Dr Frost* (2015–2016), leading him to take time out before returning in 2019 with season 4. A special investigation of the negative comments that webtoonists regularly receive, undertaken in 2019, describes the cyber environment as a "jungle thick with malicious comments" (Park 2019). The report places the blame on platforms that maintain the right to oversee and gatekeep user comments; clearly, effective editorial staff and AI software (e.g., Naver's CleanBot) that automatically filter offensive UGC remain in short supply. As a result, this problem persists today—for platforms other than Lezhin, of course.

Another element contributing to the success of Lezhin Comics is its four-pronged "artist-friendly" policy. First, Lezhin initially offered creators a much higher percentage of the platform's sales profits than nearly all other platforms. Second, Lezhin undertook to accept a wider range of adult subject matter than was available on Daum Webtoon and Naver Webtoon, introducing greater creative freedom of expression. Third, Lezhin Comics offered creators access to an editorial team with experience in the comic-publishing industry, especially with polishing stories and refining plots. As far as we know, the largest Daum Webtoon and Naver Webtoon platforms lacked such expertise and manpower, although editorial input was common among smaller platforms such as Mr. Blue, which utilized a small team of in-house producers to help coach creators and edit their content. Fourth, Lezhin Comics maintained a high level of image quality by setting the resolution of all artwork at 720 pixels (on its mobile app), while many other webtoon platforms only required a resolution of 530 pixels. For creators such as

NOTZ, a winner of the 2014 Naver Webtoon Competition and creator of the webtoon *I Throw Myself at You* (2020) on the Naver Series platform, this higher image quality accentuated the nuanced colors and details of illustrations in ways that other platforms failed to achieve. Lezhin also offered readers a choice of scrolling vertically or horizontally, catering to individual viewing preferences and offering flexibility with device screen sizes. (KakaoPage also offers readers these two viewing choices.)

As a part of its "artist-friendly" policy, Lezhin flouted industry convention by permitting creators to upload completed episodes on a weekly or ten-day basis. Breaking away (at least initially) from the strict weekly workflow deadlines demanded by Daum and Naver permitted Lezhin's creators to take a little more time to produce better quality work—part of the company's strategy for increasing traffic, sales, and registered users and thus the size of its active fan base. Writer-illustrator LEE Yul debuted on Lezhin Comics with the drama *A Compendium of Ghosts* (2013–2019), a series about mythical Korean divinities set against a backdrop of intricate traditional artwork. The color composition and traditional art illustrations in this series, which received the 2013 KOCCA Korean Content Award, are so complex that LEE required double the conventional weekly time frame to complete each episode. Because Lezhin was flexible, and appreciated the merits of LEE's style, it offered him a biweekly uploading strategy. Such generous scheduling was foreign to other platforms such as Daum Webtoon and Naver Webtoon. (As of early 2020 a registered subscriber could unlock one free episode of *A Compendium of Ghosts* each day or use three Lezhin virtual coins to read any one episode in real time.) As a result of these "artist-friendly" strategies, a small army of professional and amateur creators migrated to Lezhin Comics, eager to upload their serialized work onto its platform.

Meanwhile, in mid-2015 Lezhin began offering all creators a set payment (i.e., "minimum guarantee") each month in addition to a lower share (50/50 split) of sales profits than previously offered (i.e., a 70/30 split in favor of the artists). While this initiative had some logical basis, it actually caused considerable debate and contestation among creators and other industry representatives. Because Lezhin Comics was a paid webtoon platform, its revenue-sharing system promised creators a potential (but not necessarily larger) stream of income than was available from the Daum Webtoon and Naver Webtoon platforms. These two other platforms required that a creator (and their series) be successful in terms of readership figures—that is, that they be a "Featured" artist—before they were eligible to receive a salary and revenue-sharing payments (see chapter 4). Yet the industry's deployment of a minimum guarantee was (and still is) different from the same named system used in the film industry; film producers receiving a minimum guarantee usually keep all of these proceeds no matter how much a film earns at the box office, thereby shifting most of the risk to the distributor. In reality, even in 2020 amateur and aspiring webtoonists such as NOTZ remain skeptical of the minimum-guarantee model due to its complexities. The authors interviewed NOTZ on several occasions between 2017 and 2020, and he explained his understanding and concerns: if a webtoon's profit falls short of minimum guarantee expectations, then the creator, rather than the platform, is "liable" for the so-called loss. On the one hand, this system offers the potential for a regularized income structure for the average webtoonist. On the other, it poses a kind of debt imposed on the creator who needs to keep working for the platform until their series (or the next series) can generate enough sales to cover the minimum-guarantee payment advanced to them. Nonetheless, regardless of the "success" of their series, creators debuting on Lezhin Comics earned a basic wage, albeit a wage with conditions. In turn, this drew an expanding pool of new talent interested in developing a sustainable career in webtoons. Previously, most practitioners could have only dreamed of making a name for themselves (and some money) on Daum Webtoon and Naver Webtoon—where the competition was very high—but now had the potential to achieve both goals with Lezhin Comics. As it happens, despite its risks and complexities, by 2020 the minimum-guarantee option for webtoonists had become something of an industry standard.

Lezhin has differentiated itself from other platforms by targeting female readers in their late teens and early to mid-twenties as well as male readers between the ages of twenty-five and thirty (Summers 2013). In July 2014 women comprised of 63 percent of total registered users of Lezhin Comics. The company understood the growing importance of female consumers in the digital-contents market, which it used to cater to a demographic more willing to pay for legal content than others. According to one industry report, female consumers generally prefer mobile content with high-quality images and well-developed story arcs, and they were less likely than male consumers to download content illegally. The rise of female consumption in the digital-contents market (today over 60 percent) was noted by a variety of paid platforms, including Naver Webnovel, CJ ENM's OTT channel TVING, and SK Broadband's video-on-demand streaming service Hoppin.[7]

While the primary user demographics of Naver Webtoon and Daum Webtoon were readers in their teens and twenties, respectively, the particular demographic that Lezhin targeted enabled it to embrace the type of adult content (e.g., BL and other erotica) missing from most other platforms. As table 1.1 in the introduction chapter indicates, both Daum and Naver each featured less than 5 percent of adult titles, while around 37 percent of the titles in Lezhin Comics' catalogue were adult in nature.

Limited space prevents a detailed discussion of the numerous hit titles that soon appeared on Lezhin Comics. However, one series stands out for its transmedia trajectory: *Bad Boss*. An adult thriller (2013–2017, 69 episodes, including a prologue, epilogue, and special episodes) by Neon B, *Bad Boss* is a sexually explicit series about an innocent girl who falls in love with her boss, an ex-gigolo who is turning his life around. Her boss's sordid past reemerges after he unexpectedly runs into a former roommate, who had originally recruited him to become a male escort. The series reportedly generated more than 300 million KRW (approximately $280,000 USD) in sales revenue during its first season on Lezhin Comics (Z. Lee 2014). In 2018 *Bad Boss* was adapted into a feature-length animated film and released directly to video-on-demand streaming platforms and digital cable channels.

After stabilizing its domestic operations over the first twenty-four to thirty months, Lezhin Entertainment expanded into the Japanese and US markets in July and December 2015, respectively. Rather than set up a new entity or subsidiary to conduct its business abroad, as Naver's Line Webtoon had done in the United States, Lezhin Comics began offering multiple language services from its central website and mobile app. According to the authors' interviews in 2018 and 2019 in Seoul with Grace CHONG (Lezhin Entertainment's Korean-English translator and SNS manager), all of the company's day-to-day business dealings were handled from within Korea, including the translation and localization of its webtoon titles.[8] Lezhin's Japanese and US ventures have paid off, as the company experienced rapid growth in these markets: in 2017 Lezhin recorded 47 percent growth in Japan and 75 percent growth in the United States compared to its figures for 2016 (J. H. Park 2018). In addition, in 2018 Lezhin Comics achieved top ranking in the United States on Google Play Store's Grossing Comic Apps charts, surpassing the Marvel, DC, and Madefire apps in the first half of that year (Babeltop 2018).

In May 2017 Lezhin continued to internationalize its operations by entering the Greater China market through licensing some of its webtoon series to Tencent and Kuaikan Manhua in Chinese-language versions. This deal has earned increasing revenues for Lezhin and its Chinese partners. In 2019 the company began expanding into Europe by signing a MOU (memorandum of understanding) with French webtoon platform Delitoon, introducing French-language versions of its webtoons to a new readership.

Eager to sustain growth and increase its exposure—and also to inspire new content by local creators, especially in the US, Japanese, and Chinese (and Korean) markets—Lezhin initiated an annual World Comic Contest. First held in 2015, this event is designed to attract a range of contestants who have created fresh stories with mature content. Winners receive cash prizes and the opportunity to serialize their work on Lezhin Comics for an international readership. In the second contest, in 2016, writer-artist Koogi won first prize ($100,000 USD) for *Killing Stalking* (2016–2019), a BL psychological thriller about a stalker who unexpectedly becomes a victim after the man he is stalking begins to stalk him instead; it turns out that his intended victim is a serial killer. Violent obsession and sexual exploitation are the central themes that shape this dark story. Following publication of the webtoon series, *Killing Stalking* was also published as a print comic in Korean, English, Italian, and German. In late 2017, after achieving near-celebrity status, Koogi was invited by Italian publisher J-Pop Manga to appear at Lucca Comics and Games, the largest comics festival in Europe, to launch the Italian edition of *Killing Stalking*. *Wired Magazine* interviewed Koogi at this event, praising his work for its eye-catching graphics, creative story line, and tense psychological plot that pushes the boundaries of both the romance and thriller genres (Caruso 2017).

Every year since 2013 Lezhin has recorded significant increases in its net income—primarily due to increasing traffic. As of July 2019 traffic on Lezhin Comics (10.2 million) remains way ahead of KakaoPage (2.25 million) and slightly ahead of Daum Webtoon (ten million); these figures are monthly total visits on desktop and mobile web apps.[9] Lehzin—like Naver, Daum, and KakaoPage—has also moved toward increased vertical integration, as well as exploiting its IP for television dramas and feature films. As early as 2014 Lezhin partnered with Korean entertainment company Fantagio (founded in 2008 as NOA, "Network of Asia" Entertainment), tvN cable television network, and entertainment company CJ ENM. Following in Kakao's footsteps, in 2017 Lezhin became the largest shareholder in UL Entertainment, a talent-management company, acquiring a pool of talent for use in future transmedia projects.

Lezhin has also carried transmedia adaptation into other areas. In 2014 the webtoon *Blade & Soul: Birth of a Sorcerer*, based on the story world in NCSoft's hit online MMORPG *Blade & Soul*, was published on Lezhin Comics, introducing a character that was new to the existing story world. Both short web series and longer streaming movies adapted from webtoons have resulted from Lezhin Entertainment's widening relationships with the broader creative industries. In 2015 live-action versions of webtoons *Eating Existence* (2015) and *Nineteen* (2015) were released on digital-streaming platforms including Naver TV Cast. That same year, Lezhin Entertainment made two serialized "branded webtoons" to promote popular tvN drama series *Righteous Love* (2014) and *Let's Eat Part 2* (2015). (The branded webtoon genre is discussed in detail in chapter 7.) In 2017 Lezhin Comics' popular black comedy/slice-of-life series *Revatoon* (2015–present, 231 episodes to date) was released as a mobile phone game.

In another coup, Lezhin's first feature film, *Hit the Night* (2017), was invited to the 2017 Busan International Film Festival, where its director, JEONG Ga-young, won the Vision-Director's Award. The film was also invited to the main competition section of the 2018 Rotterdam International Film Festival. While *Hit the Night* was not closely linked to a specific webtoon on Lezhin Comics, producing this independent film gave the company invaluable experience in the film industry, which represented a new direction for the webtoon enterprise. Lezhin has continued to expand into the film business by acquiring a film investment and production company, Lezhin Studio, which is focused on adapting webtoon titles into feature films. In early 2020 it coproduced the tvN supernatural drama series *The Cursed* (2020), written by YEON Sang-ho (of *Train to Busan* [2016] and *Psychokinesis* [2018] fame). It remains too early to speculate where this bold new development will lead the company.

THE PRECARITY OF SUCCESS

While one could conclude the dynamic story behind Lezhin Comics' rise at this point, this would overlook some of the company's biggest challenges. Two significant events come to mind—a brief government shutdown of its website and, more seriously, labor disputes with creators and illustrators who argued that they were underpaid. In such online and digital worlds, precarious labor conditions are often endemic—not only in the webtoon industry but also in any digital environment where practitioners and platforms collide and coalesce in dynamic ways.

In March 2015 Lezhin came under the media spotlight when the Korea Communications Standards Commission (hereafter KCSC) blocked its website (https://www.lezhin.com/ko), along with dozens of other sites, without any warning or explanation. It later emerged that the site had been shut down for hosting "obscene content"—that is, adult material containing erotic images. Lezhin had been caught in a government crackdown despite the fact that in 2014 (as Lezhin's website acknowledged at the time) the company had won the Prime Minister's Award at the 9th Korea Internet Awards, which was cosponsored by the MSIT and the Korea Communications Standards Commission. This prestigious award had singled out Lezhin for advancing the social, business, and technological standards of the Internet in Korea. In addition, at the time of the crackdown its site enjoyed the "Clean Site Selection" seal of approval, determined by both the MCST and the Copyright Protection Center of the Korea Copyright Association. It had also been awarded Grand Prize as a Global K-Startup (2013) and KQL Venture Business Certification. Given these official accolades, the KCSC's branding of Lezhin.com as an "illegal and harmful site" was difficult to fathom, to say the least.

Facing a barrage of criticism for its actions, the KCSC overturned its decision, and access to the site was restored overnight. The incident was covered by most national media in Korea, which focused on the angry reactions to the ban from many of Lezhin Comics' paying users. It was generally agreed that the KCSC had been too hasty in shutting down the site without giving it sufficient scrutiny. As a result of the widespread press coverage, the KCSC lost face, whereas the incident gave Lezhin Comics the kind of free publicity and street credibility that money could never buy.

Nevertheless, as a result of this episode Lezhin and the whole of the industry underwent a major overhaul of operations. First, a necessary and timely industry-wide debate was reinvigorated over the need for a set of standardized self-regulatory practices (discussed at length in chapter 3). Second, access to adult content was permitted only after a user confirmed their age or by entering a personal identification number—known in Korea as the thirteen-digit resident registration number issued to every citizen. Third, the controversy made it widely known that Korea now had a range of viable platforms delivering diverse genres of webtoons. To limit similar negative attention in the future, Lezhin Comics added an "adult webtoon exposure prevention tab" on its website, augmenting the impressive list of government and industry credentials displayed at the bottom of the site.

While Lezhin was praised for its resilience in the face of government censorship, it did not fare so well when the company became embroiled in a very public and complex labor dispute in 2017. After about two years of growing frustration sparked by Lezhin's introduction of its minimum-guarantee policy—done with little or no broad consultation or explanation—in September and October 2017 practitioners aired their grievances in the press, focusing on payments, contracts, and communication problems with the company (D. H. Park 2018). In particular, creators expressed their concerns about the abrupt cessation of Lezhin's webnovel platform (which had been launched in 2015), resulting in the termination of all webnovel author contracts. Practitioners were also concerned about the perceived lack of transparency and fairness regarding overseas distribution of titles and the profit-sharing arrangements for international sales. Webtoonist Gray, creator of fantasy martial-arts series *Records of the Cold Moon* (2013–2017), was a particularly vocal critic.[10] In addition, late work—failing to upload work by a set deadline—now attracted strictly enforced incremental penalties (i.e., late fees), amounting up to 9 percent of a creator's monthly income: 3 percent in the second week overdue, 6 percent in the third week, and 9 percent in the fourth week (J. H. Lee 2017). It seemed the extra time and consideration that the company had once given LEE Yul to complete episodes of *A Compendium of Ghosts* in 2013 no longer suited Lezhin's content managers. On the contrary, webtoonists believed they were now being exploited by Lezhin and given little if any opportunity to consult and negotiate with company representatives. Lezhin's reputation as an "artist-friendly" platform was being seriously challenged by practitioners and industry interest groups who were clearly exasperated by the changes the company was making and the way that they were being implemented (H. D. Lee 2017).

In fairness to Lezhin, the reality of the business world was putting the company under pressure to make some tough decisions—decisions that were inevitably redefining its relationship with its contracted creators. Responding to protests from the Korean Webtoon Writers Association and the Korea Cartoonist Association, which had both accused Lezhin of unfair labor practices and intimidating micromanagement of contracted practitioners, Lezhin attempted to apologize by blaming operational miscalculations for causing the abrupt changes to its procedures and the seemingly arbitrary ways in which they had been implemented (O. S. Lee 2017).

Though Lezhin was apparently backing down, negative publicity surrounding the company reached a peak in December 2017 and January 2018, after a number of practitioners alleged that the company had drawn up a "blacklist" of "troublesome" creators who were blowing the whistle on unfair working conditions.[11] Whether or not such a list existed, the company subsequently fired a number of contracted creators involved in the protest, which only added fuel to the fire. In January 2018 Lezhin terminated its contracts with two well-known content creators, Eun-song and Michii, and also sued them for slander (Lee 2018). Eun-song, creator of the sixty-eight-episode action sci-fi series *Reversi* (2016) and grand prize winner of Lezhin's 1st World Comic Contest, and Michii, creator of the fantasy-mystery-romance series *340 Days* (2014), had both claimed to have been excluded from income-making opportunities generated by advertising and promotional campaigns (Shim 2018).

Outraged over this perceived injustice, over thirty content creators associated with Lezhin Comics and others supporting them created the group Solidary Against Lezhin's Unfair Treatment (SALUT) in January

2018.[12] The group used its website, as well as social media posts to individual members' Twitter and Facebook accounts, to challenge Lezhin and to inform local and international audiences about their plight. In February 2018, YOON Tae-ho, one of the country's best-known webtoonists and president of the Korea Cartoonist Association, attended a press conference organized by SALUT, where he criticized Lezhin on behalf of the industry for suing its creators before the dispute had gone to arbitration.

Faced with a deteriorating situation, and under fire in the media, Lezhin had little choice but to respond to these allegations as well as two petitions submitted by a group of anonymous creators to Korea's Presidential Blue House Petition Board, calling for an investigation into Lezhin's tax history (Jung 2017). Meanwhile, members of SALUT continued to meet and share stories about how they had been "victimized" by the company. Others staged a series of protests outside Lezhin's headquarters in Seoul. Finally, in July 2018, almost a year after the controversy had begun, Lezhin CEO and cofounder HAN issued a formal public apology for the blacklist, confirming the truth of the rumors. He announced that Lezhin was dropping its lawsuit against Eunsong and Michii. Lezhin also returned late fees it had collected from practitioners between 2015 and 2017 and promised to improve the fairness of its creator contracts (Shin 2018). However, the company's termination of its webnovel service and associated contracts would not be reversed. Nonetheless, by the end of 2018 a number of artists had begun leaving the platform, and HAN had stepped down as CEO.

There could be no doubt that these bitter and protracted labor disputes had severely undermined the "artist-friendly" reputation Lezhin had been at pains to foster since its establishment in 2013 and that had contributed to the platform's initial success. How could Lezhin Comics recover after suffering such extensive brand damage and prioritizing cost-saving measures over maintaining harmonious relationships with its content creators? After all, the company's biggest asset was its contributors, and yet it seemed a vast gulf had opened up between Lezhin and its employees. One commentator summed the situation up by describing the company as a "cultural contents dystopia, transforming artists into tools" (Wi 2018). In the end, the biggest problem proved to be a lack of communication between all parties involved, particularly Lezhin's decision to delay consultation and negotiation with its content creators.

Taking a broader view, it is clear that the company's rapid growth had contributed to operational inefficiencies and a lack of adequate human resources as well as poor communication among company staff and between them and their creators. Less than 10 percent of Lezhin's one hundred or so employees had been delegated to supervise the company's comics business—that is, manage its domestic and international operations, including translation services, and provide editorial support for content creators and the two-hundred-plus titles uploaded every week. Considering that the comics business had formed the foundation of the entire company and its plans to expand into transmedia adaptation, this can only be seen as a major oversight.

Whatever the reasons behind the crisis, it revealed an acute need for standardized webtoon contracts and employment policies—standards that would meet the approval of the government or, at least, of quasi-governmental bodies such as KOCCA and KOMACON, as well as industry groups such as the Korea Cartoonist Association and Korean Webtoon Writers Association. The challenges that Lezhin Entertainment had faced during its long-running labor dispute reflected those faced by the entire webtoon industry in the process of maturing into a robust ecosystem.[13] Many of these issues are still apparent today.

CONCLUSION

Outside of Daum and Naver, the webtooniverse is still in its early days. In particular, standard employment contracts have been relatively late in coming to the sector, and proper acknowledgement by government agencies of the webtoon business as a sustainable industry has been surprisingly tardy too. Industry organizations such as the Korean Webtoon Artists Association and the Korea Cartoonist Association continue to face challenges, especially relating to the industry's rapid transformation and internationalization, which have highlighted the sector's precarious labor conditions. For example, a recommended Standard Comics Contract Form by the Ministry of Culture, Sports and Tourism was only released in 2015. And it was only in late 2017, following a protracted labor dispute with Lezhin, that the Korean Webtoon Artists

Association and the Korea Cartoonist Association jointly released the publication *Essential Information for Webtoon Artists about Fair Contracts*, which included a reliable contract for use with any platform. The booklet also included dozens of unfair employment case studies and a checklist to prepare content creators for negotiations with a publisher. A more recent booklet published jointly by KOCCA and the Korea Cartoonist Association in December 2019 offers a three-page section called "to MG or Not to MG?," which aims to demystify this complex payment system. Obviously confusion surrounding this pathway continues to provoke debate at the time of writing in 2020 (Korea Cartoonist Association 2019).

Positive change—representative of a maturing webtoon ecosystem—is clearly on the horizon. Inadvertently both KakaoPage and Lezhin (with their advances in monetization systems) have been largely responsible for many of the changes in the sector, which probably have prevented the sector's stagnation given its dominance by two giant platforms.

This chapter has shed new light on the enterprises that have contributed most to the third (2010–2013) and fourth (2014–present) transformative stages of webtoons in Korea. We have seen that webtoon platforms come in a variety of shapes and sizes, each with a different corporate and/or entrepreneurial background. Clearly 2013 and 2017–2018 were watershed periods in terms of the emergence and transformation of webtoon enterprises and the maturity of the industry as a whole. These were pivotal moments that radically altered the ways in which readers accessed Korean-originated digital comics as well as the conditions under which artists were creating them.

Aside from these key dates, major turning points have also occurred almost every year since 2003—particularly given the governmental as well as private support for more diverse platforms and genres and the exploration of new international markets. Each new turn in the industry has surprised critics who once had trouble imagining the continuing advancement of the Korean webtoon industry. The webtooniverse continues to surprise many who believe that the industry has reached a saturation point. However, new linkages between the digital-gaming and webnovel industries are pushing webtoons into what can be seen a fourth transformative stage in terms of diversity of content, creators, platforms, readers, and markets today.

6

WEBTOONS AND TECHNOLOGICAL INNOVATION

In this chapter the authors investigate some of the major technological transformations and innovations that have shaped the current webtoon industry and its ecosystem. A brief explanation of the physical content layout adopted by the webtoon industry is offered, highlighting the distinctive features of this digital format compared to conventional digital- and web-based manga and other comics. Next, the authors explore the advanced features that set particular webtoon types apart, including horror-toon, smart-toon, cut-toon, effect-toon (aka moving-toon), inter-active-toon, and webtoon animation. The Internet company Naver and its subsidiaries Naver Labs and Naver Webtoon are responsible for many of these innovations and the continuing experimentation as well as for the research and development of webtoons and other digital and social media entertainment technologies.

Although on a much smaller scale than Naver, Daum Webtoon has also experimented with a number of smartphone innovations and viewing formats. For example, between 2014 and 2015 in-house developers experimented with three types of new digital comics. The first format called *dubbing-toons* added "dubbed" narration, music, and sound effects over a series of cuts, simulating the feeling of watching an animation. The second type, *chatting-toons*, which can be adapted to almost any genre, constructed a story through a series of seemingly private social media posts in a chat room—advanced by a user's vertical scrolling.[1] Finally, similar to Naver Webtoon's effect-toon, Daum Webtoon's *moving-toon* combined aspects of the dubbing-toon with animation effects, blurring the boundaries between a webtoon and an animated cartoon.[2] While only a few examples of each format were released by Daum Webtoon, they were mostly added to existing series rather than creating new series from scratch. As a business strategy, this reduced the risk for the company while it sought ways to attract a new cohort of smartphone users to webtoons and their augmented formats. We may never know the full impact of these innovations by Daum Webtoon because they appeared to cease in 2014, around the time of the Daum Communications merger with Kakao, which created a mega ICT enterprise called Daum-Kakao (later renamed Kakao).

On the contrary, the authors show how the webtoon industry has shifted its very foundation, as well as along the periphery, through the major technological achievements pioneered by one of the major platforms—Naver Webtoon—as well as a small number of minor enterprises. In so doing, this chapter sheds light on some of the previously unrecognized history of the webtoon industry and on the strategic linkages between Korea's webtoon, gaming, and ICT industries and the ways in which they have contributed to the expansion of the webtooniverse.

TOYING WITH NEW TOOLS

Since its humble beginnings, Korea's webtoon industry has both contributed to and applied advanced online, mobile, and digital technology across all stages of its development. This includes developing practices and infrastructure across its production, distribution, consumption, and marketing and promotion environments, at every turn exploiting Korea's mature ICT infrastructure, environment, and user culture.

Despite this sophisticated framework, webtoons are an infinitely flexible format. They can be created either by hand on paper with the most basic drawing and coloring tools (and then scanned or digitized), or they can be developed in a fully digital environment, utilizing painting software on a tablet PC or graphics tablet. The average reader can access webtoons and enjoy the regular consumption of content with the most basic apps and devices and with access to limited wired or wireless network bandwidth. Reading vertically scrolling webtoons is not like watching a movie or television show on a streaming platform such as YouTube or Netflix, as it does not depend on superfast broadband. At the other end of the scale, more advanced interactive webtoons, requiring enhanced devices and increased bandwidth, can be created as state-of-the-art experiences in an augmented reality (AR), virtual reality (VR) or mixed reality (MR) environment. Webtoons at this end of the spectrum utilize one or more multimedia elements (such as background music and sound effects), animation elements, haptic effects (such as vibration), and other interactive mechanisms that enhance storytelling techniques as well as the user's visceral experience.

Thus the webtoon industry involves a spectrum of mostly digital practices and cultures that blur the boundaries between comics and animations, games, e-books, and AR, VR, and MR experiences.

From the outset the webtoon ecosystem was developed in close association with Korea's IT industry, which by 2003 had propelled the nation to the top global position for Broadband access per 100 inhabitants (2002–2003). Korea had also become a world leader in ICT through its investment in computers, hardware components, and next-generation communications infrastructure, including high-speed broadband, Wi-Fi, voice over Internet, and video (OECD 2004). The release and rapid acceptance of iPhones in 2009 and Korean-brand Android smartphones in 2010 created the ideal digital-screen environment for Korean webtoon enterprises and their vertically scrolling content. This period also marked a remarkable shift in the broadband arena, with Korea becoming the second nation (following Japan) to roll out more fiber-based Internet subscriptions than either DSL or cable (OECD 2009).

The rapid development of Korea's larger ITC environment is crucially important to the story of webtoons and their exponential growth and commercialization—even though, ironically, webtoons can be produced and consumed using basic technology. Nevertheless, continuously since their emergence webtoons have benefitted from the rapid development of the country's advanced ITC environment, which continues to place Korea among the top nations in ITC indices (OECD 2019; ITU 2019). Chapter 3 also demonstrates how proactive policy contributed to the nation's transformations.

Apart from a few published case studies, the history of webtoons and webcomics remains largely unexplored. Even the purportedly authoritative *Routledge Companion to Comics* (Bramlett, Cook, and Meskin 2017), with contributions by some of the best-known scholars in the field and with global coverage, pays very little attention to web and digital comics, let alone webtoons, despite the fact that enthusiasts began sharing webcomics in BBS groups as early as the 1980s, uploading them on Internet portals such as America Online (AOL), Prodigy, and CompuServe in the United States and then via personal websites in the mid-1990s. A thirty-two-page report published in 1998 by Pamela P. Walatka, then a researcher working for NASA, instructed interested parties on "How to Make a WebToon"; however, the digital format described in her report is light years away from the Korean-born webtoon that we know today.

Any discussion of webtoon technology must begin with the Web 2.0 technology associated with the Korean digital-media industry. Since the birth of the modern format in 2003, webtoons have been designed to facilitate communication flows between producers and distributors on the one hand and consumers on the other. Webtoon platforms (both sites and apps) facilitate the active participation of readers by enabling them to add short comments at the end of each episode, encouraging the type of user-generated content and active audience participation lacking in traditional media channels. These comments vary in length from words and phrases—such as "masterpiece" or "no fun"—to whole paragraphs offering detailed commentary on a particular episode. Users can also "like" or "dislike" an existing comment, which, when totaled, places them up or down in display order (similar to the up/down voting feature on Reddit), differentiating webtoon platforms from other online posting forums. Sometimes readers' comments about characters or events in the story are incorporated by writers and artists. Leading webtoon creator YOON Tae-ho, known for mystery stories such as *Moss* (2007–2008), *The Insiders* (2010–2012), *Misaeng* (2012–2013), and *Pine* (2014–2015), studies comments to gauge viewer attitudes toward his work. For example, the first episode of *Moss* on Daum Webtoon attracted 37,300 comments, which YOON treated as a barometer to measure the reception of his story and characters. By enabling a robust participatory culture, these and all other webtoons are highly compatible with the broader "spreadable media" discussed by well-known popular culture theorists Henry Jenkins and colleagues (Jenkins, Ford, and Green 2013).

In terms of physical layout, a conventional Western contemporary print comic book usually comprises a thirty-two-page booklet, including twenty to twenty-six pages of story plus advertisements, but excluding the front and back cover. Although comic books (and the related graphic novels) vary in terms of style, format, and length, one of the most widely used standard formats, which has changed little since the mid-1940s, is around 10.4 inches by 6.8 inches (25.7 centimeters by 16.8 centimeters), with the content presented in a left-to-right reading, page-turning format.[3] And, according to conversations the authors had at the 2018 San Diego Comic-Con with Dave Kellett, creator-cartoonist of the daily comedy webcomic *Sheldon* (1998–present, http://www.sheldoncomics.com/) and weekly sci-fi webcomic *Drive* (2009–present, http://www.drivecomic.com/), "webcomics" display at least ten thousand different forms, functions, and styles.[4]

Vertically scrolling webtoons, which Daum innovated in 2003, form a significant contrast to these and other formats. Today the Korean-originated vertically scrolling format, generally in which episodes include an average of seventy to eighty cuts, is the cornerstone feature of the now-transnational webtoon. And associated with this vertical format is a host of other technological innovations that continue to expand this globalized digital-media format. While it is impossible to credit every experiment, there are a number of innovations that stand out.

SPECIAL THRILLER CHILLERS AND OTHER TECHNOLOGICAL INNOVATIONS FROM THE CENTER

Throughout this book we have focused on the conventional formats that most enterprises have adopted for online and mobile webtoons. However, different viewing modes, in addition to the now-conventional vertically scrolling method, have been experimented with over the years and given a variety of names, including the "cut-toon," "smart-toon," "effect-toon," "moving-toon," and "interactive-toon." A basic chronology of these alternative webtoon formats is presented in table 6.1. Naver has been responsible for most of this development, as well as for experimentation with digital and social media entertainment technologies.

The *horror-toon* was one of the earliest types of experimental webtoons; the form was trialed through a series of annual summer specials

Table 6.1.   Summary of Naver's Representative Webtoon Innovations

Year	Types	Titles	Notes
2011	Horror-toon (flash-toon)	*Oksu Station Ghost*, *Bongcheon-dong Ghost*	Flash-animation techniques embedded in webtoon artist Horang's project
2012	Smart-toon	*Space King* (2012–2016), *Buff Girl, O-ora* (2012), *Distant Sky* (2014–2018)	Best use of smartphone interface: each panel (i.e., individual drawing) presented differently: zoom in and out, moving up and down
2015	Cut-toon	*Yumi's Cells* (2015), *Red Color* (2015), *Hell Is Other People*(2018)	Slide-view system: webtoon readable horizontally by tapping mobile phone screen; readers can comment on each panel
2015	Effect-toon (moving-toon)	*No Ill Intention* (2015), *Go Go Go: Secret of Skeleton Water* (2015), *2015 Horror Special: Goosebumps, Ghost's Way* (2016)	Webtoon Effects Editor tool introduced by Naver Labs to add multimedia effects in webtoons; available only to featured artists
2017	Interactive-toon (aka romance action-toon)	*Encountered* (2017)	Using Naver Labs' facial-recognition tool, GANs, deeplearning, and AR technology
2018	Horror-toon	*No Play* series (2018)	Use of VR and AR technology
2019	Webtoon short animation	*Psycho-sociopath Nyanya* (2019)	Short animation available on website as well as app

Source: Authors' own research.

(July to August) that Naver Webtoon used to draw traffic to its parent site. *Oksu Station Ghost* (2011) and its sequel *Bongcheon-dong Ghost* (2011), both single webtoon episodes created by the artist Horang (pen name of CHOI Jong-ho), are representative examples of the use of technology to transform this webtoon genre into something unique. They are among the first known webtoons to embed Flash animations, making them a hybrid between a digital comic and a fully animated digital cartoon. Generally speaking, creators use "flash" to simulate different camera techniques (e.g., zoom, pan, dolly, truck) within individual panels or single drawings, creating a local sense of motion. Released as a part of Naver Webtoon's 2011 Mystery Special Shorts Series, *Oksu Station Ghost* and *Bongcheon-dong Ghost* were celebrated for the novel impact of their 3D-like effects on readers (Nam 2014). Their animation effects turned out to be more arresting than the stories themselves.

As individual episodes in Naver's summer thriller series, both *Oksu Station Ghost* and *Bongcheon-dong Ghost* have simple story lines. *Oksu Station Ghost,* named after the Oksu Station subway stop in Seoul, is about a man who encounters a female ghost one night while waiting to catch the last train home. *Bongcheon-dong Ghost* centers on a school-girl who is walking home in the hilly neighborhood of Bongcheon one night when she meets a confused woman who is looking for her baby. The student is chased by the mad (ghost) woman, who is later discovered to have committed suicide earlier that day. Both webtoons contain an animated jump scare created with Adobe Flash Animation software. In *Oksu Station Ghost,* a hand and bloody face suddenly pop out of the screen while the reader is scrolling down the vertical webtoon.

Word-of-mouth publicity about Horang's "horror-toons" went viral in Korea and beyond via online fan communities including Steemit, Screamer Wiki, Reddit, YouTube, and 9GAG (in Hong Kong).[5] Due to their readership outside Korea, Naver Webtoon eventually added English-language versions of each episode to its 2011 Mystery Series. Such a move was rare before the 2014 launch of Naver's English-language site Line Webtoon—where these two episodes appeared as part of a thirty-seven-episode thriller collection called *Chiller* (from 2015), represented by various individual artists.[6]

The first appearance of the horror-toon was followed by a number of *smart-toons*—a general term for any smartphone-based webtoon that departs from the vertically scrolling format, including *Buff Girl, O-ora* (2012), *Space King* (2012–2016), and *Distant Sky* (2014–2018). The latter two series have proved particularly popular among Naver's core demographic of teen readers.

Space King (2012–2016, 163 episodes) is a "space opera" about a group of characters from a regional galaxy who are campaigning to be elected galactic president. Created by PARK Seong-yong, this sci-fi webtoon features a motley cast of characters that encounters space creatures of various kinds and engages in a series of interplanetary battles. The battle scenes featured in episode seventy (containing eighty-seven panels that are numbered at the bottom of the screen), for instance, illustrate how so-called smart-toon technology can be used to manipulate the viewing experience. In this episode (and throughout the series) readers tap the screen to toggle back and forth (as opposed to scrolling) between single frames that appear (somewhat arbitrarily) from one of four positions on the screen. This format resembles ComiXology's Guided View, which was released in October 2013—about a year after Naver Webtoon's release of *Space King*. A sense of motion is created by zooming in and out of panels (often called "cuts") rather than flipping or turning pages. Through this application a practitioner can direct the viewer's attention to multiple-panel sequences in ways that are predetermined. In episode seventy, when a figure marches to the right, subsequent panels appear horizontally from the right side of the screen. When characters confront each other on the other side of the screen, the viewer's attention is directed once again through panels that appear either as close-ups or horizontally from the left side of the screen. As mentioned above, users tap anywhere on the screen to advance to the next panel (or return to the previous one). Breaking up a large scene into a cohesive series of panels in this way simulates the experience of observing sections of a panoramic scene. One resulting effect is a heightening of tension as the action progresses, increasing the readers' sense of engagement with the story.

The smart-toon techniques employed in *Space King* are hard to explain in the absence of visual aids. Simply put, the vectors of action facilitated by the mobile app version (but not the web version) play with the frame and push the boundaries of the webtoon's on-screen space in clever ways. What this format does *not* do is offer a choose-your-own-adventure reading and viewing experience in which the reader determines the direction of the story; the practitioner has total control here. Nevertheless, the extra effort needed to produce a smart-toon with such a level of immersion adds further complexity (and strain) to an artist's workflow practices, already stretched to meet the normal weekly upload timetable. Naver's venture into smart-toons and cut-toons (described later) are endeavors designed to utilize a smartphone's screen space to its full capacity—beyond the capabilities of a webtoon formatted for a website accessible from a PC.

An example of the disaster webtoon genre, *Distant Sky*—written by YOUN Inwan and illustrated by KIM Sunhee—dissects life in a post-apocalyptic Seoul. Of its five seasons, the first three included smart-toon features, while the final two seasons were released as conventional vertically scrolling webtoons. A boy named Haneul (meaning "sky") wakes in complete darkness and discovers that he is surrounded by human corpses. In this pitch-black world, which turns out to be the inside of a giant sinkhole, there is no electricity, no visible stars, and little sense of life. Unexpectedly in this deserted cityscape, Haneul meets a girl named Heyool, and they decide to explore ways of escaping this hellish world and find the distant sky. To survive, they must endure the horror of the giant sinkhole, which is filled with the rubble of crushed buildings and dead bodies, as well as hordes of blood-sucking insects and other supernatural creatures. If this were not enough, they must outwit and outrun cannibalistic predators and dodge streams of boiling lava.

This intriguing story by seasoned writer YOUN Inwan (also CEO of webtoon and digital media content production company YLab), coupled with the detailed hand drawings of KIM Sunhee, was well received by readers. Fans of the series are still waiting for the adaptation of *Distant Sky* for television, originally announced in 2016. However, fans have been able to enjoy a live-action music video—featuring Heyool wandering around in the dark—which was produced as a teaser prior to the release of *Distant Sky*'s second season, made with joint investment from Naver Webtoon and CJ ENM. As a further link between the webtoon and music industries, the video featured the song "Only" by singer-songwriter Oh Ji-eun.

Distant Sky mimics the features appearing in *Space King*—the incorporation of touch-screen elements to view the panels of a scene. A combination of extreme close-ups and jump-zooms enables the reader to feel thoroughly immersed in the story world. Optimized for the mobile environment, the *Distant Sky* smart-toon incorporates simulated flashing lights, advanced zooming features, and added navigation options through multiple-panel sequences. These effects enhance the spatial dimension of the artwork, enabling the viewer to experience modified viewpoints in ways that are much more dynamic than a conventional webtoon, which is static by comparison. Present in each full frame image in *Distant Sky*, these features offer readers an immersive experience as Haneul and Heyool journey through the nightmarish urban landscape. As the story advances, this visual presentation style reinforces the psychological sense of anxiety, doom, and fear experienced by the two protagonists.

Cut-toons display a single frame on the screen at one time. As in each of the three smart-toons discussed here, readers tap the screen to transition between individual panels. A quintessential *cut-toon* is *Yumi's*

Cells, first released on Naver Webtoon in 2015. *Yumi's Cells* had reached 480 episodes in May 2020, thereby demonstrating the type of longevity that smart-toons failed to achieve.[7] This slice-of-life romance series follows Yumi and her friends, their day-to-day lives at work, and their constant search for the perfect date. A particularly appealing feature of the series is the banter and bickering between Yumi's anthropomorphized brain cells, which constantly try to process everything that is happening to her. On the *Yumi's Cells* website, each episode contains a statement informing readers that they are seeing a cut-toon and that the platform's mobile app offers the optimal horizontal viewing experience. (Only the web version presents episodes in the traditional vertical layout.)

On the mobile app, each cut in each episode of *Yumi's Cells* invites readers to post comments before proceeding to the next cut, enhancing their potential level of interactivity and engagement with the series. An unobtrusive button at the bottom of the screen grants access to the comment feature, giving readers the choice to read and add to the comments or to ignore them and read all the panels in one uninterrupted flow. When the authors met thriller webtoon writer HWANG Sun Tae at the 2019 OZ Comic-Con in Sydney (where he was speaking on a KOCCA-sponsored Australia-Korea Webtoon Forum), he explained that this format offers different opportunities for user engagement than are offered in other styles of webtoons. HWANG also underscored how this type of webtoon differs from other series where the comment section is usually located at the end of an episode.[8] Since its initial release, the rising number of comments posted with each new episode suggests that audiences are enjoying the opportunity to respond to the work in this way. The first cut in the prologue to *Yumi's Cells*—the first panel of the inaugural episode released prior to season one—displays a little over 3,600 comments. This style of interactivity works well in a title like *Yumi's Cells*, where the compartmentalized story of Yumi's life is told through her inner-body cells, which serve as contributing voices in the narrative.

One of the most popular *effect-toons* (aka *moving-toons*), the name given to a webtoon containing embedded animation effects, is the 2015 series *Go Go Go* (aka *Go Go Go: Secret of the Skull Water*). This series was made possible with assistance from the Webtoon Effect Editor, a proprietary software program created by Naver Labs, which describes itself as an "ambient intelligence company" (https://www.naverlabs. com/).[9] The high-resolution imagery appearing in this and other webtoon series hosted by Naver Webtoon and Line Webtoon (as well as the added music and sound effects in a number of titles) were made possible through multiple (at least seventeen) innovations and patents developed by Naver Labs (Im 2015). A subsidiary of parent Naver Corp., formed in 2015 Naver Labs also researches and develops a range of products that incorporate artificial intelligence (AI), robotics, and autonomous driving. *Go Go Go* was created by HA Il-kwon, best known for the hit webtoon series *Annarasumanara* (2010), *God of Bath* (2011), and *Duty After School* (2012). *Go Go Go* is a contemporary Indiana Jones–style adventure about a grandfather, father, and son trio seeking an ancient human skull, which allegedly conceals a source of magical water. This story is intertwined with the traditional Korean legend of Wonhyo, a seventh-century Buddhist monk who became enlightened after drinking water from such a skull, teaching him how to wield the power of the mind over reality.

Utilizing Naver Labs' software, HA created a novel type of vertically scrolling webtoon that played with perspective by combining moving images and panels, embedded GIFs, and some haptic vibration effects (used to accentuate explosions, gunshots, and the like) (Kwon 2015). *Go Go Go* features flickering text and moving text on the screen, characters spinning in a ball across the panel and then dropping from the top of the screen onto a pile, and the manipulation of lighting, where the lights dim, leaving characters in the dark or in silhouette. In addition, some panels become brighter as the reader scrolls upward, scenes containing a full moon simulate its rising, and waterfalls are seen cascading. The technical term for this technique is "parallax," which enables artists to manipulate perspective by layering several pictures in one cut and alternating the scrolling speeds (Eun-soo Jin 2015). Adjusting colors and images in these ways suits the story's use of flashbacks and other plot devices, offering readers something new and exciting in a webtoon. While sound effects and music can also be utilized with the Webtoon Effect Editor, this aspect is not applied in *Go Go Go*.

However, some sound effects—including an alarm clock buzzing on a mobile phone, church bells ringing ominously, and jarring sound effects designed to startle the reader—are utilized in another popular moving-toon, *No Malice* (2015–2017). This sixty-episode thriller about a serial killer was created by Hwanjaengi (a pen name), who debuted in Naver Webtoon's Best Challenge section and is best known for his slice-of-life and war webtoon series. However, despite the many advantages of the Webtoon Effect Editor, the intensive time commitment needed to produce experimental effect-toons, such as *Go Go Go* and *No Malice*, poses challenges for many artists. The regimented weekly deadlines common within the industry—and that define platforms such as Naver Webtoon, Daum Webtoon, and KakaoPage—have dissuaded most artists from considering these technical innovations. Audience tastes are another concern; despite the many positive comments posted about particular effect-toons, horror-toons, and smart-toons, so far readers have failed to demand en masse that more special-effects-laden webtoons be made available on their favorite platforms.

Despite these challenges, experimentation continues on the fringes of the industry. Some of the most engaging webtoon formats, offering audiences the most comprehensive immersive experience, are the *AR-toon* and *VR-toon*, discussed next. *Ghost of Somi* (2016) and *Finger Ghost* (2018), which are accessible only via the Naver Webtoon mobile app, utilize augmented reality (AR) and virtual reality (VR), respectively. Each series illustrates how technology, and shocking effects in particular, can be used to maximize the intensity of horror genre stories.

IMMERSION AND EMPATHY IN VR-TOONS

Since the mid-2010s, the webtoon industry has pursued several lines of enquiry regarding the application of AR and VR techniques to the medium's standardized vertically scrolling format. Apart from the distinctive experience they offer readers, developers are attracted by the promise of monetizing this technology via new pathways, especially as mobile network speeds (and, in some cases, affordability) continue to improve around the world. In 2018 the value of the VR entertainment content market was estimated at $7.9 billion USD, and it is expected to expand into a $44 billion USD industry by 2024 (Research and Markets 2019). The 5G network infrastructure—available in Korea since 2019—will allow the production and streaming of a range of VR content, including online and mobile games, feature films, animations, and also webtoons and other types of digital comics. A number of VR webtoon startups on the edges of the industry—outside of the innovations initiated by a few of the leading webtoon platforms—offer an insight into the conditions underpinning the convergence and application of VR to webtoons.

Among these smaller enterprises, Fun Funny Brothers and ComixV (https://comixv.com/) have attempted to innovate advanced types of webtoons on the sidelines of the industry. In 2015 and 2016 Fun Funny Brothers, a small content-production start-up based in the government-sponsored Contents Korea Lab in the outer Seoul area of Gyeonggi Province, began creating a VR webtoon. A beta version of its "VR-toon" was circulated via Google Play Store in 2017; the app offered readers a 3D viewing experience by transforming (or up-converting) layered 2D webtoon images (Im 2017).

In 2016 Fun Funny Brothers' 3D/VR initiative was eclipsed by work promoted by ComixV, a new startup based in the KOMACON Manhwa Business Center, which featured 360-degree comics. ComixV and its VR-toon start-up were launched by YANG Byung-suk, an ex-Naver Webtoon and webnovel producer. YANG understood that it is cheaper to produce VR-toons than VR films and VR games and that it is easier for consumers to access VR-toons, since all they need is a smartphone and a cardboard VR headset. When the authors met YANG and other ComixV staff in 2018 and 2019, they revealed that one of their main challenges was to educate the public about the unique features of its VR-enhanced webtoon contents compared to conventional scrolling webtoons (and even plain old page-turning print comics). Compared to the passive reading modes that characterize these formats, VR developers have a much larger space to occupy with content and must find new ways to gratify the viewer's gaze. A new world of opportunities, as well as the challenge to fully utilize them, is presented by this highly active and immersive environment. Although there are some potential cost savings in creating VR-toons, merging VR technology and webtoons into a seamless whole is a very demanding creative and technical effort.

In adapting the technology for media, VR content creators are obliged to develop strategies and solutions for extending 2D content in ways that can populate the full 360-degree space, including accompanying spatial sound. This basic requirement prevents creators from simply up-converting existing webtoon images, which are usually much lower resolution than the high-definition (HD) content required for VR media. And while VR-toons potentially offer artists a larger canvas on which to illustrate, creating higher resolution images is more time-consuming and thus less ideal for the regularized workflows of the webtoon industry. Despite these drawbacks, the quest to devise an immersive and potentially empathetic experience has been one of the main driving factors behind experimenting with VR-toons from the outset.

Both the Fun Funny Brothers and ComixV launched their VR-toon enterprises around the time that VR headsets—such as Oculus Rift, owned by Facebook since early 2014—became available on the mass market and were generating a great deal of publicity. The rollout of VR suggests that the ways that images are depicted in the VR space can play a powerful role in the generation of empathy. Since the US weekly news magazine *Time* featured an image of Palmer Luckey—the then-twenty-two-year-old inventor of the Oculus Rift VR headset—on its August 17, 2015, cover, there has been vigorous debate over VR's potential as an "empathy machine." Between comments from renowned VR director Chris Milk—in his 2015 TED Talk "How VR Can Create the Ultimate Empathy Machine"—and other media justice initiatives like the VR series Project Empathy (https://www.projectempathyvr. com/), content creators and media evangelists have promoted the medium as a way of generating empathy through a first-person immersive experience (Milk 2015). Milk's VR film *Clouds Over Sidra* (2015) is set inside a Syrian refugee camp, creating an intensely emotional and intimate experience through the viewer's engagement with the suffering of the people who appear in the film and the conditions they endure.[10] With this potential for empathy in mind, a small number of webtoon enterprises are venturing into this new territory.

As a strategy for generating publicity for its VR-toons, ComixV was quick to recruit JI Gang-min, an early comics creator on the Naver Webtoon platform well known for his popular weekly slice-of-life webtoon series *Welcome to the Convenience Store* (2008–2014), which focuses on the lives of four convenience store workers and the motley crew of customers they serve on a daily basis. This highly successful series—which owes its longevity and large audience following to its strong story lines—has been adapted across multiple media formats, including print comic books (2008), a twenty-four-part animated television series (2009, jointly produced by Naver Webtoon and Tooniverse, a cartoon and anime broadcasting channel operated by CJ ENM), and a PC game (2012) and mobile game (2014).

Given JI's substantial following (also discussed as part of the "branded webtoons" phenomenon in chapter 7), recruiting him and using his and his series' name value was a smart move. However, adapting his work to VR was never going to be easy. How would JI's illustration style and his particular "comics language"—consisting of limited colors and store settings with limited detail, as well as frequent close-ups of characters' Pop!-doll faces (wide eyes and enlarged heads)—be adjusted and reformatted for the VR environment? Could the flat, one-dimensional style of his artwork and its limited depth of field between backgrounds, middle grounds, and foregrounds be readily adapted to this new transmedia-IP domain?

When the authors met JI at the KOMACON Manhwa Business Center in Bucheon (where ComixV's office is situated), he raised these and other questions and concerns about using VR and also AR technology in webtoons. JI was acutely aware that the current production system in the webtoon industry provides artists with barely enough time to complete their weekly episode(s), let alone enable them to experiment with alternative technologies and special effects—under the direction of the established platforms, which lead the implementation of this technology. Indeed, each *Welcome to the Convenience Store* webtoon episode is between ten and twenty cuts, which is roughly one-quarter the length of a typical webtoon episode in 2021, relieving JI of some of the pressure of meeting a regular five- or six-day deadline for each new episode.

The issues raised by JI were similar to the questions that the authors had asked themselves before experiencing a beta version of the *Welcome to the Convenience Store* VR-toon at the ComixV office in Bucheon. Through no fault of its creators, its limited use of the full 360-degree space and the affordances of VR technology more broadly restricted its appeal as a novelty format and thus its potential for generating empathy for JI's much-loved characters and stories. When we tried to "walk" behind the convenience store counter and reach out to food objects and read their labels, this proved impossible in the bounded world created by this particular transmedia version of the series. While this was probably a worthwhile experimental venture, it ultimately failed in the webtoon context because the full capabilities of VR were not explored and applied. This is a reasonable expectation of any VR project but a huge task for any webtoon enterprise—whether it is working at the center of the industry or at its periphery. In this case, a great story was not enough to make the *Welcome to the Convenience Store* VR-toon a sustained success. Nonetheless, ComixV has since begun developing and applying VR technology in the field of education, where VR contents are making impacts around the world.

In 2016 a new VR-webtoon enterprise began to attract attention. With financial backing from Naver Webtoon, master horror-webtoon creator CHOI Jong-ho (aka Horang) established a start-up called Studio Horang, where he began developing methods of integrating VR technology with webtoons. Prioritizing a good story over the lure of a novel technology has always been important to Horang, who has worked extensively with 3D modeling and design in the online- and mobile-gaming and software industries. In 2007 Horang debuted as a webtoonist on Daum Webtoon with the forty-two-episode mystery-romance series *Thousand Years Fairy Tale* (2007), which featured six different folk tales in an omnibus style. He became an industry star following the release of several horror webtoons on Naver Webtoon: *A Story of Cloud* (2009), followed by *Oksu Station Ghost* (2011) and *Bongcheon-dong Ghost* (2011), which are discussed above. His other titles include *Blue Bird at the End* in the *What if the Earth Were Destroyed* series (2012), *Ghost in Masung Tunnel* (2013) in the *Hometown of Ghost Tales* series (both in Korean and English), and *Tong-wall Ghost* in the *Goosebumps* series (2015).

After achieving a reputation as a horror-webtoon master, Horang began making teaser "branded webtoons" (discussed in detail in chapter 7) for numerous horror feature films, including *Hansel & Gretel* (2013), *Tunnel* (2014), *Oculus* (2014), *The Gallows* (2015), *The Quiet Place* (2018), and *Annabelle* (2019). In all of these promotional branded webtoons, Horang employed the same Flash animation technique that he had first used in the *Oksu Station Ghost* and *Bongcheon-dong Ghost* horror-toons. (Horang also worked on teaser webtoons for mobile games such as *Bloody Hunter* [2012], *Crow* [2015], and *Blade & Soul* [2016].) In addition to his reputation as a consummate horror storyteller, Horang has been recognized as a master of transmedia adaptation; or at least the style of webtoons for which he is known is in strong demand from these other industries.

In 2016 Horang created a VR cartoon production tool called Sphere-Toon Maker, and in 2017 he launched a new VR webtoon service platform called SphereToon (https://www.spheretoon.com/indexEn.html). Horang's *Finger Ghost* (2018) series on Naver Webtoon was created with the SphereToon Maker, introducing a new kind of VR-webtoon to readers. In early 2020 Horang's VR content and app were available through the Microsoft Store, Google Play Store, and Oculus.com.

By launching SphereToon, Horang had underscored the fact that one of the biggest challenges in developing VR-toon technology and content was a lack of understanding among developers of the language of comics (VR Research Center 2018). This factor explains the missed opportunities in ComixV's experiments with JI's *Welcome to the Convenience Store*, in particular in navigating the transition from the original webtoon's narrative and aesthetic sensibilities to the VR-toon environment. Studio Horang's release of the SphereToon Maker and SphereToon app offered all creators a new tool for producing VR-toons in ways that capitalized on Horang's experience as both a webtoon artist and an IT and software developer. It also provided a new commercialization option that went beyond Naver Labs' Webtoon Effects Editor tool that HA Il-kwon had used to create *Go Go Go* (2015). At the very least webtoonists now had a publicly available tool to create a new VR-toon from scratch—or up-convert their flat webtoon images into a VR-toon. On a higher plane, practitioners were being invited to think about new ideas and join the debate over the role of VR-toons and the mechanics involved in seeing their work literally from a different perspective.

In April 2019, coinciding with the increasing rollout of 5G network infrastructure and services in Korea, Studio Horang formed a new partnership with LG Telecom (LG U+), one of Korea's top three IT companies. This arrangement had two major advantages. On the one hand, it established a channel for the steady procurement and processing of high-definition content required for producing 3D webtoons. On the other hand, the partnership enabled LG Telecom to increase its footprint in the webtoon industry, as well as the wider creative industries, with the potential for developing a new stream of transmedia adaptation IP, including VR content for movies, games, and YouTube videos. Following the deal, commentators hailed this cross-industry partnership as a major boost for the cutting-edge technology underpinning the next generation of Korea's creative industries (Moon-ki Kim 2019). It also signaled new opportunities for transmedia VR adaptations of such award-winning Naver Webtoon series as HA Il-kwon's *God of Bath* (2011–2012), HWANG Joon-ho's *Forest of Humans* (2012), and Jeong-seo's *Transparent Cohabitation* (2016–2017) (Lee 2019). More recently, in March 2020 Naver launched other famous webtoons as VR contents, such as the historical action-adventure martial-arts series *Gosu* (2015–present), slice-of-life romance series *Yumi's Cells*, and psychological-horror series *Hell Is Other People* (aka *Strangers from Hell*, 2019), among others, resulting in Naver's continued interest in expanding the applications of VR technology and promoting it as a novel viewing format.

INTERACTIVE-TOONS: *ENCOUNTERED* (2017) AND THE AR SCENE

The participatory fan culture surrounding webtoons has been enhanced by major innovations in basic platform technology—notably, the comment-posting function, voting, rating, and, in the case of Line Webtoon, crowd-sourced translations of about one hundred titles in thirty-two different languages.[11] Another emerging arena in which fans are participating in interesting ways—albeit via a built-in feature on the Naver Webtoon mobile app—is the AR interface on an eight-episode high school drama webtoon series called *Encountered* (2017). In late 2017 Naver Webtoon launched this experimental series created by HA Il-kwon (of effect-toon *Go Go Go* fame), inviting readers to become their own character in the story.

Introduced as an "interactive webtoon," *Encountered* merged several real-life layers—an individual user's name, actual face (selfie), and real environment (captured via the forward-facing camera that is activated automatically after giving consent)—with the illustrated world of the webtoon. By integrating such (now basic) smartphone capabilities with Naver Labs' underlying facial recognition, machine-learning techniques, and AR infrastructure, *Encountered* creates a cartoon version of the individual user and includes their images as well as references to them in the narrative. In turn, and with the device's camera activated at specific parts of each episode, this newly self-created on-demand webtoon character appears over live images of the user's real world (similar to the layering effect in the Pokémon GO app). To enhance this interactive experience, push notifications are sent to the user after they leave the episode or app, asking where they went next.

Excited by the novel application of an immersive technology, webtoon fans flocked to *Encountered*; in the three days following its initial release in Korea it was reportedly viewed over ten million times (Sohn 2017). The seamless bond between the cutting-edge technology and the enchanting story was (and still is) this series' primary attraction. At the heart of this high school drama is a boy-meets-girl story. With the assistance of the app (and the camera), the smartphone user is placed in the role of the boy (only the boy character is offered), and this new character is incorporated into the webtoon world with its lonely high school girl character. A friendly figure, she divides her time between the story world and the real world (captured by the camera).

A new technology known as *generative adversarial networks* (GAN)—harnessed to the machine-learning process involving the analysis of over seven thousand facial images—was used to create a facial-image likeness of the user's face. This sophisticated algorithmic approach to developing a novel user experience was a first for the webtoon industry (Yu 2017). Other technological innovations used in *Encountered* include a 360-degree panoramic view of the story world's classroom setting—altered by rotating the smartphone. The moment when the female character crosses over into the real world and takes a selfie with the reader is fresh and innovative. And when the user blows on the phone, the webtoon girl's hair swirls around. In all these ways, the user experience is transformed from the kind of passive interaction conventionally found in the medium to something much more engaging—albeit experienced within the bounds of the given story line.

Naver Webtoon's *Encountered* demonstrates how various technological features can be incorporated into a webtoon series with the aim of diversifying the user's experience. At the same time, the example of *Encountered* raises important questions about how technology can be employed in ways that add to the storytelling in a webtoon rather than merely showcasing what is possible.

CONCLUSION

Our discussion of the experimental and innovative webtoons presented in this chapter is intended to give readers a sense of their aims, history, and overall role in the wider webtoon ecosystem and industry. The webtoon texts and user experiences discussed here—mostly explored from inside the industry—are all designed to augment the conventional passive experience of scrolling vertically through a webtoon episode. An evolving participatory culture is being formed, adding energy to the ongoing "digital-comic revolution" inspired by webtoons.

Limited space has prevented us from offering more detailed analyses of the differences between the horror-toon, smart-toon, cut-toon, effect-toon (aka moving-toon), interactive-toon, and VR- and AR-toon that we have researched for this chapter, as well as the "motion books" developed by Madefire—not to mention the more basic interactive digital– and webcomics (and platforms) innovated by Marvel, DC, and ComiXology. While enterprises such as ComixV have attempted to reformat an existing webtoon into a VR environment, others like Sphere-Toon are promoting the creation of VR webtoons from scratch, as well as offering the time-saving technique of converting existing webtoon images into VR texts. In sum, the experimental formats discussed in this chapter are very different from these other formats and platforms; their vertical reading format is what makes them distinctive. Having familiarized themselves with digital storytelling and digital aesthetics, including digital coloration, cut composition, and the use of blank spaces in between cuts, these new, innovative artists sought to master the effective use of digital interspace as a storytelling device. Flash animation effect, multimedia effect, and use of the smartphone interspace and smartphone functions were all slowly added to enhance the intensity of the reader's experience through the use of sound, vibration, or AR and VR images.

While these innovations add interest and pleasure for readers, webtoons with advanced technology remain low in numbers compared to the traditional webtoon series available. As we have seen, such initiatives are not undertaken lightly by artists. Producing a work such as *Go Go Go*, which exploits sound, vibration, and parallax effects, required around a year to produce, involving constant communication and experimentation between the artist and platform software developers. This is the main reason that readers rarely get to see such immersive and interactive webtoons as *Go Go Go* and other series produced on Naver Labs' in-house Webtoon Effects Editor. Simply put, there are few successful advanced webtoons that can sustain a long and absorbing narrative. Each year Naver Webtoon hosts a summer special horror-webtoon series that features embedded multimedia effects across a number of short omnibus stories; however, these effects are mainly intended as a simple device for inducing shock—a jump-scare for readers.

While readers appreciate such features, nearly all of the artists and company representatives the authors met while conducting research for this book believe that these available technologies (often requiring a team of creators) are only useful if they contribute something important to the storytelling strategies at the core of webtoons and other digital comics. Once again, this viewpoint confirms the adage that story is king (as, of course, is traffic).

7

THE BRANDED WEBTOON AND ITS
SOFT-POWER APPEAL

This chapter investigates the rise of a webtoon genre and format known as "branded webtoons," which has become a key source of soft power not only within the industry's own ecosystem but across Korea's wider creative industries as well. First, a brief history of branded webtoons as a nuanced form of narrative-based communication sets the context for further exploration of this hybrid storytelling genre and viral advertising format. Second, insights gleaned from a number of pioneering artists, including PARK Jong-won and JI Gang Min, are used to shed light on the ways in which some long-running webtoon characters (and their IP) are contributing to the expansion of the industry. PARK Jong-won is creator of the early webtoon *Midnight Rhapsody* (2005–2008, 327 episodes) and the Wony Frame character, and JI Gang Min is creator of *Welcome to the Convenience Store* (2008–2014, 600 episodes). Finally, we show how these webtoon elements are extending beyond the core webtoon platform environment and into the larger sphere of advertising. In chapter 8 these insights are applied to three branded webtoon series that explore the world of the immensely popular K-pop act BTS.

Studies of transmedia storytelling, narrative advertising, and convergence in the creative industries usually focus on the development and expansion of various character-driven multiuse strategies employed by firms and practitioners (Sheehan and Morrison 2009). In Korea the common name given to such action plans is *transmedia IP*—formerly known as the "one-source-multi-use" (hereafter OSMU) strategy. OSMU refers to the production and promotion activities that are spun off from a single creative source or program (intellectual property, or IP) utilizing a variety of intertextually linked products and tie-in campaigns that exploit the original IP. For decades this integrated marketing strategy has been one of chief mantras driving the policy initiatives and support mechanisms of Korea's Ministry of Culture, Sports and Tourism (MCST) and the quasi-governmental creative industry agency that comes under its aegis, the Korea Creative Content Agency (KOCCA). Historically projects demonstrating a clear OSMU pathway and range of linked outputs and/or adaptations were given higher priority by these bodies due to their potential for exploiting a range of media formats including films, animations, television series, web series, music, webtoons, and webnovels.

This chapter concentrates its attention on the potentials, outputs, and implications for the webtooniverse thrown up by transmedia IP and on its broader links to the creative industries. Key efforts to exploit transmedia IP involve strategies for globalizing content and characters through a gamut of licensed merchandise—goods that Asia's growing middle class is eager to consume.

It is almost a truism that in order for transmedia IP to attract audiences, and also to become profitable commercial property, it must possess a degree of competitive soft power. We borrow the term "soft power" from international relations–theory pioneer Joseph Nye (1990); his expression can be applied broadly to a creative-industries context— whether we are considering a film, novel, webtoon, or advertisement— to the extent that such texts embody the drawing power of a particular country and its popular culture. There can be no doubt that in 2021 the Webtooniverse is thriving at home and across many parts of the globe as a direct result of the genre's soft-power appeal.

THE SPREADABILITY OF BRANDED WEBTOONS

Since their inception, webtoon stories and characters have been utilized both as promotional tools and as rich sources of "spreadable" transmedia IP. For starters, and as we show in chapters 4 and 5, webtoons have served as a powerful lure for attracting Internet and mobile traffic to

Korea's two major search engines, Daum and Naver, as well as to other webtoon and related digital media platforms. This is precisely the type of "spreadable media" conceptualized in Jenkins, Ford and Green (2013). Whether presented as free or paid content, the webtoons hosted and/or promoted on all platforms (including user-generated reviews of webtoons on YouTube) are effectively advertisements for the plethora of products and services available on these online and mobile sites.

Companies and government organizations have also commissioned and co-opted webtoon characters and webtoon-formatted scrolling content for their own promotional campaigns. As a result, this type of embedded, branded, promotional entertainment content has become a distinctive webtoon genre in and of itself: the branded webtoon. By our definition, a *branded webtoon* is a form of embedded social media entertainment—in its most common form, a serialized advertising campaign containing a varying number of weekly episodes (usually between eight and sixteen, and each usually the length of a conventional webtoon episode)—that may or may not employ recognizable characters from an existing webtoon. And while in all cases a branded webtoon is free and looks and feels like a real webtoon series, its underlying purpose is to create an entertaining story world that promotes an existing brand, product, service, or message. Targeting readers in their teens and twenties, and going viral, are also primary aims. In instances where known webtoon characters are embedded, the branded webtoon extends the story world of the original IP, thus enhancing its transmedia IP domain.

A brief consideration of two very different examples may help to define the concept before delving into our primary case studies. First is the superhero mascot character Electro Man used by Emart, one of Korea's largest hypermarket chains. Episode one of the twenty-episode *Electroman* branded webtoon series on Naver Webtoon (2015–2016) portrays the crime-fighting superhero overpowering a gang of bank robbers who transform themselves into menacing beasts.[1] Out of nowhere appears Electro Man, wearing a blue and yellow mask and a dark blue cape—a clear reference to Marvel's fictional super villain Electro. He saves the day by defeating the perpetrators—all while finishing a prepackaged container of his favorite instant noodles, available from Emart stores as one of its best-selling Electro Man–branded products. In mid-

2018 Emart announced that it was producing a film (yet to be completed and released as of early 2021) featuring Electro Man (Yim 2018).

The second example concerns three webtoons featuring familiar characters from Naver Webtoon's longest-running (1,209 episodes as of February 2020) slice-of-life webtoon series *The Sound of Your Heart* (CHO Seok, 2006–present),: the eight-episode series *Flour Invasion* (2016), the eight-episode series *How to Use You* (2018), and the thirty-two-episode series *Please Call My Name* (2018–2019).[2] These three branded webtoons directly reference and build on the story world of *The Sound of Your Heart*, which is an example of the transmedia IP discussed in this chapter. It has been adapted into a web series (2016, Naver TV Cast), a television drama series (2016, KBS), a Netflix series (2017, season 2), an animation series (2016, Animax cable channel, 26 episodes), a printed comic books, and a mobile game (2016). In addition, the original *Sound of Your Heart* IP has been used for various character merchandise (e.g., plush toys, key chains, cups, hats, stationery, pencil cases, backpacks) and snack foods (e.g., potato chips and ramen). Traversing different media platforms and adapting an original webtoon's story line and characters—based on a specific media format—are fundamental to a conventional transmedia IP strategy.[3]

In their different ways, *Electroman*, *Flour Invasion*, *How to Use You*, and *Please Call My Name* all exemplify how webtoon-inspired or webtoon-formatted content has become part of the larger transmedia IP arena. By exploiting this content and associated ideas, webtoon platforms have gradually increased their power and reach as viral vehicles for delivering promotional messages that extend beyond the conventional tactic of using paid banner advertisements for publicizing a brand on a website. As of early 2020, this industry subsector included over 170 (both historical and current) branded webtoon series on the Naver Webtoon platform alone. This group includes commercial advertisements, public-service announcements, company promotions, and product endorsements.

Similar to Naver, Daum Webtoon has hosted webtoons with embedded product-placement content that falls into the banded-webtoon category. In 2009 the inclusion of illustrations drawn from the iRiver Disciple electronic dictionary in single episodes of *Momore, Princess of Hell* (2008–2012) and *Banquet Box* (2009) on Daum Webtoon were hailed as fresh and innovative by industry commentators (*Next Daily*

2009). Before this date, most companies had few digital or electronic options outside their own websites, blogs, and Facebook accounts for hosting and publicizing branded content. Now producing a branded webtoon and adding a webtoon platform to a company's overall promotional branding strategy makes it look in-step with the times and popular culture. Other companies using branded webtoons—all made in collaboration with Daum Webtoon—include Ildong Pharmaceutical, Ahn Lab security software, and 3M Korea.

Another example of a stand-alone webtoon campaign is the 2010 mixed-media series produced by the Korean branch of the UK Diageo Whisky company, which developed a cross-platform marketing campaign for its Windsor Whisky brand involving both a webtoon and a web series. As a strategy for increasing its brand recognition, Diageo produced and released a six-episode mystery/time-travel fantasy/romance webtoon series called *The Influence* (with two episodes each created by well-known webtoonists HA Il-kwon, PARK Sang-seon, and KIM Yeong-oh). Diageo augmented this campaign with a four-part web series featuring Korean cinema star LEE Byung-hun. In something of a novel move, the series was hosted solely on the Diageo Whisky company website—rather than sitting on a webtoon platform, such as Daum Webtoon or Naver Webtoon. *The Influence* went viral, generating considerable attention from marketing professionals, the general public, and, of course, Korea's young webtoon readers—who had previously had little reason to visit such corporate websites. In other words, hosting conventional-looking webtoons on a company website had the effect of driving traffic to that site in the same way as webtoon series on the Naver Webtoon and Daum Webtoon sites serve to direct traffic to the parent search engines. In addition, word-of-mouth promotion added momentum to this and other brand campaigns, contributing to the kind of marketing success that money alone cannot always buy. (Diageo Korea eventually folded, and its webtoon *The Influence* all but disappeared with it.)

Because branded webtoons constitute a popular form of advertising, webtoon enterprises are increasingly exploiting the monetization opportunities afforded by global digital-advertising budgets—estimated at $333.25 billion USD in 2019 and pegged to increase to $517.51 billion USD—across all Internet-connected devices.[4] More to the point, well-established platforms such as Daum Webtoon and Naver Webtoon offer the distinctive advantage of hosting such content long after a conventional advertising campaign ends, extending the shelf life of this particular promotional content.

WEBTOON CHARACTERS AND STORIES IN ADVERTISING

The history of webtoons and webcomics more generally offers numerous examples of cross-promotions and tie-ins as well as embedded advertisements and the placing of real-life entertainment stars in their story worlds. In other words, webtoons have played a transmedia IP role from the beginning, albeit in a modest form at the start. In the industry's early days the basic webtoon episode was seldom used as a vehicle for advertising and product placement. Rather, a small number of popular webtoon creators was invited to license or lend their characters to promote consumer products and services.

In 2007 Naver began leveraging the IP of some popular webtoons on its platform through advertising collaborations that targeted the typical demographic of its webtoon readers: people in their teens and twenties. Between 2007 and 2013 the number of consumer product tie-ins and cross-promotions gradually increased both within and outside of the webtoon platform environment; these comprised a mix of commercial and public service–branded webtoons featuring either existing webtoon characters or newly created ones. Table 7.1 lists some early examples of commercial product endorsements, represented by series of between six and twenty episodes. The novelty factor in all these series was the vertically scrolling webtoon format rather than their use of familiar characters.

Public-service campaigns utilizing the webtoon format and recognizable webtoon characters and content have been directed at smoking cessation, prevention of industrial accidents, copyright awareness, and suicide prevention, among many other issues. A few examples of somewhat-experimental branded webtoons using familiar characters and made for the corporate and government sectors are listed in table 7.2.

As one of the first creators of webtoons as well as branded webtoons, writer and artist PARK Jong-won—responsible for the very popular 357-episode webtoon series *Midnight Rhapsody* (2005–2008)—was

Table 7.1. **Examples of Representative Branded Webtoon Series as Advertisements**

Branded webtoon series	Artist(s)	Subject of advertisement
Crazy Waiting (2007–2008, 20 episodes)	KIM Yun-ju	Feature film *Crazy Waiting* (2008)
I Love Olympic Games (2007, 6 episodes)	Gwigwi, KIM Kyu-sam Myeong-hyeon	Olympic Games
Plants over Flowers (2009, 10 episodes)	SEO Narae et al.	Madecasol Ointment
In a Word (2010, 8 episodes)	KIM Yang-su	SK Telecom
Goodbye TB (2011–2012, 12 episodes)	Reva et al.	CDC Korea
Let's Go Heroes (2013, 10 episodes)	HA Il-kwon	Lego Hero Factory

Source: Authors' own research.

well equipped to produce the type of commercial content that would appeal to corporate clients. *Midnight Rhapsody* is a micro-sized slice-of-life webtoon (four to eight cuts per episode) that centers on a cranky but witty character called Wony, a stylized gray wolf. Wony, who is in his twenties, faces the challenges and questions the enigmas of everyday life. As a representative of his generation, he worries about money and his below-average university and English-language test scores. He also spends time drinking with friends, while completing his military service (compulsory in Korea). Due to its strong following among readers in their teens and twenties, *Midnight Rhapsody* was one of the first webtoons to be featured in English when Naver Webtoon launched Line Webtoon in mid-2014.[5]

When the authors interviewed him on multiple occasions in Seoul between 2016 and 2019, PARK identified two main advantages in employing the vertically scrolling webtoon format for promotional purposes. First, it enabled advertisers to reach readers in their teens, twenties, and thirties—that is, the general demographic of webtoon readers. Second, he noted that this webtoon genre had initially gained momentum through its use by governmental bodies that were interested in promoting "edutainment"—content that is simultaneously educational and entertaining. In 2008, as webtoons were becoming popular, PARK

Table 7.2.   Exemplary Branded Webtoon Series with Established Characters

Branded webtoon	Artist(s)	Source of character(s)	Commissioning body
Sound of Employment (2008, 8 episodes)	CHO Seok, PARK Jong-won	*The Sound of Heart* (2006–present); *Midnight Rhapsody* (2005–2008)	Ministry of Employment and Labor
Anytime Brunch (2011, 8 episodes)	KIM Kyu-sam	*Jungle High School* (2006–2011)	Hollis Coffee
Nam Kihan Getting a Job (2012, 8 episodes)	Miti	*Making Nam Kihan an Elite* (2008–2011)	Ministry of Employment and Labor
Welcome to One ID (2012–2013, 8 episodes)	JI Gang-min	*Welcome to the Convenience Store* (2008–2014)	SK Planet Co.
God of Cookie (2016, 8 episodes)	HA Il-kwon	*God of Bath* (2011–2012)	Cookie Run mobile game app

Source: Authors' own research.

and fellow artist CHO Seok (known for his creation of the popular series *The Sound of Your Heart*) cocreated an eight-episode branded webtoon series named *Sound of Employment*, part of a public-service campaign commissioned by Korea's Ministry of Employment and Labor. As its unique point of engagement, *Sound of Employment* featured the well-known characters Wony the wolf and Cho Seok with his distinctive square-shaped head, created by PARK and CHO, respectively. Both characters appeared in separate episodes, humorously explaining the various types of youth employment services available and how to apply for different support initiatives. Both Wony and Cho Seok appear in the series as unemployed twenty-somethings seeking gainful employment—the very predicament that Wony had faced in the *Midnight Rhapsody* series.

While quantitative data relating to this campaign are difficult to find, the reader comments and feedback that PARK shared with us (also available on WebtoonGuide and Webtoon Insight) reveal the positive reception for this government-sponsored branded webtoon. Not only did it reach its target audience, it is also likely that the two high-profile webtoon characters (Wony and Cho Seok) featured in it played a significant role in not only attracting viewers but also spreading viral word-of-mouth promotion for *Sound of Employment*. Today many of these early branded webtoon series still seem informative and relevant, if less entertaining than conventional webtoons from the same period.

Finally, branded webtoons have been used to promote new feature films (as also discussed in chapter 4 with *Avengers: Electric Rain* (2014) and *Star Wars: The Force Awakens* (2015), as well as in chapter 6 with Horang's promotional horror-toons). In October 2007 a movie tie-in webtoon called *Crazy Waiting*—a twenty-episode series written and illustrated by KIM Yun-ju—was released in weekly installments over the two-month period preceding the release of the romance-comedy feature film of the same name. The movie depicts the complicated lives of four young couples striving to keep their relationships alive as the male partners complete their mandatory two-year military service. While the film deals with the characters' current conflicts and dramas, including the challenges of serving in the army, the webtoon spins off an empathetic backstory for each couple. In the series' epilogue, artist KIM pleads with the viewer to "Please love this movie as much as you love my webtoon," thereby stimulating its potential for going viral.

Given the synergies between the illustrated characters in the webtoon and the live-action characters in the film, it is easy to understand how the branded webtoon—which achieved a rating of 9.76 among readers—is likely to have contributed to domestic-audience figures of 441,000 and worldwide box office takings of $3 million USD for the film.[6] Based on a cursory glance at the thousands of reader comments at Naver Webtoon, both the webtoon and the film mirrored the real-life experiences of many young couples in Korea.[7] Many of the comments on Naver Webtoon refer to the reader's intention to watch the movie, while viewer comments on Naver's movie-review site register a keen interest in reading the webtoon. The synergies involving *Crazy Waiting* and its viral transmedia IP are all too evident.[8]

Another representative example of the early use of a branded webtoon is webtoon artist JI Gang Min's *Welcome to the Convenience Store*, launched on Naver Webtoon in July 2008. (A VR adaptation of this title is discussed in more detail in chapter 6.) This slice-of-life series, with its comedic and heart-warming content, is set in a neighborhood convenience store. JI's original IP was used for a number of transmedia adaptations, including a web animation series (2009), a television animation series (2010), and social-gaming mobile apps (in 2012 and 2014). One licensing agreement proved to be unique. About a year after its debut on Naver Webtoon, 7-Eleven convenience stores in Korea began featuring JI's characters on their store-branded chocolate and strawberry Welcome Milk products. The same characters were featured again in the summer of 2011 on 7-Eleven ice cream bars. JI's webtoon brand had a powerful appeal to readers of all ages that extended beyond convenience store products, and the *Welcome to the Convenience Store* characters were used to promote other licensed products including stationery items for kids.

Following the series of 7-Eleven campaigns, JI created two new but related branded webtoons in 2012 that promoted SK Planet, an Internet e-commerce, online-to-offline, and digital-marketing company and also the mobile-commerce platform established in 2011 by the giant SK Telecom company. In September 2012 *Welcome to the Planet* (12 episodes) was released on Naver Webtoon. In it, JI's familiar convenience store characters discuss the range of map/navigation, music streaming, cloud-file sharing, video (VOD) streaming, and e-commerce services available on SK Planet. They also playfully debate their apparent misperceptions of the company. In November 2012, two months after the launch of *Welcome to the Planet*, Naver Webtoon featured another new offering from JI, *Welcome to One ID* (eight episodes), which was linked directly to the previous series and promoted SK Planet's new ID system. Here JI's familiar cast of characters praises the benefits of the platform's trouble-free log-in system for accessing all of its services. By releasing weekly episodes of both branded webtoons over the same extended period—and enabling readers to access them for free, twenty-four hours a day, seven days a week (as of mid-2020, they were still available)—the campaign enjoyed a synergy and longevity unattainable by most media campaigns.

Apart from JI, a few other webtoonists have successfully exploited their creative work in the 2010s for marketing campaigns. Webtoon characters have been featured on T-shirts by various clothing brands. Relevant titles include PARK Yongje's *God of High School* (Naver) for NII, Soonkki's *Cheese in the Trap* (Naver) for Tate, and HA Il-kwon's *God of Bath* (Naver) for Polham. In 2014 recognizable webtoon characters were used to promote canned coffee (Lotte's Let's Be), as well as paper cups, beer mugs, and notebooks for the GS25 convenience store. All these items feature iconic characters from the coming-of-age office drama *Misaeng* by leading webtoonist YOON Tae-ho, who made a name for himself on Daum Webtoon.

REFRESHING COMPANY PROFILES USING BRANDED WEBTOONS

By 2013 the soft-power appeal of webtoons, combined with the exploitation of their transmedia IP, swelled the number of branded webtoons produced after major firms outside of the creative industries began to capitalize on the potential of the expanding webtoon market. Branded webtoons were seen as a cost-effective format and media channel for promoting a brand, product, service, or campaign, complementing the conventional artwork used in company websites, blogs, Facebook accounts, and other social media outlets. Advertising executives grasped that branded webtoons are cheaper, easier, and quicker to produce than television advertisements, for instance, and are readily accessible online or via mobile apps long after an eight- or sixteen-episode series has been released.

According to Naver Webtoon, which acts as both a webtoon distributor and an agency that represents artists, the process of developing an eight-episode branded webtoon regularly involves three months of preproduction before the first weekly episode is ready for uploading. After being selected for the job, the webtoon artist creates a detailed story line and presents samples of their visual style, which are all then approved by the company. At least three episodes of the series are completed before the launch, when the artist shifts to a weekly deadline for the remaining five episodes.

For an eight-episode branded webtoon to be featured on Naver Webtoon, the going rate in 2020 was 50 million KRW (approximately $43,000 USD).[9] Daum Webtoon and KakaoPage have a different pricing strategy, charging 3 million KRW (approximately $2,600 USD) for each episode produced. An additional fee of between 2.5 million KRW and 15 million KRW (between $2,150 and $12,900 USD) per episode is paid to the artist(s), depending on their name value and the length of each episode (Yuk 2017). Obviously A-list artists command the highest commissions. The cost of producing and hosting a branded webtoon series on one of Korea's largest webtoon platforms is a fraction of the cost involved in producing and airing a thirty-second television spot on a prime-time free-to-air network show—between $200,000 and $665,000 USD for an ephemeral production that may never surface again after its scheduled run (Poggi 2018).

One company that has successfully pursued the branded webtoon path is Hanwha Chemical (part of the Hanwha Group conglomerate). Known as a long-established if unfashionable company, Hanwha Chemical had ambitions to become a global leader in the chemical industry. For many years the company had struggled to recruit bright young talent for its primary business-to-business operation. Despite being virtually unknown among the youth demographic, in July 2013 the twenty-two-episode series *Hanwha Chemical: The God of Salary*—created by the artist Miti, and produced by YLab, one of Korea's largest and best-known webtoon agencies—was released on Naver Webtoon. At the time, it was one of the first extended narrative promotional branded webtoons to be hosted on any platform. In sponsoring the production of *The God of Salary*, Hanwha Chemical aimed to not only increase the awareness of its corporate brand among the general public but also reposition itself as a trendsetting organization that would be attractive to a new generation of university graduates. Could a rebranding campaign wrapped inside an entertaining webtoon meet this objective? On this occasion, the answer was yes.

The main character in the series was YEON Bong-shin (meaning "god of salary" in Korean), a confident and forward-thinking rookie employee who devises clever solutions for overcoming workplace conflicts. He also displays great mental agility when facing the challenges posed by new projects. With his relentless gung-ho spirit, YEON wins a pitch for a major chemical contract (in season 1) and then oversees the building of a large-scale solar power plant in Africa (in season 2). The office dramas involving YEON and his colleagues reveal a number of power conflicts played in soap-opera style, as well as an international industrial spy intrigue. A hint of a romance between YEON and one of his female colleagues makes the story all the more complicated and interesting.

Despite the disclosure in the first episode that *The God of Salary* was created specifically to promote Hanwha Chemical (and the chemicals industry more generally), an identification repeated in successive episodes, readers found the series highly entertaining and eagerly awaited each new weekly episode. Based on the waves of fresh university graduates applying for jobs at its Seoul-based headquarters, Hanwha Chemical deemed *The God of Salary* a success. As a result of this positive viral response to the series, which many applicants acknowledged during their interviews, Hanwha Chemical commissioned a second and third season to build on its campaign (Yeom 2016).

At the time, series one fell within the top 30 percent of webtoon titles featured on Naver Webtoon (Jin-hyeok Lee 2014). The next series, the forty-eight-episode *Working Hero* (2015)—more than double the length of *The God of Salary*—ran for one year. It depicted an exciting world where company employees are disguised as superheroes. Pitting their wits against evil monsters, a trio of Hanwha Chemical workers with superhuman powers fights to save the world—and their loved ones. Launching *Working Hero* in 2015, the company acknowledged the success of the branded webtoon campaign in raising and refurbishing the company's image. The first series alone had attracted over fifty million accumulated page views, equivalent to an average of 1.13 million page views for each episode (Hong 2015).

Although both *The God of Salary* and *Working Hero* appear in Naver Webtoon's Featured section, they offer clear disclaimers about their status as advertising. This has enabled the series' stakeholders to maintain transparency for readers, prompting them to decide whether or not to keep reading this branded material on its own terms. In other words, this strategy has provided readers with the power to ignore the promotional content, thus clarifying the level of acceptance (and praise) that readers show toward this type of webtoon. As late an 2020, and as if to illustrate the staying power of the branded webtoon genre, both *The God of Salary* and *Working Hero* were still accessible for free on Naver Webtoon and also on the company (now Hanwha Solutions) website. The extended shelf life of the campaign and its soft-power appeal beyond the average television, print, or search-engine brand advertisement is remarkable, making *The God of Salary* and *Working Hero* two of the most memorable and successful examples of their kind.[10]

Produced by Seoul-based Creek and River Entertainment, a subsidiary established in 2001 by the Japanese creator-agency of the same name, *Working Hero* received the Golden Branded Webtoon Award at the 2017 Bucheon International Cartoon Festival.[11] Following this initial success, branded webtoons have burgeoned as a genre, gradually created by individual artists through webtoon agencies rather than by teams of artists. This distinctive format has contributed to the rise of new enterprises in the Webtooniverse, including production studios and agencies like Nulook Media, Jaedam Media, Tooneed, Creek and River Entertainment, and YLab, which negotiate between writers and artists on the one hand and platforms on the other. In 2017 giant gaming company NCSoft (creator of Lineage, the popular massive multiplayer online role-playing game or MMORPG) invested 3 billion KRW (approximately $2.6 million USD) in one of these companies, Jaedam Media—once again demonstrating the Korean gaming industry's long-term interest in facilitating synergies between the webtoon and online and mobile video gaming industries and their potential to develop joint transmedia IP.

Among these enterprises, YLab stands out because its webtoons are published by Naver Webtoon, Daum Webtoon, Kuaikan (China), Comico (in Korean, Japanese, Chinese, Thai, Indonesian, and Spanish), Kadokawa, Kodansha, Shueisha, Shogakukan, and Square Enix (all in Japan). YLab is also fast becoming a diversified entertainment company, positioning itself to compete with the likes of Naver's StudioN and KakaoPage's Kakao M. YLab was founded in 2006 by experienced comic book writer YOUN Inwan, who debuted in 1996. YOUN is also well known for collaborating with illustrator YANG Gyeong-il. Together the pair has created two comic book series: *Blade of the Phantom Master* (2001–2007, first published in Japanese) and *Island I* (1997–2001). They are also responsible for multiple webtoon series, including *Island I* (2016), *Island II* (2016–2018), *Blade of the Phantom Master* (2017–2019), and *Kingdom of the Gods/Burning Hell* (2019). With the exception of *Island II*, these projects were all adapted from original comic books; and *Kingdom of the Gods* provided the inspiration for Netflix's first original Korean series, the globally popular historical horror-thriller zombie series *Kingdom* (2019, 2020).

According to most (if not all) of the Korean webtoon industry personnel that the authors interviewed while researching and writing this book, YLab's sustained productivity, growing size, and financial success in Korea and abroad is largely the result of the investment that it has received from Naver, including a 2017 cash injection for its Japanese branch, YLab Japan. In fact, over the past decade YLab has maintained a close relationship with Naver, releasing the majority of its webtoons on the Naver Webtoon platform. For example, both Naver Webtoon and Webtoon—previously known as Line Webtoon—feature the horror-disaster smart-toon *Distant Sky* (2014–2018), written by YOUN and illustrated by KIM Sunhee; it is discussed in greater detail in chapter 6.

Partly modeled on the Marvel Cinematic Universe and DC Comics' Multiverse, YLab has created what it calls its "Super String blockbuster IP," in which characters across YLab's portfolio of properties appear within a unified story world. In this sci-fi universe, Earth is on a collision course with Jupiter, which has mysteriously been knocked out of its orbit and has already destroyed Mars. Central character Mi-ho, female CEO of the fictitious Daehan Group, attempts to save humans by transporting them to another dimension using a superstring theory application—loosely based on the real-world superstring theory of particle physics. After discovering that this interplanetary disaster was caused by a sinister group called White White, Mi-ho goes into battle against them with the band of "Super String" superheroes that she has recruited. In 2020 YLab's slate of Super String–related webtoon series include the dystopian disaster *Distant Sky*, the music healing drama *Westwood Vibrato* (also written by YOUN and illustrated by KIM, 2011–2012), the fantasy-action *Blade of the Phantom Master* (see above), the sci-fi action *Terror Man* (2016–2020), and nine additional series (as of March 2020). On its platform, Naver Webtoon offers a special section called Super String, featuring all these interconnected webtoons, accompanied by announcements outlining its plans to develop feature films, television dramas, and games based on the Super String IP.[12]

In addition to its Super String webtoons, YLab has produced the high school coming-of-age feature film *Fashion King* (2014) and the ten-episode (each of ten minutes) romance drama web series (on Naver TV Cast) *Prince's Prince* (2015)—both based on webtoons of the same name. YLab has also produced a number of branded webtoons for a variety of corporate clients including Jin Airlines, Nexon video games, the Seoul Housing and Communities Corporation, the National Museum of Korea, and the Ministry of Health and Welfare. It has also created promotional material for the US supernatural horror feature films *Incarnate* (2016) and *Annabelle: Creation* (2017) and for the Korean historical action drama *The Fortress* (2017). With this impressive portfolio, YLab continues to play an important role in the development of branded webtoon campaigns and in extending the boundaries of transmedia adaptation.

In the next section we build on many of the synergies discussed above by showing how branded webtoons are also being employed in the music industry. In particular we introduce the role of the webtoon industry in helping generate massive fan engagement for the iconic K-pop group BTS. This sets the scene for the fuller discussion of webtoons promoting the group in chapter 8.

THE BTS UNIVERSE: ORBITING THE WEBTOON ECOSYSTEM

As of 2020 Naver Webtoon, Webtoon, and Naver, their parent company, remained an unrivaled force that is shaping the direction and expansion of the Webtooniverse. With their potential to offer strong narrative trajectories, branded webtoons are a small but integral part of this success story. In particular the BTS Universe—the transmedia story world surrounding the phenomenally popular K-pop group BTS (aka Bangtan Boys)—has prompted what is by far the most ambitious branded webtoon series that Naver Webtoon has codeveloped: *Save Me*. *Save Me* is also the most successful series in terms of exposure and the realized potential for expanded transmedia adaptations to go viral.

BTS is a K-pop singer-writer act formed in 2010, comprising seven attractive young men, all born between 1992 and 1997: RM (formerly Rap Monster, KIM Nam-joon), Jin (KIM Seok-jin), Suga (MIN Yoon-gi), J-Hope (JUNG Ho-seok), Jimin (PARK Ji-min), V (KIM Taeh-yung), and Jungkook (JEON Jeong-guk). The group debuted in mid-2013 with the single album *2 Cool 4 Skool*; since then the group has become one of the most significant globally facing representatives of the K-pop industry as well as one of the new faces of Korea's broader creative industries.

Each member has proven music-writing and -producing skills, and the group's musical style is a blend of genres. Beginning with hip-hop in 2013, they have since explored pop-rock, rock, electronic dance music, punk, ballads, and also Latin. Most of their songs contain catchy melodies that mediate stories about growing up and facing the challenges of youth, including school bullying, mental-health issues, questions of self-identity, and the search for love. Beneath the group's upbeat surface and their catchy melodies is a range of socially engaged concerns including LGBTQ rights, women's emancipation, and personal development and independence. Unlike many other K-pop groups, as well as Western idol groups, BTS avoids songs about puppy love, romantic relationships, and partying—enabling both BTS and their management company Big Hit Entertainment (established in 2005) to retain a distinctive place within the larger Korean and global music industries.

To a greater extent than most Korean and international groups, BTS has maintained an active digital presence across major domestic and international social media entertainment and networking platforms. Its creative and commercial empire has contributed an estimated $4.65 billion USD to Korea's gross domestic product (GDP)—"enough to put it in the same league as Samsung and Hyundai" (Abramovitch 2019). The group's enormous fan base is more than partly responsible for this commercial and cultural achievement.

BTS's colossal fan following, amassing since 2013, has generated comparisons between this K-pop phenomenon and mid-twentieth-century Western supergroups the Beatles and (to a lesser extent) the Monkees.[13] The group's astounding success comes down to BTS's ability to connect with a global millennial generation. The group's active use of the Internet and mobilesphere for sharing content and mobilizing fans has ushered in a new era of global fandom that no other Korean musical act has previously enjoyed—at least not to nearly the same extent. In addition to its omnipresence on the official BTS Big Hit Entertainment websites, the group also utilizes Twitter, Facebook, YouTube (its official channel is BangtanTV), Instagram, Blog, and V Live (a live video-streaming service operated by Naver: Channel BTS).

As of March 2021 the official BTS Twitter account (@BTS_twt) had 33.3 million followers—10.8 million more than the authors noted in November 2019. Although BTS has fewer followers on Twitter than other acts such as the all-male pop group One Direction—which formed in the United Kingdom in 2010 and has a slowly receding total of 31.5 million followers—BTS has amassed an enormous weekly total number of messages. According to the online music analytics firm Next Big Sound, which tracks musicians' performance on social networks, streaming services, and radio, BTS attracted over 12.4 million mentions during the week beginning November 11, 2019, while Taylor Swift's eighty-five million followers produced a mere 565,100 mentions (Vultaggio 2019). BTS members appear as hyper-users of social-networking platforms, posting casual biographical snippets, including behind-the-scenes images and comments. This high level of activity and engagement with fans has made their utilization of social media entertainment platforms more extensive and effective than the efforts of other K-pop stars and chart-toppers such as Super Junior, TWICE, EXO, PSY, and Black Pink. But it doesn't stop there. BTS has a secret weapon in its media arsenal that sets it apart from its rivals: a global legion of fans known as the BTS ARMY, which was officially formed in July 2013, a month after BTS's debut.

According to one journalist who specializes in international music, media, and Asian pop culture, "Without ARMY [an acronym for Adorable Representative M.C. for Youth], there is no BTS. Without BTS, there is no ARMY" (Herman 2017). It was ARMY fans who voted en masse for BTS in the Top Social Artist category at the Billboard Music Awards in 2017, 2018, and 2019, enabling the group to retain this major international award for three years in a row. As of May 2020 the official @BTS_ARMY Twitter account, as well as around sixty-nine international ARMY Twitter accounts, boasted a combined total of over seven million followers. Many of these hyper-fans create an ever-expanding galaxy of grassroots viral content, which supplements the content produced by BTS and Big Hit Entertainment. In this way, BTS fans produce and circulate vast amounts of user-generated content, playing a key role in the BTS Universe (also known as the Bangtan Universe, or BU).

A comprehensive campaign of transmedia IP, comprising highly orchestrated live and filmed events, music videos, and social media entertainment content, the BTS Universe was born in April 2015 with the release of the music video for "I Need U." At base, the BTS Universe encapsulates an expanding, fictional, transmedia story world and character set manifested through the seven members of the group, who are presented as inhabiting an alternate reality. Sustained across their songs, music videos, and short films and all the mixed-media, press, and fan-generated publicity surrounding them, this evolving story portrays the anxieties and challenges of the group (and their webtoon avatars) and their aspirations for a better future.

The symbiotic relationship between BTS and their fans, as well as the large use of social media throughout the BTS Universe, demonstrates the powerful influence of fans in the K-pop industry. In the entertainment worlds of fans and transmedia storytelling, value is created through the "high relational exchange" between both parties (Davis 2013). It is precisely this value that continues to underpin the ongoing expansion and success of the BTS Universe and the galaxy of transmedia IP surrounding it. BTS's branded webtoon *Save Me* has emerged from this larger domain.

As we will see in the next chapter, three branded webtoons have been produced to activate the BTS Universe. Our case study exposes previously unrecognized soft-power aspects of the webtoon industry and its transmedia storytelling, merchandizing power, and crowd-sourced viral transportability. We highlight some of the wider synergies between the webtoon industry and its strategies for leveraging and profiting from transmedia IP on the one hand and the larger creative industries on the other.

8

K-POP WEBTOONS AND THE TRANSMEDIA IP NEXUS IN THE BTS UNIVERSE

This chapter investigates the development and impact of three unique branded webtoon campaigns that have played a catalytic role in the formation of the BTS Universe—introduced in chapter 7—and the larger K-pop industry. It shows how three webtoon series about the K-pop boy band BTS—*We On: Be the Shield* (2014), *Hip Hop Monster* (2014), and *Save Me* (2019)—offer an intimate exploration of the world of BTS in the service of a commercial imperative. Departing from the standard narrative advertising strategy, these three branded webtoon series are a form of narrative advertising designed to transport readers into a story world in which the hosting platforms (as well as the viral promotional content) appear fashionable, innovative, and strongly oriented toward contemporary youth culture. As an experiment—partly the result of the limited number of existing branded webtoon series—this strategy has created a strong connection between BTS and the popular webtoon format. In exploring these linkages, this and the previous chapter highlight some of the wider synergies between the webtoon industry and its strategies for leveraging and profiting from transmedia IP on the one hand and the larger creative industries on the other.

BRANDED WEBTOONS AND THE NEWFOUND
TRANSPORTABILITY OF THE BTS UNIVERSE

As we have seen, the branded webtoon concept draws on perceptions of narrative-based communication as a sophisticated and hybrid entertainment-marketing technique—a strategy that involves using narrative elements gleaned from popular-entertainment contents (e.g., in a television program, film, or online or mobile video game) as a cross-promotional vehicle for advertising and marketing a brand or product (Balasubramanian 1991). Put simply, branded webtoons offer a new collaborative opportunity for tie-ins involving products and brands while distinguishing this type of promotional transmedia IP from the traditional product-placement strategies found in legacy media.

Reflecting on the opportunities afforded by branded webtoons, recent studies acknowledge the value of presenting a core message in a subtle way—here in the context of popular entertainment (Lee and Hwang 2017). In what follows, we draw on this kind of analysis to evaluate how such as strategy is being employed in one of the creative industries' most active domains, Korean popular music (aka K-pop), and we explore how one act in particular, at the top of the K-pop and world music charts, is leveraging the popular culture and viral potential of webtoons.

In an early attempt to shape the BTS Universe (aka Bangtan Universe, or BU)—or at least as a teaser prior to its formal inauguration—in 2014 Big Hit Entertainment commissioned two branded webtoons, *We On: Be the Shield* and *Hip Hop Monster*. Both were originally released on SK Communications' Internet search portal, Nate.com, at one time a competitor of Daum and Naver. Formerly Korea's number-three webtoon platform following Naver Webtoon and Daum Webtoon, Nate lost its position in 2013 after the industry was swamped by a flood of new paid platforms. After gradually losing market share, Nate ceased its webtoon service in December 2018. The release of the two BTS webtoons was part of a marketing strategy aimed to coincide with the 2014 release of BTS's debut studio album *Dark & Wild*. In conjunction with Big Hit Entertainment, CJ ENM produced *We On: Be the Shield*, a sci-fi webtoon written by LEE Sun-gi and illustrated by PARK Jong-seong (August 2014–April 2015, 29 episodes). It tells the story of a group of seven high school students, known collectively as "Be the

Shield" (aka BTS), who attempt to save the world from alien monsters. Equipped with superpowers, they fight together as a team.

Next, building on the viral word-of-mouth promotion that had created a following for *We On: Be the Shield*, Jaedam Media produced and released *Hip Hop Monster*, a comedic slice-of-life webtoon written and drawn by Grinemo (September 2014–July 2015, 44 episodes). *Hip Hop Monster* is about seven students who attend the fictitious Bangtan High School. All seven boys (Jin, Suga, J-Hope, Rap Monster, Jimin, V, and Jungkook), plus an eighth character who represents an amalgamation of the group, are active members of the school's hip-hop club. Thus the series loosely mirrors the story of BTS, who began as a hip-hop act. Each appears as a cute animal-like character in both work (band practice) and play scenes. All eight of the characters featured in *Hip Hop Monster* have been merchandized by CJ ENM in a range of trinkets, figurines and dolls, key rings, notebooks and stationery, computer and mobile phone peripherals, and other collectable items. Given that *Hip Hop Monster* predated Line Friends' launch of the official BTS-BT21 merchandising line in October 2017—the group's official chain of character merchandise—the webtoon served as a kind of prequel to the full unfolding of the BTS Universe.

It is instructive to compare the webtoon strategies used to market BTS with those promoting a rival group, Got7. In August 2014, around the time that *We On: Be the Shield* and *Hip Hop Monster* were released, JYP Entertainment—one of Korea's "big three" music companies (with SM Entertainment and YG Entertainment)—posted the branded webtoon *Gottoon* (20 episodes, each released at fortnightly intervals) on the group's own site (https://got7.jype.com/). *Gottoon* featured a new seven-member idol boy group, Got7, which made its debut in January 2014 with the release of *Got It?*, an EP (extended album). The *Gottoon* series focused on the group's origin story, their daily lives, and the relentless practicing of what would become their signature martial arts tricking and street-dancing moves. However, unlike *We On: Be the Shield* and *Hip Hop Monster*, which were posted alongside other web comics hosted on the Nate platform, the stand-alone *Gottoon* series was accessible only via the JYP website, giving it limited potential to reach the growing numbers of readers attracted to webtoon-dedicated platforms.

In February 2018 JYP released a second webtoon, *GET* (February–June 2018), right before the release of Got7's eighth EP, *Eyes On You*. In *GET*, we meet Mark, a US student recently transferred to J High School of Performing Arts. After joining a quirky rapping and martial arts club (called GET), Mark befriends the members of the soon-to-be group Got7 and participates in a series of music-audition programs with them. Learning from its mistakes with the release of *Gottoon*, this time JYP worked directly with KT's webtoon platform Ktoon, exposing the series to Ktoon's wider webtoon readership. However, despite JYP's attempts to innovate something similar to BTS's three webtoon series, *We On: Be the Shield*, *Hip Hop Monster*, and *Save Me* (see below), with *Gottoon* and *GET*, JYP and its partnering webtoon platform failed to produce a promotional product that was in the same league as those featuring BTS.

When the *We On: Be the Shield* and *Hip Hop Monster* were released, BTS was already on the path to celebrity. Their debut single *2 Cool 4 Skool* and EP *O!RUL8,2?* were released in June and September 2013, respectively, and their second EP, *Skool Luv Affair*, which completed their "school trilogy," had been available since early 2014. By the end of 2013 the group was receiving attention in Korea as a "new artist of the year" after winning the Melon Music Awards, Golden Disc Awards, and Seoul Music Awards. Despite this domestic recognition, and although *Hip Hop Monster* was available in Japanese and English as well as Korean, their two promotional webtoons were still largely unknown outside Korea. ARMY fans would soon help rectify the situation, undertaking their own viral promotion of the webtoons.

While the original forty-four-episode webtoon series is no longer available on Nate.com, *Hip Hop Monster* was released in English on Line Webtoon between March 2017 and February 2019; each episode was called a "track."[1] During their absence from the Nate platform, images from both *We On: Be the Shield* and *Hip Hop Monster* were rediscovered by ARMY fans—the cartoon characters of each member were especially cherished—and circulated on Koreaboo, a website specializing in K-pop content, as well as on other BTS fan sites and a number of domestic and international Twitter accounts. ARMY members were also busy posting a range of other images and content related to the group on their own personal social media networks on a daily basis. Thus the ARMY has played an important promotional role in the transmedia IP environment outside formal licensed platforms—a key feature of both the BTS Universe and the webtooniverse in general.[2]

Whatever their immediate impact, *We On: Be the Shield* and *Hip Hop Monster* continue to attract a following. Fans all over the world continue to post thousands of comments on reposted images of *We On: Be the Shield* on the social media entertainment storytelling platform Wattpad (and to a lesser extent for *Hip Hop Monster* on Line Webtoon). The branded content of these webtoons represents an important early initiative to generate buzz for BTS and its youthful members as well as for the fictional Line Friends BT21 story world and its line of merchandise. This wealth of transmedia IP, and the real and fictitious (i.e., alternate world) stories of which it is a part, has been a major contributor to the BTS Universe.[3]

BTS'S *SAVE ME* WEBTOON AND THE REVERSE VIRAL PROMOTION OF THE WEBTOON PLATFORM

Before the official launch of the name and concept in 2017, the BTS Universe was known as HYYH—an abbreviation of the phrase *Hwa Yang Yeon Hwa,* meaning the most beautiful or happiest time of one's life. The name HYYH first appeared in April 2015 following the release of the song and music video "I Need U," the lead single on BTS's third EP, *The Most Beautiful Moment in Life, Part 1.* In the alternate universe portrayed in the video, the seven BTS members appear as their alter egos. This trope was reprised in subsequent BTS music videos including, "Run," the lead single on their fourth EP; *The Most Beautiful Moment in Life, Part 2* (2015); "Young Forever," the title song of the group's first compilation album, *The Most Beautiful Moment in Life: Young Forever* (2016); and "Fake Love," the lead single on BTS's third studio album, *Love Yourself: Tear* (2018).

The ever-expanding BTS Universe received a major boost following the release of the group's third and most sophisticated branded webtoon, *Save Me,* originally a song title from their first compilation album, *The Most Beautiful Moment in Life: Young Forever* (2016). For this 2016 compilation album, BTS received the Album of the Year award at the Korean Melon Music Awards, a major music-industry event sponsored by the Kakao M entertainment company and its online music store and music-streaming service, Melon.

After a five-year hiatus following the releases of *We On: Be the Shield* and *Hip Hop Monster*, *Save Me* was a very accomplished production; it was also the series to make the most impact on the BTS Universe. This dark drama wrapped in a webtoon was published between January and April 2019 (17 episodes, including a prologue). The completed series appeared simultaneously (for free) on Naver Webtoon (in Korean) and on Naver's global Line Webtoon platform in six languages: English, Japanese, Simplified Chinese, Traditional Chinese, Indonesian, and Thai. (These were all authorized translations on what we call Naver's sister sites.) In addition, twenty-five unofficial translations into other languages by registered volunteer fans—what we have elsewhere called "transcreators" (Yecies et al. 2020)—were soon posted on Line Webtoon (renamed Webtoon in September 2019). All but two of these multilanguage versions (Danish and Lithuanian) had yet to be completed as of March 2020. At the time of writing, the complete series is available in Spanish, Turkish, German, Arabic, Russian, Romanian, Portuguese, French, Polish, Italian, Greek, Swedish, Malaysian, Vietnamese, Czech, Filipino, Hindi, Ukrainian, Persian, Bulgarian, Dutch, and Bengali, in addition to the authorized translations. Their work shows the extent to which these volunteer fan translators have contributed to the transnational expansion of the BTS Universe.

Big Hit Entertainment provided the story content for the *Save Me* webtoon. This was derived from images and plotlines featured in BTS music, music videos, short films, social media messages, and a series of published materials produced since the release of *The Most Beautiful Moment in Life, Part 1* in 2015—the birth moment of the BTS Universe. One of Naver Webtoon's production subsidiaries, LICO (Life Is Comic), was responsible for the artwork. Established in mid-2017, LICO is a digital-content production company that produces a diverse range of digital media content, including animation and webtoons.[4] As a corporate production, rather than a series created by an identifiable writer/artist combination, *Save Me* differs from most webtoon series. This unconventional approach has enabled the series to promote the Webtoon platform rather than the usual route of the platform promoting the series.

On both Naver Webtoon and Webtoon, *Save Me* has gone on to become a viral sensation, bolstered by buzz generated on Twitter and Facebook and, of course, via a multitude of blogs and websites belonging to ARMY and other BTS fans. Judging by the number of likes accrued, *Save Me* was successful even before the series had reached the half-way mark. It attracted over two million likes on Webtoon and 113,198 user comments—figures that surpass most other branded webtoons on the Webtoon platform. Within this data set of user-generated content, which continues to expand, the *Save Me* series has attracted a total of 3,338,687 likes. The episode with the largest number of likes (354,197 as of January 2020, and 360,334 as of March 2020), as well as comments (13,950 as of January 2020), is the series prologue.

The prologue sets the brooding tone for the series and explains the double meaning of the title—all while evoking iconic imagery that is recognizable from a range of the group's existing mediasphere (i.e., the BTS Universe). Seok-jin (usually known by his stage name Jin), the oldest member of BTS, is the lead character and narrator in the webtoon. The opening images in this introductory episode reveal pools of splattered blood on the ground, as well as on Seok-jin's hands and face. Due to the webtoon's mature themes, it would have been appropriate to show the same warning here that appears in the final episode: "This episode contains violence. Reader discretion is advised" (although it is absent from the Korean-language version on Naver Webtoon). This is no sci-fi or comedy—nor a story for the faint-hearted. One of the group members is in jail, and another is about to commit suicide by jumping off a high rise building. A third member of the group has had a lethal fall in a stairwell, while a fourth is trapped in a motel room that he's set ablaze in a fit of depression. A fifth band member is in a hospital room with an intravenous drip, dying from a chronic illness. Although it is difficult to identify each member of the group in this first episode, they are clearly all in need of help.

Although the series uses the group member's real names, the remaining episodes flesh out the alternate world that is an integral part of the BTS Universe. At the start of the series, Seokjin returns home from a two-year stay in the United States after graduating from high school. Feeling anxious about being home, he drives around the neighborhood and passes his old high school. A glimpse of one of his high school friends, Jungkook, evokes joyful memories of the past. Flash back to seven students in detention after school, spending time together and having fun—in the only place they could "relax and laugh inside that stuffy school." Returning home, Seokjin sees Namjoon (aka RM) working at a gas station, but he continues without stopping to say hello. Later that night, Seokjin has a nightmare in which he and his six best friends are drowning and he is helpless to save them (and himself). After awaking abruptly, he looks at his phone, which reads May 22—a date that corresponds to a fictitious diary entry made by Jungkook (May 22, 2022, headed "The Most Beautiful Day of Our Lives") in *The Most Beautiful Moment in Life: The Notes.* Jungkook's ironically titled journal entry in this alternate universe conjures a shocking, near-death experience, culminating in the rhetorical question, "Living will be even more painful than dying—but, even so, do you still want to live?"[5]

Some time later, Seokjin stops at the gas station where Namjoon is working, but he finds it awkward to start a conversation. Seokjin is clearly finding it difficult to fit back into his hometown after being away. What happened between them? How do Namjoon and the others feel about seeing Seokjin? Did he abandon them, and, if so, are they holding a grudge against him? Readers never really discover the answers to these questions. Feeling guilty, Seokjin returns to the gas station the next day, only to learn that Namjoon has been taken to jail for fighting with a customer. Regretting their missed encounter, Seokjin visits him in jail, where he realizes that he probably could have prevented the fight and Namjoon's incarceration if he had intervened the previous night. Furthermore, he is shocked to learn about the suicides of his friends Jeonggook and Yoongi (aka Suga). Adding to this growing misery, Hoseok (aka J-Hope) has been hospitalized following an accident, and as he leaves the jail Seokjin sees Taehyung (aka V), a victim of domestic violence at the hands of his father; Taehyung is entering the building in handcuffs. Jimin's whereabouts are unstated, but he's probably in strife like all of Seokjin's other friends. Seokjin speculates that everything might have been different had he simply said hello to Jeonggook and Namjoon when he'd had the chance.

At the end of episode one, Seokjin is mentally transported back to June 12 (the date appears on a photo and was the date of the group's official debut in the United States in mid-2013) , to a beach where he and his six best friends are relaxing and enjoying their carefree lives. They truly seemed united. But where did it all go wrong, and why did everyone end up being so miserable? What led this tight-knit group of friends to part company? Such questions pervade his (and the reader's) thoughts. Finally, an omniscient voice—ostensibly emanating from a strange white cat circling his legs—asks Seokjin, "If you could turn back time, do you believe that you could straighten out all the errors and mistakes and . . . save everyone?" Seokjin replies that he "would do anything" to achieve that goal.

This is the point in the webtoon at which the "Groundhog Day" scenario begins. When Seokjin awakes from his wild nightmare (at the very end of episode one), it is April 11, which is the date that the new album *Map of the Soul: Persona* is scheduled to be released. This is an "intertextual gift" for alert readers. The challenge is revealed: with their help, Seokjin must save his friends from their impending doom, in the process reliving the same day over and over again.

In this nightmarish fictional world, Seokjin strives to become a hero. Nonetheless, the fates of all seven friends are sealed, as the series reveals with brutal directness. (Hence the warning to readers in the final episode.) No matter how hard he tries, Seokjin fails to save his friends, becoming trapped in an unending cycle of sorrow and frustration. Seokjin's solitary efforts to save each of his friends in turn are thwarted by unforeseen circumstances. This underlines the moral of this story: one should accept fate and avoid trying to alter the course of one's life but also strive and live life to the fullest. As it happens, Seokjin does save some of his friends, but he loses his own life in the process—after Taehyung stabs him in a rage sparked by Taehyung's hatred of his abusive father.

In the final episode (episode fifteen), the recurring omniscient voice tells Seokjin, "You won't make it out here alone . . . given this entangled destiny." To which Seokjin responds in thought, "Yes. No matter how many times I tried, I could never have saved them all on my own." Holding the photograph of the group's memorable day on the beach, Seokjin looks up at the reader as the final words in the series appear on the screen: "Together with you . . ."—suggesting that the fate of BTS rests with the fans, the ARMY, the readers.

Suggestively, the phrase "together with you" also appears in the English translations of two BTS songs, "Just One Day" and "A Supplementary Story: You Never Walk Alone," from the albums *Skool Luv Affair* (2014) and *You Never Walk Alone* (2017, a repackaged version of their *Wings* album from 2016), respectively. The former song is about a busy young man who regrets lacking time to get to know a girl, while the latter is about longing for someone special to rescue a man who has reached the end of the long and lonely journey that he has followed in life. The life imagined in the stories shared by these two songs and the *Save Me* webtoon is one filled with an intense yearning for youthful innocence and contentment.

As it happens, the end of the series coincided with the April 2019 release of BTS's sixth EP, *Map of Soul: Persona*, which, according to Big Hit Entertainment's website, marks the launch of a new trilogy and the beginning of a brand new story line. In this new story BTS will explore more upbeat themes—finding love and reaching out to the world with peace and understanding.[6] If and when season two of the *Save Me* branded webtoon is released, it will very likely unfold along these lines.

GOING VIRAL AND GOING BIG

Before the end of its sixteen-week run, *Save Me* had reportedly accumulated fifty million views—no small feat for a webcomic of any kind (Hwang 2019). Hence, when Big Hit Entertainment released the BTS album *The Most Beautiful Moment in Life: The Notes 1* in March 2019, fans' appetite for the latest addition to the BTS Universe had already been whetted by the recently published webtoon. Placed as a clue for alert fans, the date "12 June" on the beach photo was a reference to the group's official debut in the United States (in 2013). Looking back, and considering all of the user-generated content that had accumulated around it, *Save Me* generated the kind of buzz that Big Hit Entertainment could leverage for the release of *Map of the Soul: Persona*, which reached number one on the Billboard 200 charts in April 2019. As the group's third consecutive number one album on the Billboard 200, *Map of the Soul: Persona* made BTS the first group since the Beatles to achieve so many number-one albums within a twelve-month period.

As we have seen, *Save Me* has played a major role in both the expanding BTS Universe and the webtooniverse. The Webtoon platform has been central to this "soft-power success story." Although like many webtoons *Save Me* lacked embedded music and sound effects,

Big Hit Entertainment collaborated with Spotify to publish an official twenty-one-song *Save Me*: BTS webtoon playlist.[7] The addition of this feature further differentiates *Save Me* from the two previous BTS-branded webtoons released in 2014.

Today Webtoon's English-language interface hosts the most extensive global fan-translation area of any platform in the mediasphere. Given this powerful marketing and user-generated-content tool, any branded webtoon published on Webtoon has the potential to reach global audiences through the work of transcreators facilitating a given series' transportability. Although only a limited number of English-language webtoon series on Webtoon are available for fan translation—fewer than eighty-five by our count in March 2020—*Save Me* (and the larger BTS Universe) has benefitted immensely from this crowd-sourced and viral-like capability. Unlike most of the branded webtoons discussed in the previous chapter, *Save Me* is contributing directly to the constructed BTS Universe in ways that *We On: Be the Shield* and *Hip Hop Monster*, as well as Got7's *Gottoon* (2014) and *GET* (2018), had been unable to match.

However, rather than giving Webtoon and the platform's transcreators all of the credit for promoting *Save Me*, one could argue that *Save Me* has functioned as an effective viral promotional tool for Webtoon. This new perspective challenges the conventional understanding of the power dynamic operating between webtoons and BTS. In other words, thanks to the soft power and super-celebrity status that BTS had accumulated prior to and after the release of *Save Me* in 2019, it would be fair to say that at the time of writing in 2021 BTS is promoting Naver as a kind of viral phenomenon, rather than the other way around. At the very least, theirs is a symbiotic relationship worth exploring in greater detail.

As a key element in the BTS Universe, *Save Me* is a good example of transmedia IP and its enhancement through participatory culture. The series visualizes the alternate BTS Universe in ways that are very different to the music videos and short films put out by the group. It focuses on the growing-up stories and everyday challenges faced by the teenage characters, even though all seven band members were past their teens when the webtoon was released in 2019. Their struggles and anxieties, as well as their hopes and dreams for the future, are recurring themes in the series and also form a core part of the self-branding strategies of their larger-than-life avatars. In these ways, the seven illustrated characters in this transmedia story world contribute to the transportability and expression of the larger BTS Universe. Thus, whether consciously or subconsciously, readers and fans are enabled to engage with the transmedia narrative embodied across the wider universe of BTS consumables (music videos, Twitter comments, short films on YouTube, feature-length filmed concerts and documentaries, published books, branded clothing, other consumer goods, and the like) as if they were all interlocking pieces in a great puzzle.[8]

While Big Hit Entertainment represents a much smaller number of acts than Korea's "Big Three" music giants (SM, YG, and JYP), it has successfully exploited the same media channels that the Big Three have used to internationalize their musical acts and create value for their brands. (In 2020, in addition to BTS, Big Hit Entertainment represented soloist LEE Hyun and a second major all-male K-pop idol group, TXT, as well as an all-female group called GFriend.) BANG Si-hyuk, founder of Big Hit Entertainment, is a well-known composer who goes by the nickname Hit Man. He gained valuable industry experience after joining JYP when it was established in 1997. BANG trained under JYP's CEO PARK Jin-young, learning about and making his own contributions to Korea's booming contemporary-music scene. Thus, while Big Hit Entertainment's business strategy has elements in common with those of Korea's Big Three, as a latecomer to the industry BANG sought to innovate and differentiate himself from the competition.

For example, BANG and his company treated K-pop trainees differently than their larger rivals, encouraging their artists' independence and motivating them to develop their own musical style—in marked contrast to the regimented approach followed by SM, YG, and JYP with their trainees (Doré and Pugsley 2019). BANG also sought to boost the company's promotional activities by actively using social media in order to communicate with fans; he credits BTS's success in the United States to "loyalty built through direct contact with fans" (Bruner 2019). Big Hit Entertainment's next step was the shaping of the BTS Universe, which encapsulated the company's utilization of IP branding and IP storytelling as a unitary promotional tool and a key vehicle for reaching fans with the BTS concept, merchandise, and "brand power" (Ingham 2019). Big Hit Entertainment's foray into webtoons was part of this larger IP nexus—and one that has set it apart from its competitors. In

June 2019 the company was reportedly worth 2.3 trillion KRW ($1.95 billion USD), surpassing the combined economic value of SM, YG, and JYP and making Big Hit Entertainment a start-up "unicorn"—an unlisted or privately held enterprise with an estimated value of more than $1 billion USD.[9]

The *Save Me* webtoon is a quintessential example of the company's IP branding and storytelling nexus, extending the often-dark story world revealed in the group's previously published multimedia materials. By adding *Save Me* to the transmedia IP mix, the BTS Universe experienced a major boost that has sparked a burgeoning number of fan comments on Webtoon, as well as on Twitter, and a variety of blogs and online discussion forums. Moreover, using a branded webtoon in this way has enabled Big Hit Entertainment to achieve a level of innovation that differentiates it from its major competitors, SM, YG, and JYP.

ANOTHER WATERSHED MOMENT FOR THE K-POP GALAXY

While the (now-aging) example of PSY's "Gangnam Style" single from 2012 shows how K-pop's international popularity has spread through viral online word-of-mouth transmission (e.g., YouTube), it wasn't until early to mid-2017, following the unprecedented reception given to super idol group BTS, that K-pop "finally broke in the United States" (*Rolling Stone* 2018). In 2017 BTS grabbed the Top Social Artist Award at the 2017 Billboard Music Awards, preventing Justin Bieber from winning this award for a seventh consecutive year. Overnight BTS became the top musical act on Billboard's Social 50 chart, which ranks acts by their fans' activity level and engagement on social media entertainment and networking platforms. In November 2017 BTS grabbed additional global attention after performing their hit song "DNA" live at the American Music Awards, dazzling the live audience as well as viewers on television—not least the BTS ARMY.

Shortly before this event, BTS had launched the Love Myself antiviolence campaign (tied to the September 2017 release of their album *Love Yourself: Her*) in partnership with UNICEF and its #ENDViolence initiative to raise funds in support of victims of violence. These high-profile events, including BTS member RM's (aka Kim

Nam-joon) speech on self-love in September 2018 to the United Nations General Assembly, enhanced the group's profile in ways that no one could have imagined.[10]

Few observers would disagree that Big Hit Entertainment's success with BTS is a result of the company's ability to nurture overseas music markets, especially in the United States and in Europe and, of course, throughout Asia. However, its biggest success has been its ability to create a popular digital culture that continuously builds on the company's existing store of digital content that is directed to audiences at home and abroad. In sum, Big Hit Entertainment has succeeded in developing the type of transmedia IP that has enabled it to become a content-centered corporate platform. In March 2019 the company further expanded its media universe with the debut of a five-member all-male idol group called Tomorrow X Together (abbreviated as TXT) and the release of its first EP, *The Dream Chapter: Star*. Presumably TXT will benefit from the lessons learned and the commercial and cultural terrain captured during the BTS saga.

The release of *Save Me* in January 2019 enabled BTS members to reach out to existing fans and also to recruit new followers. However, the content of *Save Me* is very different from the superhero-save-the world sci-fi *We On: Be the Shield* and the comic *Hip Hop Monster* webtoons that Big Hit Entertainment released in 2014. While these previous webtoons were designed primarily to promote the then-new all-male idol group, *Save Me* was likely intended as a key element of the company's transmedia IP portfolio, designed to maintain the group's more serious edge while also building bridges between the K-pop and webtoon industries.

Adding to the IP branding and storytelling nexus, and building on the hype surrounding the *Save Me* webtoon as well as the group's multi-album releases, in mid-2019 Netmarble Games, Korea's largest mobile-gaming company, launched the story-based free-to-play game *BTS World*.[11] Within hours of its release in June 2019, the game gained top place on Apple's App Store charts in twenty-five countries, including Korea, Japan, and other Southeast Asian markets; it also hovered in the top five apps downloaded in thirty-six other countries (Spangler 2019).

Through the game's interactive experience, users role-play as a simulated BTS manager. The object of this visual novel-style game is to enable users to shape Big Hit Entertainment's IP business strategies including managing the process of BTS's debut in 2012. Here "leveling up" involves advancing through numerous career stages and facing their associated challenges. During their career journey, leading up to 2019, players assume the role of a BTS manager, encountering unexpected twists and turns along the way. Those with the best chance of excelling in the game are ARMY fans, bringing to it their extensive knowledge of BTS's real-life journey. Yet even for relatively uninformed fans the game's high level of interactivity with all seven band members—via simulated texts, phone calls, Instagram posts, and images and with one hundred previously unreleased short videos and some new songs added to the game's soundtrack—is nonetheless stimulating and potentially addictive (Tassi 2019).

Although BTS-inspired games have previously been released and successfully received across Asia, including the music-themed rhythm action game *SuperStar BTS* by Dalcomsoft (in early 2018), few if any K-pop-related video games have enjoyed the extensive global take-up that *BTS World* has achieved. Netmarble's success in this arena is yet another demonstration of the group's continuing soft-power appeal and the transportability of the transmedia IP that has accumulated around the BTS Universe.

CONCLUSION: BRANDED WEBTOONS AND THEIR SOFT-POWER APPEAL

Through the two hundred–plus branded webtoon series available on Naver Webtoon and other platforms, the genre continues to strengthen Korea's creative industries and their pursuit of exploitable transmedia IP. Nonetheless, only a small proportion of webtoons contain a story world and character set that can be successfully transported (viral or otherwise) across various media channels and adapted into films, web series, television series, and licensed merchandizing. Through its place in the larger BTS Universe, and its distinctive contribution to Big Hit Entertainment's transmedia IP portfolio, *Save Me* sheds light on some lesser-known aspects of the webtooniverse and its economic and cultural appeal.

As the authors have argued throughout this book, the type of user-generated content facilitated on webtoon platforms such as Naver

Webtoon, Webtoon, and Daum Webtoon is a core element of the webtooniverse. The analysis of *Save Me* and its evolving global reception probably needs more attention than we have attempted here in order to highlight this webtoon series' full transportability. Such analysis can be exploited in a variety of ways by creators, marketers, and other stakeholders in the webtoon industry and in the larger creative industries.

Today many webtoon enterprises are aggressively seeking to win new audiences through the orchestration of intertextual and viral linkages, adding to the success of an economy and culture driven by transmedia IP. In turn these intertextual linkages foster the economies of scope (as opposed to economies of scale) that can potentially increase the economic value of the original IP and its attractiveness to consumers. In many ways dependent on the already-established BTS Universe story world, *Save Me*'s success illustrates the commercial soundness of this approach. The sophisticated intertextuality, firmly established characters, and settings—down to the minor narrative elements and props scattered over the whole narrative—are all features that have elevated this branded webtoon to the highest level in the transmedia IP cosmos.

Commercially oriented and viral webtoons like the various series discussed in both chapter 7 and chapter 8 are among the latest types of digital media to join and accelerate the broader Korean Wave. They are enabling the webtooniverse to remain at the forefront of international and glocalized trends that signal a new stage in the development of regional soft power in a highly competitive environment. In many ways the BTS Universe and the *Save Me* webtoon series stand out as strong contenders in this ongoing soft-power struggle.

CONCLUSION: WEBTOONS—A "DIGITAL COMICS REVOLUTION"?

The research for this book started in 2017, after the authors began noticing the accelerating (albeit conspicuous) globalization of webtoons—in particular by means of the expanding number of volunteer fan translators contributing to Naver's globally facing Line Webtoon platform (renamed Webtoon in September 2019).

In early 2015 Webtoon launched an innovative crowdsourced translation service, inviting anyone to participate and to connect their work with friends and colleagues and worldwide webtoon fans—without having to download any complicated software. As explained in the introductory instructional video posted by the platform on YouTube on March 2015, anyone can register and then log in to the online translation portal (via Line, Facebook, Twitter, or Chinese Weibo social media app sign-in details) and then use the simple tools provided to select a favorite webtoon series, nominate a language, and begin entering translated text in the designated areas of a particular episode (Line Webtoon 2015). It is as simple as that. The names of all the participating translators and their chosen avatars, as well as the size (percentage) of their contributions, are displayed beneath each episode, fostering a sense of community and pride in one's work. (Some translators have contributed to dozens of webtoons.) The video also encourages contributors to add links to their work on blogs and other social media entertainment platforms, resulting in additional (and economically advantageous) electronic word-of-mouth promotion for the webtoons concerned and the

Webtoon site. This feature has saved Webtoon enormous expenditure, given that in 2017 the average cost of translating sixty cuts (including typesetting) was between 300,000 KRW and 400,000 KRW (approximately $280–$375 USD at the time) (Kang 2017, 72).

Virtually overnight, this revolutionary crowdsourced UGC feature on Webtoon—a distinctive feature of the webtoon industry as a whole (Jang and Song 2017; and Shim et al. 2020)—gave invaluable publicity to a number of Korean webtoons that had been growing in popularity with domestic readers over the previous few years. This development is part of the rise of the webtooniverse and the broad advancements in Web 2.0 and ICT that have facilitated the exchange of knowledge, the sharing of interactive tasks, and the mobilization of expertise between individuals and groups via online and mobile platforms (Malone and Bernstein 2015). Some of the earliest beneficiaries of this new "collective intelligence" include (in number of million likes as of May 1, 2020) *Tower of God* (25.6), *Noblesse* (14.3), *The God of High School* (12.1), and *The Gamer* (10.6), as well as *Cheese in the Trap* (6.7), *Dice* (6.6), *Girls of the Wild's* (5), and *unTouchable* (4.4).

As a result of this intermediation or "transcreation" process, Naver disrupted the traditional agency once commanded by legacy media companies and their highly controlled archives of analogue content. (Nonetheless, at the time of writing only eighty-four webtoon creators had given their explicit—that is, required—consent to Naver to include their series on Webtoon's fan-translation service.) While this aspect of the webtoon industry is not covered in this book, it is likely to herald a new epoch in the ongoing digital comics revolution. The globally facing Webtoon platform can be seen as an early adopter of a key globalization and glocalization strategy, pointing Korea's diverse stable of webtoon enterprises in the direction of so-called borderless markets and global readerships.

By our count, at the end of 2017 there were 29,500 individuals and loosely organized teams localizing thirty-two different language versions of serialized content on Webtoon, activity which has had the result of energizing the platform's official Simplified Chinese, Traditional Chinese, Thai, Indonesian, and Japanese sister sites (discussed in chapter 4). By mid-2019 this number had grown to 51,680 fan translators, and about a year later, in May 2020, it had increased again to 63,572, signaling the sustained interest and energy in this area—and in webtoons more generally.

On the one hand, a relatively small proportion of creators on the platform has so far consented to exposing their original Korean webtoons to this "unofficial" fan-translation system, despite its seeming to provide a reasonable level of expertise across the various languages. On the other hand, this unique feature of this platform is serving to reduce the incidence of illegal distribution (i.e., piracy) of other forms of fan-translated materials, which still plagues the industry. As the result of incidents of piracy tracked between January 2017 and 2018, the webtoon industry experienced accumulated losses of 1.86 trillion KRW (around $1.524 billion USD), impacting on the distribution of around four thousand webtoon titles. Piracy had a negative impact on the production of new webtoon titles, too, which dropped 14 percent during the same period (KOCCA 2018a, 111).

Might the systematized fan-translation infrastructure on Webtoon offer a positive path forward? Apparently the answer is yes, and at the very least it can help to reduce the potential for the type of downturn that Korea's print comics industry experienced in its heyday as a result of the illegal practice of digital scanlation.

In mid-2019—in an about-face that was probably inevitable, but nonetheless marked a striking departure from its practice of featuring free webtoons—Webtoon began charging fees and offering "fast-track" passes for the latest webtoon episodes as well as for some of the most popular older (archived) series. Although it is too early to tell how much revenue this latest upgrade to Naver's PPS monetization system will generate, this decision altered its exclusive focus on the "loss-leader" strategy it had followed from the outset (discussed in chapter 4). Previously, in mid-2018, Webtoon had initiated an advertising revenue-sharing program for eligible creators, with ads appearing beneath episodes of series classified as "popular"— those that had attained over forty thousand monthly page views in the United States and over one thousand total subscribers. Similar to Naver Webtoon's successful monetization approach in Korea (since 2013), its initial loss-leader strategy utilized outside of Korea was effectively switched to a PPS monetization structure. But this was only after Webtoon had used its "all-free" content to establish a strong foothold in the digital comics market. As a significant sign of the maturing of the industry, this relatively new scheme is bolstering the financial stability of its owner-creators (who can participate in the PPS program if they qualify) at the same time as it is increasing the platform's revenues.

The point here is that the whole industry is involved in a process of continual evolution—not just leading enterprises such as Webtoon and its parent company, Naver, and Daum Webtoon, which introduced KANG Full's vertically scrolling *Love Story* series in 2003, marking the birth of the medium as we know it. Since 2003 the webtoon industry has constantly been on the move, advancing a range of issues across the spectrum, including technical (mobile) innovation, policy intervention, content classification, monetization, transmedia IP projects, globalization, and creators' welfare. The rapid expansion of Webtoon's globally facing translation service and progressive monetization strategies are only two examples of the rate and depth at which many parts of the webtooniverse have changed since the start of this book project. While we have done our best to capture these and many of the other transformations affecting it, the industry is a fast-evolving domain of globalized media that will always be challenging for commentators to keep pace with.

We return to our discussion of the prehistory of webtoons in chapter 2 to reinforce our second concluding point. In a study of Japanese cultural policy and the phenomenon of "Cool Japan"—the global wave of Japanese popular culture that preceded the Korean Wave—Casey Brienza (2014) asks the disarmingly simple question: "Did manga conquer America?" While the short answer is no, the question itself and its timing raises some important questions about the production, circulation, and reception of popular culture and how it can be shaped by government intervention. As we argue in chapter 2, Japanese manga had a significant impact on Korea's comics industry, ironically at a time when almost all Japanese popular-culture products were officially banned in Korea. Between Korea's liberation from Japanese occupation in 1945 until 1998, when the policy was revoked, the government maintained a strict ban on Japanese popular magazines, books, comic books, television shows, and films. Despite this ban, which was primarily enacted to protect the local market, both industry and government stakeholders struggled to control the underground flow of Japanese manga and other products into Korea. Hence Japanese comics had been widely circulated for several decades before Korea officially lifted the ban.

While it would be inaccurate to say that Japanese manga "conquered" Korea, however, as an unintended consequence Korean content creators effectively became unsanctioned cultural intermediaries, localizing Japanese comics for the Korean market, which in turn kept comics culture alive in terms of readership and artistic practices. It was much easier for Korean creators and publishers to replicate Japanese manga than to create original Korean comics from scratch, and such plagiarized content made quick profits. This is a practice that mirrors some of the challenges faced today by Korea's domestic and international webtoon industry through unchecked piracy. At the same time—and unlike the policy-driven competitions and awards run today in conjunction with KOCCA and KOMACON, and platforms such as Daum Webtoon and Naver Webtoon (discussed in chapter 3)—little was done to encourage the development of stories and styles that reflected a sense of "Koreanness," despite Korean readers' general antipathy toward Japanese-inspired content. These historical conditions and practices—albeit in violation of basic copyright and protectionist laws—had the benefit of nurturing new and advanced skills for some domestic practitioners. Nonetheless, the comics industry paid a heavy price for failing to fully adapt to the digital age, and thus it struggled to remain solvent for many years to come.

However, as we show, many print comic publishers eventually *did* seek ways to take advantage of the digital wave and to weather the disruption to the publishing industry that followed by hosting some digitized versions of their own comics online. But they were outmaneuvered by the birth and rise of the webtoon as an alternative form of comics. The attempted transition of many traditional players to the webtoon industry only occurred much later, in the mid-2010s, after acknowledging that webtoons offered an avenue to remain solvent in the mainstream comics (and publishing) industry. For the most part, their efforts were too little and came too late. Traditional publishers had failed to learn important lessons from the late 1990s, when the KIM Dae-jung government's push to develop the Internet domain spawned the unauthorized reproduction or "scanlation" of comics—an illegal process by which fans digitally scan whole comic books and distribute them for free through the Internet. Publishers such as Seoul

Media Group, Daewon Media/Daewon Culture & Industry, and Haksan Publishing simply missed the opportunity to profit from this frenzy of online activity and interest and refashion it as a legal and monetized venture. Scanlation eventually became so widespread that it threatened to cripple the comic book industry and make *manhwabangs* (comic book rental shops) redundant. These shops slowly lost their status in Korean youth culture, especially after Internet and gaming spaces or *PC bangs* proliferated and became alternative spaces in which teenagers could loiter and consume increasing numbers of digital comics.

At the time of writing, a small number of legacy comic book publishers has finally begun to integrate themselves into the webtoon industry, particularly as content providers. In September 2018 KakaoPage invested 40 billion KRW (approximately $35.96 million USD) to acquire around 20 percent of the shares each belonging to Korea's three leading comic book publishers, Seoul Media Group, Daewon Culture & Industry, and Haksan Publishing, in a bid to guarantee a continuing supply of comic book IP for its webtoon series (and webnovels) (Ahn 2018). As a result, these three leading publishing companies from the 1990s are now enjoying a newfound vitality and viability in the contemporary webtoon industry, where their vast knowledge, experience, and longstanding accumulated artist networks are generating new value. While developing new titles, these companies have also provided part of their vast store of comics IP to some of the most active webtoon platforms, including KakaoPage and Naver Webtoon, feeding the demand of the webtooniverse for new sources of "Super-IP" inspiration.

In addition to comic book publishers, traditional book publishers have also demonstrated an interest in participating in the rapid growth of the webtoon industry. For example, Wisdom House Media Group—the largest book publisher in Korea—initiated its own webtoon platform called Justoon in May 2018, shortly after the successful publication of YOON Tae-ho's *Misaeng* book collection, which was adapted from the *Misaeng* webtoon. An unexpected bestseller, *Misaeng* opened Wisdom House Media Group's eyes to the lucrative potential of the burgeoning webtoon market.

The rise of the webtoon out of a dying print comics industry, during a previous era of protectionism, and the export of webtoons to new markets is a dynamic story spanning over two decades. The webtoon industry continues to maintain its distinctiveness from other webcomics, which are mostly digitized versions of paper comics published online (e.g., ComiXology and Marvel.com in the United States). Webtoons can be briefly characterized as a full-color, vertically scrolling digital "snack culture" read on personal computers and (mostly now) mobile devices. As we show in chapters 3 and 4, although a few basic types of webtoon-like comics were published by a number of entrepreneurial Internet enterprises in 2000, it was not until 2003 and 2005 that Korea's giant search engines Daum and then Naver perfected and popularized the vertically scrolling format and genres with which we are now familiar. As we show in chapter 5, new enterprises such as KakaoPage and Lezhin Comics emerged in 2013, rapidly becoming serious competitors to pioneers Daum Webtoon and Naver Webtoon. Given more time and resources, a second (and probably third) book could be written about the remaining thirteen highly active and forty-eight lesser-known Korean webtoon enterprises, not to mention the increasing number of international companies (e.g., Graphite—the "Netflix-meets-Spotify-meets-YouTube for free comics" platform) that are now competing in the domestic and global webtoon and webcomic markets.[1]

Put simply, webtoon platforms come in a variety of shapes and sizes, each with a different corporate or entrepreneurial background and agenda. Each of the platforms discussed in this study has adopted or at least explored a monetization model, including "fast-pass," pay-per-view of episodes, and freemium "free-if-you-wait" viewing options, as well as a range of rewards systems, enabling viewers to share content with their social networks via other social media platforms such as Twitter, Instagram, and Facebook. These various monetization and loyalty models have gradually become significant revenue-generating channels—particularly for platforms that feature specific types of content (e.g., adult, BL, and GL) and appeal to a narrow reader demographic. These broader linkages are being further strengthened for content creators through their own individual crowdfunding campaigns on Patreon or Kickstarter.

These various developments are the latest interventions to enrich the webtoon ecosystem, which in our analysis has passed through four distinctive stages. The first stage (1998–2002) saw the emergence of amateur web comics and experiments with distributing digital comics via the Internet (i.e., N4 and Comics Today). The second (2003–2009) saw the online birth and early transmedia adaptation of webtoons. The third (2010–2013) saw the creation of a mobile-centered ecosystem launched via the rapid proliferation of smartphones and novel monetization strategies. And the fourth (2014–present) saw an accelerating internationalization push through globally facing platforms.

This last phase includes the gradual expansion of "branded webtoons," a commercial variant that has become a key source of soft power not only within the industry's own ecosystem but also across Korea's wider creative industries. As we describe in chapter 7, this subsector includes hundreds of archived and currently running webtoon series—created specifically for commercial advertisements, public-service announcements, company promotions, and product endorsements—which include supporting marketing materials for promoting new films and television series. In chapter 8 we explore three distinctive branded webtoon series involving BTS, one of the most globally recognizable and successful K-pop acts ever to have been seen on stage or accessed across the digital mediasphere. The group's promoters have created remarkable synergies between the webtooniverse and the BTS Universe—the transmedia story world surrounding BTS that is largely responsible for driving its phenomenal global popularity. Our treatment of these previously unrecognized soft-power aspects of the webtoon industry and its transmedia storytelling power, merchandizing success, and crowdsourced transportability exposes some of the ways that webtoons are being used to leverage and profit from transmedia IP.

This book has taken major steps to providing some significant details and analysis of the complex history and diversity of webtoons and the larger industrial ecosystem that they inhabit—and that the authors have dubbed the *webtooniverse*. Especially in chapters 6, 7, and 8 they demonstrate how the industry has continuously facilitated and embraced a major push toward the creation and exploitation of innovative technology and transmedia IP. For those even remotely aware of the existence of and expanding opportunities for webtoon adaptations, webtoons have become a kind of petri dish for nurturing the development of a single story source or "transmedia IP engine" for driving different media formats (e.g., films, television series, webcomics, webnovels, and web series) and a variety of platforms (e.g., big-screen cinema, IPTV, web portals, and mobile streaming on demand). More traditional industry producers—such as the international film production company G-Base, which has begun nurturing its own webtoon series *Caster* (2018–2019) on Webtoon as a potential IP engine—are beginning to realize the promise of the rapidly evolving webtoon format outside of Korea. Although unmentioned in its publicity materials, *Caster* is a small but important example of the mainstream film industry's foray into webtoons—as well as its adoption of the "effect-toon" format (discussed in chapter 6), which utilizes embedded music and sound effects over a series of cuts, simulating the feeling of watching an animation (Line Webtoon 2017).

Boasting an original song and score from Academy Award and Grammy and Emmy Award winner actor-singer and rapper Common, *Caster* is an original multimedia star vehicle for Common, who plays the lead title character. The series was created by seasoned IP creator and digital media entrepreneur Austin Harrison in collaboration with comic book illustrator (and Eisner Award nominee) Zach Howard and veteran writer and graphic novelist (and former Marvel Comics editor) Mike Raicht—the three principals at the IP development and marketing company Noble Transmission—as well as artist Jason Masters.

This high-energy action series features the exploits of a globetrotting antiques collector who becomes ensnared in an international cloak-and-dagger operation. *Caster* has by far the longest credits of any comparable webtoon, including several companies and individuals involved in the series' production and distribution and original music rights (including Naver Webtoon founder KIM Junkoo, Webtoon global head and innovator KIM Hyungil, and head of content Tom Akel, who are listed as the "Webtoon executive producers"). Of these, G-Base is a film production company run by actor Gerard Butler and Alan Siegel (coproducer with Butler of *Law Abiding Citizen*, 2009; *Olympus Has Fallen*, 2013; *London Has Fallen*, 2016; *Den of Thieves*, 2018; and *Hunter Killer*, 2018, among other series), who have the rights to produce a live-action adaptation of the series. In sum, *Caster* is the epitome of the "IP-engine" concept (Yecies et al. 2020) whereby the original webtoon represents a potential multiplatform character and transmedia story that can be exploited across mobile devices, streaming platforms, and on the big screen in cinemas.

While attempting to frame webtoons as a new type of graphic narrative, Cho (2016) draws upon the term "collective innovation" as a way to differentiate Korean webtoons from other conventional digital comic formats from the United States and Japan. Cho's assertion that the capacity for webtoon platforms to coalesce aggregates of authors and artists "versus individual innovative webcomic forms, which are not recognized as a major cultural tendency of creating comics on the digital platform," rightfully credits webtoons for becoming a "mainstream popular culture form in Korea." Our book has extended these ideas by showing how a spectrum of webtoon industry players are involved in multiple interconnected processes of collective innovation across the webtooniverse. In all the ways emphasized in each chapter, webtoons and webtoon enterprises are becoming enmeshed within the global mediasphere, pushing media convergence across the creative industries in new directions. Perhaps more than any other digital medium, webtoons exemplify the notion of "collective innovation" as well as representing a "digital comics revolution" for their ability to circumvent the cultural, geographic, and economic barriers to entry (i.e., costs) associated with traditional media production and distribution channels. Whatever the case, this book has attempted to give new meaning to the concept of "collective innovation," which may sound clichéd but is nonetheless part of the process of creating both cultural and economic value between producers (creators and publishers) and consumers (readers) in the digital comics industry. It is precisely the ways in which the spectrum of webtoon industry players investigated in this book are challenging the dominant companies across the global mediasphere that make this story a timely contribution to the field as well as to our understanding of Korea's rapidly transforming digital economy. Online and mobile webtoons are now part of the most visible and highly profitable face of Korea's evolving digital media and creative industries—not only for their impressive viewership statistics and increasing sales but also for their synergies across various media formats and platforms, as well as the foundation they are providing for transmedia (and transnational) adaptations in the television, film, gaming, live theater, publishing, music, and web drama industries.

Today the older, conventional view of comics as a form of "low culture" and thus harmful to youth, a prejudicial perspective originating in the 1960s, has gone out the window. The success of the contemporary webtoon industry has been built on a sustained readership base made up of both old and young—a group that has maintained its interest in a comics culture that was at one time subjected to severe social and political censorship. The other side to this rosy-colored portrayal, however, are the hurdles that the industry has faced along the way. As we discuss in chapter 5, in early 2015—without warning and in an apparently random act of discrimination—the Korea Communications Standards Commission (KCSC) shut down the Lezhin Comics website for allegedly distributing "obscene" content to adolescents. Catching industry observers by surprise, this move occurred a considerable time after this pay-to-view webtoon enterprise (along with peer platform Toptoon) began featuring adult content and demonstrating market strength and international expansion. However, following public and industry protests, KCSC reversed its decision just one day later (Gwon 2015). Lezhin—and arguably the then-nascent webtooniverse as a whole—benefitted from the unexpected publicity, not least because of the robust advocacy initiatives aimed at protecting freedom of expression that followed. The week after the rescinding of the ban, Lezhin launched a special "appreciation" sale to reward its customers for their support. Thanks to the KCSC, since this incident Lezhin—and the webtooniverse, we would argue—has never looked back.

Have webtoons, then, conquered the globe? Although it may sound cliché, a better question, which this book answers, is, How did the birth of webtoons in 2003, and their ongoing evolution, represent a watershed "soft-power" moment not only for Korea's creative industries but also for the globalization of Korean-born webtoons and the glocalization of Korean-inspired webtoons? The material analyzed in the book has provided some answers, given that webtoons are now available in dozens of translated languages, plus the fact that increasing numbers of practitioners in many parts of the globe have begun making their own webtoons. The short answer to the question posed above is that, more than any government policy initiative, the webtooniverse (as conceptualized in these pages) has been instrumental in advancing the overall development and global reach of Korea's creative industries, which in turn has added fuel to a revolution of a kind—the digital comics revolution.

NOTES

1. INTRODUCING WEBTOONS AND THE EXPANSION OF KOREA'S CREATIVE INDUSTRIES

1. BONG's 2013 sci-fi action-drama *Snowpiercer* was adapted from the French graphic novel *Le Transperceneige* (1982) by Jacques Lob and Jean-Marc Rochette.

2. However, Kim's (2014) chapter in *The Korean Popular Culture Reader* does offer more details on webtoon's related precursor history of print comics.

3. Generally speaking, webcomic artists working in the Anglophone have struggled to bring new readers to their sites as a result of competition from social-networking services (SNSs), such as Facebook, which dominate online and mobile traffic. There is a consensus among webcomic creators that the web no longer holds the opportunity for growth. See Dale 2015.

4. See Korea Creative Content Agency (KOCCA) 2018b.

5. Initially written to explain how Tapastic operated, the following analogy could be expanded to cover webtoon platforms in general; see Serafino 2015.

6. Data taken from Webtoonguide: Webtoon Analysis Service, at https://was.webtoonguide.com/dashboard (accessed 1 May 2020).

7. https://www.comichron.com/.

8. Data taken from Webtoonguide: Webtoon Analysis Service, athttps://was.webtoonguide.com/dashboard (accessed 1 May 2020).

9. See Grand Comics Database (GDC) 2020.

10. Bufftoon's mother company, NCSoft, is Korea's number one game-making and -publishing company and is known for the widely popular role-playing games *Lineage* and *Lineage II*. Bufftoon began in 2013 as a webzine and

digital-comics service published by NCSoft, and in mid-2018 it was launched as a webtoon platform.

11. Before 1996, all domestic film scripts needed to be approved at the preproduction stage and all foreign films examined by the Performance Ethics Committee, which had maintained these powers since its establishment in the late 1970s.

12. Popular titles (rated by number of views) can earn creators an exclusive contract from a platform, averaging between $2,000 and $5,000 USD per month. See iResearch 2018.

2. CONCEPTUALIZING THE IMPACT OF JAPANESE MANGA IN KOREA AND THE PREHISTORY OF WEBTOONS

1. For more on the long history of comics (aka manga) in Japan, see Ito 2005.

2. KO's *Im Kkokjong* series is a Robin Hood–type drama based on a real historical figure. Set in the sixteenth century during the Chosun Dynasty, *Im Kkokjong* follows the life and exploits of a justice-seeking bandit. KO's contributions were a success, and the circulation of *Daily Sports* was duly boosted. See Park 2013.

3. Iwabuchi (2002) offers a parallel framework through his analysis of the complex contemporary process of localization by which Japanese media companies and technology firms (e.g., Sony) seek to expunge the explicit marks—which he likens to an "odor"—of Japanese culture in order to increase their penetration of international markets.

4. For an overview of censorship concerns and conditions in Japan, see McLelland 2015, Allison 1996, and McLelland 2011.

5. See Jang 2012.

6. See *Dong-a Ilbo* 1966 and *Kyunghyang Shinmun* 1968b.

7. For more on the history of the US Comics Code Authority, see Adkinson 2008 and Nyberg 1998.

8. See Deputy Director of *Dong-a Ilbo* Department of Social Affairs 1983; and see So 1984.

9. See the press release issued by Korea's Truth and Reconciliation Commission (2010).

10. Figures from KMDb (accessed December 1, 2019), https://www.kmdb.or.kr/db/kor/detail/movie/K/03967.

11. LEE Hyun-se was an especially prolific artist, who has published a total of 686 books (including series), as well as three webtoon series on Naver Webtoon and Daum Webtoon (since 2015). Among his other credits are thir-

teen transmedia adaptations (ten films and three television dramas), including the films *The Report of Daughter-in-Law's Rice Flower* (1989), *Armageddon* (1995), and *Terrorist* (1996) and the television dramas *Police* (1994), *2009 Alien Baseball Team* (2009), and *Birdie Buddy* (2011).

12. For more on these film censorship cases, see Yecies and Shim 2016 and Shim and Yecies 2016.

13. LEE's legal battles are chronicled in Choi 2006.

14. See Kim and Kim 2012.

15. KIM Pung and Kian84 stand out for their success in the wider entertainment industry. KIM Pung was one of the regular chef contenders in the variety cooking show *Please Take Care of My Refrigerator* (2014–2019). Kian84 (aka KIM Hee-min) eventually became a celebrity on Naver Webtoon with the high school slice-of-life comedy webtoon *Fashion King* (2011–2013, and its 2014 adapted film), the webtoon series *Bokhak King* (2014–present, a sequel to *Fashion King*), and his frequent appearances on the reality-variety television series *I Live Alone* (2013–present).

3. POLICY INTERVENTION AND THE FORMATION OF THE WEBTOONIVERSE

1. Korea's broadband policy originated in the government's launch of four major initiatives—the first and second Basic Plan for Administrative Computerization (1978–1982; 1983–1987) and the first and second Basic Plan for a National Backbone Network (1987–1991; 1992–1996). For full details concerning these and other related policy instruments, see Korea Internet and Security Agency (KISA) 2015.

2. Which can be accessed online at https://archive.org/.

3. See Noh 2002.

4. See Song 2001.

5. As of mid-2020, *Love Story* was available at http://webtoon.daum.net/webtoon/viewer/221. The first three episodes, including the epilogue, can be viewed for free, and the remaining episodes are available for 100 WON each (approximately 80 US cents).

6. These and other policy documents are available on the Korean government policy information site POINT, at https://policy.nl.go.kr/search/searchDetail.do?rec_key=SH2_PLC20190242479.

7. The Promotion of Cartoons Act received the Presidential Enforcement Decree in August 2012. See Korea Law Translation Center 2012b.

4. DAUM AND NAVER: THE SEARCH PORTALS UNDERPINNING KOREA'S TRANSNATIONAL WEBTOON IP ENGINES

1. See http://www.kobis.or.kr/kobis/business/mast/mvie/searchMovieList. do and http://www.boxofficemojo.com/title/tt1694019/?ref_=bo_se_r_1.

2. See Yonhap News Agency 2009.

3. See the congratulatory video footage on the launch of *Avengers: Electric Rain* featured at the end of the webtoon's prologue, at http://webtoon.daum. net/webtoon/viewer/27101.

4. See http://www.crunchbase.com/organization/tapas-media.

5. See http://www.tapas.io.

6. For more details on the CIC system, see Kim and Ryu 2017.

7. In August 2013 Naver's parent company, NHN, was separated into two separate entities: NHN Entertainment Corporation (the new name for Hangame) and Naver Corp. However, the parent company's name reverted to NHN in April 2019. Today NHN's subsidiaries include Line Corporation, Naver's global outpost established in Japan in 2001, which has operated the Line Messenger social-networking platform since 2011. While the Korean market is dominated by competitor Kakao's Kakao Talk messenger app, Line Messenger is one of the top seven messenger apps in the world, becoming even more popular in Japan, Taiwan, Thailand, and Indonesia than it is in Korea.

8. Initially, in 2014, Japanese translations of Naver webtoons appeared at www.webtoons.com/ja. Then in late 2016 all translated and original webtoons from Japan were transferred to a new site, XOY (http://xoy.webtoons.com/ja), which was terminated in January 2019. As of mid-2020, the official Japanese site for Naver's webtoon service in Japan was LINE Manga (https://manga.line. me).

9. See *Forbes* 2014.

10. The statistics in this paragraph appear on Naver's official corporate relations blog (Naver Corporation 2019b).

11. Other platforms that also initiated a pay-per-view model, and were inspired by Daum and Naver, include Ktoon (2015, Olleh Market Webtoon), Comico (2015 in Korea and 2016 in Japan), and Bufftoon (2018).

5. ASIA'S NEW TITANS OF PAID CONTENT: SECOND-GENERATION WEBTOON PLATFORMS KAKAOPAGE AND LEZHIN COMICS

1. In mid-2012 the KakaoTalk app had reportedly been installed by 97 percent of smartphone users in Korea, a figure driven by the app's embedded photo-centered social-networking service KakaoStory (launched in early 2012). See Rong 2012.

2. In early 2011 KakaoPage received an initial cash injection of three billion KRW (approximately $2.67 million USD) from Korean venture capital firm Smilegate Investment—a major underwriter of Korean Internet and gaming companies. And by the beginning of 2012 KakaoPage had received another 3 billion KRW in funding from Samsung Venture Investment. This level of investment reflects the wider linkages between the webtoon and other industries as well as their confidence in the webtoon industry's potential for continued growth and expansion.

3. See Hyeong-joon Yun 2013.

4. Current rankings are available at http://www.appbrain.com. And see AppBrain 2020.

5. The series is available at https://piccoma.com/web/product/3557.

6. For the views of Naver Webtoon's popular artist HA, who debuted in 2006 with the comic drama *Sambong Barber Shop*, see Kim 2011. Neon B is the creator of Lezhin's hit adult thriller–romance series *Bad Boss* (2013–2015) and also writer of popular romantic slice-of-life comedy-drama webtoon *Dieter* (2011–2011, illustrated by Caramel). Neon B's views on the issue are prominently displayed in the epilogue of *Bad Boss*, available at https://www.lezhin.com/en/comic/badboss_en/e1 (registration required).

7. See Lee and Park 2014.

8. As of 2020 the English-language Lezhin Comics iOS app offered content in eighteen languages: English, Basque, Czech, Dutch, Finnish, French, German, Italian, Japanese, Korean, Norwegian, Polish, Portuguese, Russian, Slovak, Spanish, Swedish, and Vietnamese. The operating language on the Android app—either Korean, English, or Japanese—is determined by the user after downloading a file.

9. These data according to a basic search on SimilarWeb for www.lezhin.com, www.page.kakao.com, and www.webtoon.daum.net (accessed October 15, 2019).

10. Gray's experiences with Lezhin are chronicled on her Twitter account, at https://twitter.com/yousowol.

11. The list, which was contained in an apparently leaked internal Lezhin e-mail, was confirmed by Korean broadcaster SBS. See Sim 2018.

12. Solidary Against Lezhin's Unfair Treatment's website details these controversial issues, as well as the group's engagement with Lezhin Comics. See http://www.legyuyeon.com/blank-4.

13. As the industry marked its ten-year anniversary, other platforms were also experiencing labor issues. Shortly after its formation in 2013, Kiwitoon (no known relation to New Zealand) faced legal action for unfair contracts with its creators, claiming full copyright of webtoons, pocketing 100 percent of advertising profits, and manipulating the upload durations of particular webtoon titles. Kiwitoon artists issued a protest statement, the Korea Cartoonist Association intervened on their behalf, and the company sued those artists who had signed the statement for breach of contract. However, Kiwitoon eventually withdrew from the case, and all its artists canceled their contracts; the company filed for bankruptcy the following year. See O. S. Lee 2017.

6. WEBTOONS AND TECHNOLOGICAL INNOVATION

1. The contemporary "chat-fiction" webnovel, accessible via mobile apps such as Hooked, Eavesdrop, and Cliffhanger, resembles Daum Webtoon's early experiment with chatting-toons.

2. In 2014 Daum Webtoon introduced its own type of moving-toon, or short-animation format but only via the Daum Webtoon smartphone app. However, this innovative format was too costly to maintain, especially after it failed to attract the sustained interest of readers. For an example, see the series *The American Ghost Jack: Moving-toon*, available at: http://m.webtoon.daum.net/m/webtoon/viewer/31254.

3. For a detailed history of the modern comic book industry in the United States, see Gabilliet 2010.

4. Kellett is also one of the coauthors of the book *How to Make Webcomics* (Guigar et al. 2011).

5. A few of the numerous examples include https://steemit.com/horror/@ninzacode/horror-webtoon-ep01-ok-su-station-ghost-by-horang, https://wiki.screamerfanbase.com/Ok-su_Station_Ghost, https://www.reddit.com/r/horror/comments/rde8y/oksu_station_ghost_sequel_to_bongcheondong_ghost/, and https://9gag.com/gag/azAYwAj/bongchong-dong-ghost.

6. See https://www.webtoons.com/en/thriller/chiller/list?title_no=536.

7. The original Korean-language version of *Yumi's Cells* on Naver Webtoon is available at https://comic.naver.com/webtoon/list.nhn?titleId=651673.

8. Writer HWANG is well-known in Korea for the Daum Webtoon *I Killed My Wife* (2010, adapted as a feature film in 2019) and the Lezhin Comics webtoon series *Bloody Festival* (2015) and *Gok Du* (2015), as well as for his 2018 book *Crowdsourcing Webtoon Storytelling* (Keuraudeu-sosing weptun seutoritelling) (Seoul: Communication Books).

9. In 2018 Naver Labs' deep-learning and machine-learning department, particularly for webtoon research, was transferred to Naver Webtoon and re-named W Research.

10. For more on VR as an "empathy machine" and its application to the short film *Bloodless* (2017), produced by Gina Kim, see Buckmaster and Yecies 2019.

11. For more on Line Webtoon's "transcreators," see Yecies et al. 2020.

7. THE BRANDED WEBTOON AND ITS SOFT-POWER APPEAL

1. Available at https://comic.naver.com/webtoon/list.nhn?titleId=663752.

2. These three branded webtoon series are available, respectively, at https://comic.naver.com/webtoon/list.nhn?titleId=687130, https://comic.naver.com/webtoon/list.nhn?titleId=718023, and https://comic.naver.com/webtoon/list.nhn?titleId=713334.

3. While this chapter focuses mostly on Naver's branded webtoons, many other webtoon platforms have also produced a number of these types of pro-motional series. For instance, in 2014 Lezhin Comics released a two-episode branded webtoon (https://www.lezhin.com/ko/comic/gundo) to promote the release of the historical-action feature film *Kundo: Age of the Rampant* (2014), starring HA Jeong-Woo. Also in 2014 Daum Webtoon published a thirteen-episode branded webtoon with and for the Ministry of Unification, called *Calm Down! Cheong-Doong!*, which features an anthropomorphized (migrating) bird from North Korea who goes to Seoul in search of a job following reunifica-tion. Once in Seoul, Cheong-Doong struggles to integrate into society. Howev-er, he perseveres and eventually succeeds, though he still misses his family and home in the North. (See http://webtoon.daum.net/webtoon/view/unification.)

4. See Enberg 2019.

5. *Midnight Rhapsody* is available in English on *Webtoon* at http://www.webtoons.com/en/slice-of-life/midnight-rhapsody/list?title_no=116&page=1.

6. See IMDb 2021.

7. See https://comic.naver.com/webtoon/list.nhn?titleId=24952.

8. User comments on the film can be found at https://movie.naver.com/movie/bi/mi/basic.nhn?code=64195.

9. See Naver Webtoon 2016.

10. Another Hanwha Group–branded webtoon favored by readers (and thus a successful series) is the fantasy-disaster series *2024* (2014–2015, 50 episodes over two seasons). Produced for Hanwha Life Insurance, *2024* is set in a postapocalyptic era in which the entire Korean peninsula is under threat of a massive volcano. Other examples include *Pitch Like Me* (2015, 28 episodes) and *Orange Moment* (2016, 25 episodes), two brand webtoons that promote the Hanwha Eagles baseball team.

11. Initially Creek and River concentrated on television broadcasting and film projects; however, in the early 2010s they expanded into branded webtoons, and in 2020 they began producing their own webtoon series, such as the historical drama *Eyes of the Dawn* (2020)—a transmedia adaptation of the serialized novel (1975–1981) and famous television series from 1991. The webtoon is currently published on Naver Series.

12. See https://comic-superstring.naver.com.

13. See Caulfield 2019.

8. K-POP WEBTOONS AND THE TRANSMEDIA IP NEXUS IN THE BTS UNIVERSE

1. See https://www.webtoons.com/en/challenge/hip-hop-monster/list?title_no=67213&page=1.

2. See *Koreaboo* 2019. And see https://www.wattpad.com/story/113698168-we-on-be-the-shield-season-1-webtoon-bts.

3. Line Friends is a brand of characters developed in Korea in 2011 and released in 2015 by Naver's Japanese subsidiary Line Corporation as a series of icons and emoji stickers for its mobile messenger app LINE. Today Line Friends is a massive merchandising agglomerate, including retail stores in major cities in Mainland China, Hong Kong, Japan, Taiwan, Thailand, North America, and, of course, Korea. The success of the BTS-BT21 merchandising line has contributed directly to Line Corporation and parent company Naver's annual profits. During the period spanning January 1 to September 30, 2019, revenues of 14,048 million Yen (approximately $128.9 million USD) were generated by Line Friends, primarily from sales of character merchandise. See LINE Corp 2020.

4. LICO's other webtoon series include *Ghost Theater* (2019–2020), the horror *Ghost Teller* (as QTT, 2017–2020, 92 episodes), and the drama *Refund High School* (2018–2019, 135 episodes), on both Naver and Webtoon, as well as the serialized animation *Psycho-sociopath Nyanya* on Naver Webtoon (2019–2020, 105 episodes).

5. The date May 22 (in Korea) is the same day that BTS received the Top Social Artist Award at the 2017 Billboard Music Awards ceremony held in Las Vegas (May 21 in the United States).

6. See https://ibighit.com/bts/eng/discography/detail/map_of_the_soul-persona.php.

7. The *Save Me* webtoon playlist is found at https://open.spotify.com/playlist/40VgHWhi70m3WHg2mfBUK1.

8. See further, Scolari 2009; Granitz and Forman 2015; and Davis 2013.

9. According to Korean stock exchange figures from June 5, 2019, the stock/share values of the Big Three are SM at 1.6 trillion won, or $1.36 billion USD; JYP at 929.6 billion won, or $787.8 million USD; and YG at 580.5 billion won, or $491.95 million USD. See Han 2019.

10. While limited space precludes us from treating other notable points on the BTS time line, one event in particular is worth noting: the March 2018 release of the documentary *BTS: Burn the Stage* on the YouTube Red premium streaming channel. This eighty-five-minute film, which was also shown in Korean cinemas on CGV's ultrawide Screen-X format (a 270-degree panoramic format utilizing a central screen plus two side screens), showcased the 2017 BTS Wings Tour, as well as other key moments for the group in 2017.

11. Founded in 2000, Netmarble has developed a number of immensely popular and profitable titles, including *Seven Knights*, *Marvel Future Fight*, *EvilBane* (known as *RAVEN* in Korea and Japan), *Cookie Jam*, *Lineage 2 Revolution*, and *Everybody's Marble*.

CONCLUSION: WEBTOONS—A "DIGITAL COMICS REVOLUTION"?

1. See the June 2019 launch of Graphite covered in Johnston 2019.

REFERENCES

Abramovitch, Seth. 2019. "BTS Is Back: Music's Billion-Dollar Boy Band Takes the Next Step." *The Hollywood Reporter*, October 2. https://tinyurl.com/s4f3so8.

Adkinson, Cary D. 2008. "*The Amazing Spider-Man* and the Evolution of the Comics Code: A Case Study in Cultural Criminology." *Journal of Criminal Justice and Popular Culture* 15 (3): 241–61. https://static1.squarespace.com/static/5b0ee82df793927c77add8b6/t/5b90691340ec9ab3a95e4388/1536190740798/1+Adkinson+2008.pdf.

Ahn, E. S. 2013. "Thursday Column: Did KakaoPage Fail" (Mogyoil achime: Kakaopeijineun silpaehaenna). *Seoul Economy*, August 28. https://tinyurl.com/s4vxrv5.

Ahn, H. J. 2020. "KakaoPage Reveals the OST of Their Webtoon *The Legendary Moonlight Sculptor* on 20th" (Kakaopeiji 20il weptun dalbitjogaksa OST eumwon gonggae). *ZDNet*, January 20. http://www.zdnet.co.kr/view/?no=20200120090952.

Ahn, J. S., and S. W. Yi. 1997. "Public Security—Chilling Effect on Cultural Community" (Munhwagye deopchin gongan chanbaram). *The Hankyoreh*, July 25, p. 11.

Ahn, Sung-mi. 2018. "Mobile & Internet: KakaoPage Invests W40b in 3 Comic Publishers." *The Korea Herald—The Investor*, September 28. http://www.theinvestor.co.kr/view.php?ud=20180928000419.

Allison, Anne. 1996. *Permitted and Prohibited Desires: Mothers, Comics, and Censorship in Japan*. Berkeley: University of California Press.

AppBrain. 2020. "Google Play Rankings." Accessed March 1. https://tinyurl.com/s3aqwo3.

Babeltop. 2018. "Lezhin Comics Beats Marvel and DC on U.S. Google Play." *Venture Square*, April 19. https://www.venturesquare.net/world/lezhin-comics-beats-marvel-dc-u-s-google-play/.

Baek, Byung-yeul. 2014. "Korea's 'Webtoon' Industry: Boom or Bust?" *The Korea Times*, February 20. https://www.koreatimes.co.kr/www/news/culture/2014/02/203_151973.html.

———. 2019. "New Kakao M CEO to Challenge Netflix, CJ ENM in Original Content." *The Korea Times*, January 2. http://www.koreatimes.co.kr/www/tech/2019/01/133_261355.html.

Balasubramanian, Siva K. 1991. *Beyond Advertising and Publicity: The Domain of Hybrid Messages*. Working paper no. 91-131, January 1. Cambridge, MA: Marketing Science Institute.

Bhargava, Jayant, and Alice Klat. 2016. *Content Democratization: How the Internet Is fueling the Growth of Creative Economies*. [New York]: Strategy&, PricewaterhouseCoopers. https://www.strategyand.pwc.com/gx/en/insights/2017/content-democratization/content-democratization.pdf.

Bockstedt, Jesse C., Robert J. Kauffman, and Frederick J. Riggins. 2006. "The Move to Artist-Led On-line Music Distribution: A Theory-Based Assessment and Prospects for

Structural Changes in the Digital Music Market." *International Journal of Electronic Commerce* 10 (3): 7–38.

Bramlett, Frank, Roy T. Cook, and Aaron Meskin. 2017. *The Routledge Companion to Comics*. New York: Routledge.

Brienza, Casey. 2014. "Did Manga Conquer America? Implications for the Cultural Policy of 'Cool Japan.'" *International Journal of Cultural Policy* 20 (4): 383–98.

Brouillette, Sarah. 2014. *Literature and the Creative Economy*. Redwood City, CA: Stanford University Press.

Bruner, Raisa. 2019. "The Mastermind behind BTS Opens Up about Making a K-Pop Juggernaut." *Time*, October 8. https://time.com/5681494/bts-bang-si-hyuk-interview/.

Buckmaster, Luke, and Brian Yecies. 2019. "Docu-reality and Empathy in *Bloodless* (2017): A Manifesto for Transnational Virtual Reality Cinema." In *Asia-Pacific Film Co-productions: Theory, Industry and Aesthetics*, edited by Dal Yong Jin and Wendy Su, 275–92. New York: Routledge.

Cartoonists Emergency Committee Against KCSC. 2012. "Signing a Business Agreement between the Comics Community and the Korean Communications Standards Commission" (Manhwagyewa bangsongtongsinsimuiwiwonhoeui eommuhyeobyak chegyeol). *Cartoonists Emergency Committee Against KCSC Blog*, April 8. https://blog.naver.com/nocut_toon.

Caruso, E. 2017. "Koogi: 'I Didn't Want *Killing Stalking* to Seem like a Romantic Story'" (Koogi: "Non volevo che *Killing Stalking* sembrasse una storia romantica"). *Wired.Italy*, November 3. https://www.wired.it/play/fumetti/2017/11/03/koogi-killing-stalking/.

Caulfield, Keith. 2019. "BTS Meets the Beatles and the Monkees in Billboard Chart History with 'Map of the Soul: Persona.'" *Billboard*, April 21. http://www.billboard.com/articles/columns/chart-beat/8507983/bts-beatles-monkees-billboard-chart-history.

Chae, Myungsin (Veronica), and Byungtae Lee. 2005. "Transforming an Online Portal Site into a Playground for Netizens." *Journal of Internet Commerce* 4 (2): 95–114.

Cho, Heekyoung. 2016. "The Webtoon: A New Form for Graphic Narrative." *The Comics Journal*, July 18. http://www.tcj.com/the-webtoon-a-new-form-for-graphic-narrative/.

Choi, E. Y. 2012. "Success Factors for Thriller Webtoon Moss—Everything about Yoon Taeho" (Janhokan seurilleo weptun ikki seonggong yoineuntt—yuntaeho jakgaui modeun geot). *Channel Yes*, August 30. http://ch.yes24.com/Article/View/20492.

Choi, Young-jin. 2006. "Lee Hyun-Se, President of the Korean Cartoonist Association, Is Busy Creating Manhwa Hallyu" (Manhwa hanryu mandeulgie yeonyeomi eopneun hanguk manhwagahyeophoe-jang ihyeonse). *Lady Kyunghyang*, October. http://lady.khan.co.kr/khlady.html?mode=view&code=4&artid=8655.

Choo, Kukhee. 2010. "Consuming Japan: Early Korean Girls Comic Book artists' Resistance and Empowerment." In *Complicated Currents: Media Flows, Soft Power and East Asia*, edited by Daniel Black, Stephen Epstein, and Alison Tokita, 6.1–6.16. Melbourne, Australia: Monash University ePress.

Chosun Ilbo. 2000. "The Webtoon, a New Genre Unfolds" (Weptun sae jangneu pyeolchinda). April 27. http://biz.chosun.com/site/data/html_dir/2000/04/27/2000042770418.html.

Chou, J. H., and J. G. Yi. 1997. "Fears of School Bullying—Iljin Association" (Hakgyopongnyeok iljinhoe gongpo). *Kyunghyang Shinmun*, June 29, p. 1.

Chua, Beng Huat. 2012. *Structure, Audience and Soft Power in East Asian Pop Culture*. Hong Kong: Hong Kong University Press.

Chua, Beng Huat, and Kōichi Iwabuchi. 2008. *East Asian Pop Culture: Analysing the Korean Wave*. Hong Kong: Hong Kong University Press.

Cinarel, Ceyda, and Byoung-Tak Zhang. 2017. "Into the Colorful World of Webtoons: Through the Lens of Neural Networks." In *Proceedings of the 2017 14th IAPR International Conference on Document Analysis and Recognition*, 35–40. Kyoto, Japan, November 9–15.

Cine21. 2002. "Future of Internet Comic Business" (Inteonet manhwasaeobui apgireun). January 3. http://www.cine21.com/news/view/?mag_id=6532.

Cunningham, Stuart. 2015. "The New Screen Ecology: A New Wave of Media Globalisation?" *Communication Research and Practice* 1 (3): 275–82.

Cunningham, Stuart, and David Craig. 2019. "Creator Governance in Social Media Entertainment." *Social Media + Society* 5 (4): 1–11. https://journals.sagepub.com/doi/full/10.1177/2056305119883428.

Dale, Brady. 2015. "The Webcomics Business Is Moving on from Webcomics." *Observer*, November 16. http://observer.com/2015/11/webcomics-changing-business-model/.

Davis, Charles H. 2013. "Audience Value and Transmedia Products." In *Media Innovations: A Multidisciplinary Study of Change*, edited by Tanja Storsul, and Arne H. Krumsvik, 175–90. Göteborg, Sweden: Nordicom. https://www.nordicom.gu.se/sites/default/files/publikationer-hela-pdf/media_innovations._a_miltidisciplinary_study_of_change.pdf.

Deputy Director of *Dong-a Ilbo* Department of Social Affairs. 1983. "An Imbalance in Public Relations" (Hongboui bulgyunhyeong). *Dong-a Ilbo*, November 2, p. 4

Djuna. 2006. "What Were the Problems of Korean Horror Films in 2006" (2006 Hanguk horeo yeonghwa mueosi munjeyeonna). *Cine21*, September 8. http://www.cine21.com/news/view/?mag_id=41111.

Dong-a Ilbo. 1966. "Over 10,000 Pornographic and Low Quality Comics Incinerated" (Oeseol yuhaemanhwadeung moa 1mangwonsogak). June 3, p. 4.

———. 1978. "Yujeong Association Says Comic Shops Are the Home of Children's Crimes" (Yujeonghoe jijeok manhwagagega eorini beomjoe onsang). May 27, p. 7.

Doré, Philippa, and Peter C. Pugsley. 2019. "Genre Conventions in K-pop: BTS's 'Dope' Music Video." *Continuum* 33 (5): 580–89.

Enberg, Jasmine. 2019. "Digital Ad Spending 2019, Global." *eMarketer*, March 28. http://www.emarketer.com/content/global-digital-ad-spending-2019.

Entertainment Team. 2002. "Silent Protest of Comic Artist Who Became Speechless and Motionless" (Sonbareul ilko hal mareul ireun manhwaindeurui chimmuksiwi). *Joongang Ilbo*, February 23. https://news.joins.com/article/682613.

EY. 2015. "Cultural Times: The First Global Map of Cultural and Creative Industries." Study, December 8. Text available online at https://ficdc.org/wp-content/uploads/2019/11/CISAC-Cultural_Times_2015.pdf.

Forbes. 2014. "Gallery: Next Gen Innovators 2014." August 20, p. 2. http://www.forbes.com/pictures/mfl45eleeh/next-gen-innovators/ - d451e19c462d.

Gabilliet, Jean-Paul. 2010. *Of Comics and Men: A Cultural History of American Comic Books*. Translated by Bart Beaty and Nick Nguyen. Jackson: University Press of Mississippi.

Goggin, Gerard. 2011. *Global Mobile Media*. London: Routledge.

Grand Comics Database (GDC). 2020. "Statistics by Country, Ordered by Number of Issues Indexed. Grand Comics Database." Accessed May 1. https://www.comics.org/international_stats_country/.

Granitz, Neil, and Howard Forman. 2015. "Building Self-Brand Connections: Exploring Brand Stories through a Transmedia Perspective." *Journal of Brand Management* 22 (1): 38–59.

Guigar, Brad, Dave Kellett, Scott Kurtz, and Kris Straub. 2011. *How to Make Webcomics*. Berkeley, CA: Image Comics.

Gwon, O-sang. 1997. "Youth Protection Committee Listed 5 Million Comic Books from 1,700 Series as Harmful Contents" (Manhwa 1cheon7baekjong 5baekmangwon Cheongsonyeonbohowi Yuhaepanjeong). *The Hankyoreh*, July 16, p. 26.

Gwon, Sun-taek. 2015. "Lezhin Comics, Lucky to Avoid Its Site Blocked, but How About Deliberation Process of the Site?" (Uni Joa 'Jeopsokchadan' cheolhoedoen rejinkomiks, tongsinsimui munjeneun?). *MediaUS*, March 27. http://www.mediaus.co.kr/news/articleView.html?idxno=47563.

Han, Gwang-deok. 2019. "Big Hit Entertainment Worth More than US$1 Billion." *The Hankyoreh*, June 12. http://www.hani.co.kr/arti/english_edition/e_entertainment/897576.html.

Hanguk Kyungje. 2000. "Hankyungje Report: An Abundance of Cyber Manhwabang" (Hangyeongje ripoteu saibeo manhwabang suduruk). September 6. https://news.naver.com/main/read.nhn?mode=LSD&mid=sec&sid1=101&oid=015&aid=0000275303.

Han, S. H. 2013. "The Rise of Artists Making 100 Million KRW—Focus on Lezhin Comic's Experiment" (encheo weptun peullaetpomeseo eokdae yeonbong jakga naonda - ejinkomikseu silheom jumok). *ETnews*, October 30. https://www.etnews.com/201310300477.

Herald Economy. 2005. "Bookshop Communication: Numbers of Self-Publishing Enterprises, Empty Statistics" (Chaengmaeul tongsin: 1in chulpan algobomyeon sokbingangjeong). October 17. https://news.naver.com/main/read.nhn?mode=LSD&mid=sec&sid1=001&oid=016&aid=0000188324.

Herman, Tamar. 2017. "Meet the Fans of BTS: Profiles of American Army." *Billboard*, September 29. http://www.billboard.com/articles/columns/k-town/7981702/meet-fans-bts-profiles-american-army.

Hjorth, Larissa. 2003. "Cute@keitai.com." In *Japanese Cybercultures*, edited by Nanette Gottlieb and Mark McLelland, 50–59. New York: Routledge.

Hjorth, Larissa, Jean Burgess, and Ingrid Richardson. 2012. *Studying Mobile Media: Cultural Technologies, Mobile Communication, and the iPhone*. London: Routledge.

Hjorth, Larissa, and Olivia Khoo. 2015. *Routledge Handbook of New Media in Asia*. Abingdon, UK: Routledge.

Hockx, Michel. 2015. *Internet Literature in China*. New York: Columbia University Press.

Hong, Ji-min. 2012a. "K Comics Leads New Hallyu #6 Talking about Webtoon" (K-Komikseu sinhallyu ikkeunda #6 Weptuneul malhada). *Seoul Newspaper*, May 27. http://www.seoul.co.kr/news/newsView.php?id=20120528014004.

———. 2012b. "Leading the New Hallyu, K-Comics #3: A Few Words about Comics in the 1970s and 1980s" (K-komikseu sinhallyu ikkeunda #3 1970~80 nyeondae manhwareul malhada). *Seoul Newspaper*, May 7. https://www.seoul.co.kr/news/newsView.php?id=20120507018001.

Hong, J. P. 2015. "Hanwha Chemical—Starting the 3rd Season of Its Branded Webtoon, *Working Hero*" (Hanwhakemikal, beuraendeu weptun sijeun3 wiking hieoro yeonjae). *Money Today*, January 15. https://tinyurl.com/sufpfdw.

Hong, J. W. 2008. "Why the Film Remakes of Kang Full's Webtoons Fail: A Double-Edged Sword of Having Many Readers" (Gangpul wonjak yeonghwahwa silpae iyu: dokja maneunge yangnarui geom). *Newsen*, December 5. http://www.newsen.com/news_view.php?uid=200812051146521003.

Hun, S., and E. Yu. 2017. "Issue Insight: Evolution of Community, Transforming Byeongmat Code" (Issue Insight: Keomyunitiui jinhwa byeongman kodeudo bakkuda). *N Content*, September–October, pp. 30–33.

Hutchinson, Rachael. 2019. *Japanese Culture through Videogames*. New York: Routledge.

Hwang, Hye Jin. 2019. "BTS's Webtoon *Save Me* Ends with 50 Million Views." *Newsen*, April 12. https://channels.vlive.tv/B938BF/celeb/0.10680578.

Im, B. 1993. "Focus: Comic Market #3. Distribution Channels Changed, Putting Korean Comic in Danger" (Jipjungchwijae manhwa sijang 3 yutonggujo byeonhae hangungmanhwa byeorang). *The Hankyoreh*, October 29, p. 9.

IMDb. 2021. "*Crazy Waiting* (2008) (Kidarida michyeo)." Accessed January 15. http://www.imdb.com/title/tt1233482/.

Im, Hong-seok. 2017. "Diverse Ventures for VR Webtooon, Fun Funny Brothers Launch Ssoltoon" (Vrweptuneul wihan dayanghan dojeon, peonpeonibeuradeoseu ssoltun gonggae). *VR New Network*, March 17. http://www.vrn.co.kr/news/articleView.html?idxno=5618.

Im, J. S. 2015. "Goosebumps, Webtoon with Shrieking Special Effects" (Kkyak teuksuhyogwa chijanghan weptun, soreumdonne). *The Hankyoreh*, June 30. http://www.hani.co.kr/arti/economy/economy_general/698269.html.

Ingham, Tim. 2019. "BTS Label Big Hit Entertainment Turned Over $166m in H1 2019—Close to Its Revenues in the Whole of 2018." *Music Business Worldwide*, August 21. https://www.musicbusinessworldwide.com/bts-label-big-hit-entertainment-turned-over-166m-in-h1-2019-close-to-its-revenues-in-the-whole-of-2018/.

International Telecommunication Union (ITU). 2019a. *Digital Transformation and the Role of Enterprise Architecture*. Geneva: International Telecommunication Union. https://www.itu.int/dms_pub/itu-d/opb/str/D-STR-DIG_TRANSF-2019-PDF-E.pdf.

International Telecommunication Union (ITU). 2019b. *Measuring Digital Development: Facts and Figures, 2019.* Geneva: International Telecommunication Union.

iResearch. 2018. "The 2018 Report on Chinese Webnovel Writers." May. http://report.iresearch.cn/wx/report.aspx?id=3208.

Ito, Kinko. 2005. "A History of Manga in the Context of Japanese Culture and Society." *The Journal of Popular Culture* 38 (3): 456–75.

Iwabuchi, Kōichi. 2002. *Recentering Globalization: Popular Culture and Japanese Transnationalism.* Durham, NC: Duke University Press.

Jang, Sang-yong. 2012. "1960s and 1970s: #3 The Best and Worst Monopoly System" (1960 nyeondae~70 nyeondae: (3) Choegoija choeagui dokjeom cheje). *Digital Manhwa Gyujanggak*, April 23. http://dml.komacon.kr/webzine/38/1221.

Jang, Wonho, and Jung Eun Song. 2017. "Webtoon as a New Korean Wave in the Process of Glocalization." *Kritika Kultura* 29: 168–87. https://journals.ateneo.edu/ojs/index.php/kk/article/view/KK2017.02908/2562.

Jenkins, Henry. 2006. *Convergence Culture: Where Old and New Media Collide.* New York: New York University Press.

Jenkins, Henry, Sam Ford, and Joshua Green. 2013. *Spreadable Media: Creating Meaning and Value in a Networked Culture.* New York: New York University Press.

Jeong, C. H. 2016. "Heated Debate over Violence and Obscenity in Webtoons vs Freedom of Expression" (Do neomeun pongnyeoktpseonjeongseong weptun gamnoneulbaktt simui ganghwavs pyohyeonjayu useon paengpaeng). *Digital Times*, July 6. https://n.news.naver.com/article/029/0002352230.

Jeong, S. 1997. "Juvenile Violence, Homosexuality . . . *Enjo-kōsai* . . . the Harm Done by Japanese Manga Is Spreading" (Cheongsonyeon pongnyeok . . . dongseongae . . . wonjogyoje ilbonmanhwa haeak imi peojyeo). *The Hankyoreh*, October 22, p. 27.

Jeon, S. C. 1995. "Comics via PCs—Advent of the Internet Manhwabang" (Manhwaneun PCreul tagotttongsin manhwabang soksokdeungjang)." *Kyunghyang Shinmun*, September 26, p. 29.

Jeon, S. H. 2000. "Comics: Sound Effects Coming from Comics in N4, Internet Manhwa Webzine" (Manhwa inteonet manhwawepjin N4 manhwaeseo hyogwaeumi deulline). *DongA.com*, March 20. http://www.donga.com/news/article/all/20000330/7521386/1?=.

Jin, Dal Yong. 2016. *New Korean Wave: Transnational Cultural Power in the Age of Social Media.* Urbana: University of Illinois Press.

———. 2020. *Transmedia Storytelling in East Asia: The Age of Digital Media.* New York: Routledge.

Jin, Eun-soo. 2015. "Webtoon Artists Get Special Effects Help from Naver," *Joongang Daily*, June 23. http://koreajoongangdaily.joins.com/news/article/article.aspx?aid=3005707.

Jin, Min-Ji. 2015. "Cartoonist Addresses Cyberbullying." *Joongang Daily*, August 14. http://mengnews.joins.com/view.aspx?aid=3007879.

Jo, Euna. 2014. "Successful Formula for Paid Webtoon Service Lezhin Comics" (Rejinkomikseuui yuryo weptun seonggong bigyeol). *Business Post*, August 14. http://www.businesspost.co.kr/BP?command=naver&num=3743.

Jo, G. H. 1969. "Chaos Tainting Innocence of Children" (Dongsimi sideuneun mubunbyeorui hyeonjang). *Dong-a Ilbo*, May 3, p. 3.

Johnston, Rich. 2019. "Graphite Launches as a Netflix-Meets-Spotify-Meets-YouTube for Comics for Free—or $4.99 per Month Ad-Free." *Bleeding Cool*, June 11. https://bleedingcool.com/comics/graphite-launches-as-a-netflix-meets-spotify-meets-youtube-for-comics-for-free-or-4-99-per-month-ad-free/.

Jung, Bora. 2013. "Like a Mirage—The Last 8 Months of KakaoPage" (Singiru kakaopeiji, jinan 8gaeworui gwejeok). *Bloter*, July 14. http://www.bloter.net/archives/158056.

Jung, M. K. 2017. "Ongoing Exposure of Lezhin's Power Trip: Why Is It Happening?" (Kkeunimeopsi teojineun rejinkomikseu gapjil pongno…Wae?). *Media Today*, December 14. https://tinyurl.com/vo5xwx2.

Kang, Tae-jin. 2017. "Study on the Globalization Strategies of Webtoon Platforms." National IT Industry Promotion Agency. Report no. 17-05, December

Keane, Michael. 2016. *The Handbook of China's Cultural and Creative Industries*. Cheltenham, UK: Edward Elgar Publishing Limited.

Keane, Michael, Brian Yecies, and Terry Flew, eds. 2018. *Willing Collaborators: Foreign Partners in Chinese Media*. London: Rowman & Littlefield International.

Kim, D. H. 2006. "A Totally Different Variation of Kang Full's Original, *Apt.*" (Gangpurui wonjakgwaneun jeonhyeo dareun byeonjugok, apateu) *Cine21*, July 4. http://www.cine21.com/news/view/?mag_id=39731.

Kim, G. H. 2000. "New Manhwa Boom in Cyber Space" (Jigeum saibeosesangen manhwa yeolpung). *Dong-a Ilbo*, August 20. https://news.naver.com/main/read.nhn?mode=LSD&mid=sec&sid1=103&oid=020&aid=0000022145.

Kim, G. U., and D. H. Kim. 2012. "40 Million Copies of WHY Series Hits the Jackpot—Did Cartoonists Get Rich, Too?" (4000 manbu daebak WHY sirijeu, manhwagado donbangseok?). *Money Today*, January 19. https://news.mt.co.kr/mtview.php?no=2012011812553901811&outlink=1&ref=https%3A%2F%2Fsearch.naver.com.

Kim, G. Y. 2011. "Ha Ik-kwon, I Want to See How My Manhwa Has Changed through Live Theater" (Hailgwon, Yeongeugeuro bakkwil je manhwa, jeodo bogo sipeoyo). *CNB Journal*, November 28. http://weekly.cnbnews.com/news/article.html?no=107726.

Kim, H. J. 2015. "Lezhin Comics Speak Out in Obscenity Controversy" (Eumnanseong domae oreun rejinkomikseuui toro). *Premium Chosun*, May 10. http://premium.chosun.com/site/data/html_dir/2015/05/04/2015050402330.html?csmain.

Kim, H. S. 2000. "First Book Published Collecting Internet Comics" (Inteonenmanhwa danhaengbon cheot chulpan). *Hanguk Kyungje*, August 4, https://news.naver.com/main/read.nhn?mode=LSD&mid=sec&sid1=102&oid=015&aid=0000263720.

Kim, Il-ju. 2007. "Nostalgia for Old Boys: The Resurrection of *Babel II*" (Oldeuboiui hyangsu babel2seui buhwal). *The Hankyoreh*, January 28. https://www.hani.co.kr/arti/culture/book/186994.html.

Kim, Jihoon. 2019. "Korean Popular Cinema and Television in the Twenty-First Century: Parallax Views on National/Transnational Disjunctures." *Journal of Popular Film and Television* 47 (1): 2–8. https://www.tandfonline.com/doi/full/10.1080/01956051.2019.1562815.

Kim, Ji-Hyeon, and Jun Yu. 2019. "Platformizing Webtoons: The Impact on Creative and Digital Labor in South Korea." *Social Media + Society* 5 (4): 1–11. https://journals.sagepub.com/doi/full/10.1177/2056305119880174.

Kim, Moon-ki. 2019. "In the 5G Era, LG Breaks New Ground with AR and VR" (Jigeumeun 5gsidae LGU, 'Vr-Ar'ro seungbusu saepanjjanda). *inews24*, July 8. http://www.inews24.com/view/1190616.

Kim, Myung-Bae, Bong-Ju Kwon, Sang-Hee Lee, GwangYong Gim, and Jong-Bae Kim. 2016. "A Study of the Effects of Webtoon Contents and Cooperative Characteristics on Open Collaboration Platform Usage." *International Journal of Software Engineering and Its Applications* 10 (9): 51–64.

Kim, Kyu Hyun. 2014. "Fisticuffs, High Kicks, and Colonial Histories: The Ambivalence of Modern Korean Identity in Postwar Narrative Comics." In *The Korean Popular Culture Reader*, edited by Kyung Hyun Kim and Youngmin Choe, 34–54. Durham, NC: Duke University Press.

Kim, Kyung Hyun, and Youngmin Choe, eds. 2014. *The Korean Popular Culture Reader*. Durham, NC: Duke University Press.

Kim, Kyung-hun. 2012. "School Violence Problem? Then Attack Webtoons!" (Hakgyopongnyeok munje? geureotamyeon weptuneul gonggyeokanda!). *Oh My News*, February 28. http://www.ohmynews.com/NWS_Web/view/at_pg.aspx?CNTN_CD=A0001702829.

Kim, Seong-min. 2012. "Furious Elementary School Students—Do You Know This Violent Webtoon?" (Yeolhyeolchodeunghakgyo i pongnyeok weptuneul asimnikka). *Chosun Ilbo*, January 7. http://srchdb1.chosun.com/pdf/i_service/pdf_ReadBody.jsp?Y=2012&M=01&D=07&ID=2012010700099.

Kim, Y. D. 1997. "My Youth, My Love. Comic Artist HUH Young-man #4: How Long Are You Going to Be Drawing Girls' Comics?" (Naui jeolmeum,naui sarang manhwaga heoyeongman (4) Eonjekkaji sunjeongmanhwaman geurilgeonya). *Kyunghyang Shinmun*, March 18, 31.

Kim, Yoo-chul. 2018. "Naver to Invest $135 Million in Online Cartoons." *Korea Times*, June 26. http://www.koreatimes.co.kr/www/tech/2018/12/133_251296.html.

Kim, Young-hwan. 2012. "Korea's First Comic Book 'Rabbit and Monkey' Released." (Gungnae choecho manhwa danhaengbon "tokkiwa wonsungi" gonggae). June 21. http://www.hani.co.kr/arti/culture/culture_general/539079.html.

Kim, Young-Kyu, and Min-Ho Ryu. 2017. "Towards Entrepreneurial Organization: From the Case of Organizational Process Innovation in Naver." *Procedia Computer Science* 122: 663–70. Text downloadable from https://www.sciencedirect.com/science/article/pii/S1877050917326698.

Koreaboo. 2019. "BTS's Forgotten Webtoon Has Resurfaced and ARMYs Are Shook." January 14. http://www.koreaboo.com/stories/bts-forgotten-webtoon-resurfaced/.

Korea Creative Content Agency (KOCCA). 2009. *Long-Term Development Plan for the Comics Industry: 2009–2013* (Manhwasaneop jinheung jungjanggigyehoek). Seoul: KOCCA.

———. 2013. *2012 Cartoon Industry White Paper*. Seoul: KOCCA.

———. 2018a. *Comic Webtoon Illegal Circulation Status Report* (Manhwa weptun bulbeobyutong siltaejosa). Report no. KOCCA18-27. Seoul: KOCCA.

———. 2018b. *2017 Graphic Novel Industry White Paper* (2017 Manhwa Saneop Baekseo). Seoul: KOCCA Industry Support Department.

———. 2019. *Comics Industry Development Plan Research* (Manhwasanop baljon gyehwek surip yongu). KOCCA report no. 18–51. Naju: KOCCA.

Korea Internet and Security Agency (KISA). 2015. *2015 Korea Internet White Paper*. Seoul: KISA. https://www.kisa.or.kr/eng/usefulreport/whitePaper_List.jsp.

Korea Law Translation Center. 2012a. Enforcement Decree of the Promotion of Cartoons Act. Presidential Decree No. 24038, August 13. https://elaw.klri.re.kr/eng_mobile/viewer.do?hseq=42674&type=lawname&key=Promotion+of+Cartoons+Act.

———. 2012b. Promotion of Cartoons Act. Act No. 11311, February 17. https://elaw.klri.re.kr/eng_mobile/viewer.do?hseq=25593&type=part&key=17.

Korea Cartoonist Association. 2019. "Comic Webtoon Fair Contract Guide" (manhwa weptun gongjeong gyeyak gaideu). Seoul: Korea Cartoonist Association. Available for download at https://tinyurl.com/ydxah3ab.

Korea.net. 2013. "Government Collaboration Leading to the Success of 'Paid Webtoon Service.'" December 2. http://www.korea.kr/news/policyNewsView.do?newsId=148770632&call_from=naver_news.

Korea's Policy Briefing. 2013. "Government Collaboration Led to Success of Paid Webtoon Service" (yuryo weptun seobiseu seonggong ikkeun jeongbu hyeobeop). December 2. http://www.korea.kr/news/policyNewsView.do?newsId=148770632&call_from=naver_news.

Korea's Truth and Reconciliation Commission. 2010. "Press Release regarding the Consolidation of the Press and the Journalists Who Were Forced to Quit in 1980" (1980 nyeon eollon tong pyehap mit eollonin gangje haejik sageon bodojaryo). January 7. http://www.jinsil.go.kr/Information_Notice/article2/read.asp?num=190&pageno=3&stype=&sval=&data_years=2015&data_month=.

Kozinets, Robert V., Andrea Hemetsberger, and Hope Jensen Schau. 2008. "The Wisdom of Consumer Crowds: Collective Innovation in the Age of Networked Marketing." *Journal of Macromarketing* 28 (4): 339–54.

Kruse, Zack. 2017. "Overwhelmed by a Cloak of Darkness: Steve Ditko's Dark Karma and Cosmic Inner Space." *Inks: The Journal of the Comics Studies Society* 1 (3): 267–87.

Kwang, Choi. 2014. "Daum, Launching the Animated Webtoon 'Moving Toon' Service (Daeum, aenimeisyeonhyeong weptun 'mubingtun' seobiseu gaesi)." *JoongAng Ilbo*, April 1. https://news.joins.com/article/14318373.

Kwon, Hyemi. 2015. "Flinch, Flinch: How Naver's Effect-Toon Was Created" (Umjjirumjjil neibeo hyogwatun, ireoke mandeureosseoyo). *Bloter*, September 15. http://www.bloter.net/archives/238763.

Kwon, Seung-Ho, and Joseph Kim. 2014. "Cultural Industry Policies of the Korean Government and the Korean Wave." *International Journal of Cultural Policy* 20 (4): 422–39.

Kyunghyang Shinmun. 1968a. "Children's Cartoons" (Eorini manhwa). October 30, p. 7.

———. 1968b. "8,000 Bad Quality Comic Books Burned at Namsan" (Namsanseo bultaewo bullyangmanhwa 8cheongwon). May 22, p. 7.

———. 1970. "Comics Pollution Eating Children's Minds" (Dongsimeul jommeongneun manhwagonghae). November 28, p. 5.

———. 1971. "Cartoon Purification Derailed" (Talseonhan manhwajeonghwa). June 30, p. 5.

———. 1978. "Can We Get Rid of Low Quality Comics? Yujeonghoe Seminar" (Bullyangmanhwa eopsael su eomna yujeonghoe semina). June 2, p. 7.

Lee, H. D. 1997. "Japanese Manga Are Textbooks for Violence: Status and Causes of School Violence" (Ilbon manhwaneun pokryeok gyogwaseo hakgyopokryeok siltae—Wonin). *Dong-a Ilbo*, July 4, p. 37.

———. 2017. "Is This the End for Artist-Friendly Business Operations at Lezhin Comics?" (Rejinkomikseu jakgajuui gyeongyeong… hangyee bongchakan geosilkka). *Digital Daily*, December 11. http://www.ddaily.co.kr/news/article/?no=163501.

———. 2018. "Artist Yoon Tae-ho—Lezhin's Suit against Artists Unprecedented in the Comics Industry" (jakga gosohan rejine yuntaeho jakga, Manhwagye choyu satae gyutan). *Digital Daily*, February 13. http://www.ddaily.co.kr/news/article/?no=165858.

Lee, H. E. 2004. "Kang Full's Love Story Goes Offline" (Gangpul sunjeongmanhwa opeuraineuro). *The Hankyoreh*, February 12. https://entertain.naver.com/read?oid=028&aid=0000045222.

Lee, Jae-min. 2019. "Webtoon Technology Interview #5: SphereToon's Horang, No Limit to the Power of Manhwa" (Weptun Gisul Inteobyu #5: Seupieotun horang jakga Manhwaui himeneun hangyega eopda). *Webtoon Insight*, April 3. https://www.webtooninsight.co.kr/Forum/Content/5832.

Lee, J. H. 2017. "Lezhin, What Is the Late Fee" (Rejin jigakbiga mueosigillae). *iZE Magazine*, December 10. http://www.ize.co.kr/articleView.html?no=2017100913267231281.

Lee, Jihyun, and Jang-sun Hwang. 2017. "Characteristics of Branded Webtoon and Consumer Responses" (Beuraendeu weptunui teukseonggwa sobija baneung)." *Advertisement Studies*, no. 1mtv15: 246–95.

Lee, Jin-hyeok. 2014. "Hanwha Chemical—Release of Season 2 of *God of Salary* Webtoon" (Hanwhakemikal, weptun 'yeonbongsin sijeun2' yeonjae). *Chosun Biz*, January 14. http://biz.chosun.com/site/data/html_dir/2014/01/14/2014011401496.html.

Lee, K. M., and Park, S. R. 2014. "Marketing to Female Consumers to Sell Mobile Contents" (Yeoseong jabaya mobail kontencheu pallinda). *ETnews*, July 20. http://www.etnews.com/20140718000190.

Lee, O-Joun, and Jason J. Jung. 2020. "Story embedding: Learning distributed representations of stories based on character networks." *Artificial Intelligence* 281 (103,235): 1–32.

Lee, O. S. 2008. "When Readers Tell Me My Work Is Boring, I Will Quit My Job" (Dokjadeuri nae manhwa jaemieopda hamyeon baro ttaeryeochiul geot). *SisaIN*, December 23. http://www.sisain.co.kr/news/articleView.html?idxno=3479.

———. 2017. "Webtoon Frontline—The Penalty Fees Issue" (jigakbi nollaneuro bon weptun jeonseon). *SisaIN*, December 25. http://www.sisain.co.kr/news/articleView.html?idxno=30835&utm_source=dable.

Lee, Jong Yoon, Jae Hee Park, and Jong Woo Jun. 2019. "Brand Webtoon as Sustainable Advertising in Korean Consumers: A Focus on Hierarchical Relationships." *Sustainability* 11 (5): 1364–74. https://www.mdpi.com/2071-1050/11/5/1364/htm.

Lee, Seung-hwan. 2015. "History of Korean Webtoon Platforms and Enterprises" (Hanguk weptun peullaetpomui yeoksawa geu daepyojakdeul chongjeongni). *PPSS*, November 19. https://ppss.kr/archives/61780.

Lee, Soo-Ki, Eun-Jee Park, and He-Yu Kim. 2019. "Kakao Finds Success in Japan with Manga App." *Joongang Daily*, June 5. http://koreajoongangdaily.joins.com/news/article/article.aspx?aid=3063913.

Lee, Z. 2014. "Seven Ingredients for Successful Paid Content" (Kontencheu yuryohwa se-onggong moderui 7 gaji gongsik). *Hankyoung Business*, September 22. https://tinyurl.com/la8o4ad.

Line Corp. 2020. *(Revised) 3Q 2019 Quarterly Report (IFRS)*. October 28. https://d.linescdn.net/stf/linecorp/en/ir/all/FY20Q3_QuarterlyReport(IFRS)_3.pdf.

Line Webtoon. 2015. "Introducing Official Translation Service, 'Webtoon TRANSLATE.'" Video file. Webtoon YouTube Channel, March 9. https://www.youtube.com/watch?v=1uht0tLUU6s.

———. 2017. "Academy-Award Winner Common Joins Forces with LINE WEBTOON and Noble Transmission for Groundbreaking Comic Series—CASTER." *Notice*, November 15. https://www.webtoons.com/en/notice/detail?noticeNo=590&webtoon-platform-redirect=true.

Lynn, Hyung-Gu. 2016. "Korean Webtoons: Explaining Growth." *Institute of Korean Studies Annual* 16: 1–13. Text available at https://apm.sites.olt.ubc.ca/files/2016/02/HG-Lynn-Korean-Webtoons-Kyushu-v16-2016.pdf.

McNamara, Dennis L. 2009. *Business Innovation in Asia: Knowledge and Technology Networks from Japan*. New York: Routledge.

Maeil Kyungjae. 1977. "The Effect of Bad Comics on Children" (Bullyangmanhwaga eoriniege michineun yeonghyang). January 31, p. 8.

———. 2001. "Comics Today Publish Print Comic Book, Mythology of the Heavens by Lee Hyun-se" (Komikseutudei, ihyeonse cheonguguisinhwa danhaengbon pyeonae). November 7. https://news.naver.com/main/read.nhn?mode=LSD&mid=sec&sid1=101&oid=009&aid=0000163345.

Malone, Thomas W., and Michael S. Bernstein, eds. 2015. *Handbook of Collective Intelligence*. Cambridge, MA: MIT Press.

Martens, Marianne. 2016. *Publishers, Readers, and Digital Engagement: Participatory Forums and Young Adult Publishing*. London: Palgrave.

McLelland, Mark . 2011. "Thought Policing or Protection of Youth? Debate in Japan over the 'Non-existent Youth Bill.'" *International Journal of Comic Art* 13 (1): 348–67.

———. 2015. "Sex, Censorship and Media Regulation in Japan: An Historical Overview." In *Routledge Handbook of Sexuality Studies in East Asia*, edited by Mark McLelland and Vera. Mackie, 402–13. Oxford: Routledge.

Milk, Chris. 2015. "How Virtual Reality Can Create the Ultimate Empathy Machine." Video. TED2015, March 18, Vancouver, Canada. http://www.ted.com/talks/chris_milk_how_virtual_reality_can_create_the_ultimate_empathy_machine.

Ministry of Culture and Tourism. 2003. *Five-Year Development Plan for the Comics Industry: 2003-2007* (Manhwasaneop jinheung 5gaenyeon gyehoek: 2003–2007 nyeon). Seoul: Ministry of Culture and Tourism Ministry of Public Information.

Ministry of Public Information. 1970. *Burning Bad Quality Comics, Porn Books, Etc.* (Bullyang manhwa, oeseolseojeok deung sogak). File# CET0057991, May 27. Seoul: National Archives of Korea.

Murray, Simone. 2018. *The Digital Literary Sphere: Reading, Writing, and Selling Books in the Internet Era*. Baltimore: Johns Hopkins University Press.

Nagaike, Kazumi, and Raymond Langley. 2019. "Practicing Shōjo in Japanese New Media and Cyberculture: Analyses of the Cell Phone Novel and Dream Novel." In *Shōjo Across Media: Exploring "Girl" Practices in Contemporary Japan*, edited by Jaqueline Berndt, Kazumi Nagaike, and Fusami Ōgi, 109–32. London: Palgrave Macmillan.

Nakamura, Lisa. 2013. "'Words with Friends': Socially Networked Reading on Goodreads." *PMLA* 128 (1): 238–43.

Nam, Eun-ju. 2014. "When Scrolling Down, a 'Bloody Hand' Comes Up: 'Moving-Toons' that Will Spook Us This Summer" (Seukeurol naeryeotdeoni 'Pimudeun son'i 'Sseuk' . . . ol yeoreum deunggoreul ossakage hal 'mubingtun'). *The Hankyoreh*, July 6. http://www.hani.co.kr/arti/culture/culture_general/645612.html.

Nam, H. Y. 2019. "Lee Hyun-se: I Had to Fight Because My Junior Comic Artist Colleagues Were Watching Me" (Ihyeonse hubaedeuri jikyeoboni ssawoya haetda). *Byline Network*, October 14. https://byline.network/2019/10/14-65/.

Naver Corporation. 2019a. *2018 Naver Annual Report*. Seoul: Naver Corp. https://www.navercorp.com/navercorp_/ir/annualReport/2019/NAVER_AR_2018_Eng.pdf.

———. 2019b. "World's No. 1 in 100 Countries' Naver Webtoon Achieves Global Annual Transaction Value of 600 Billion Won." Press release. *Naver Official Blog*, September 24. https://blog.naver.com/naver_diary/221658121266.

Naver Webtoon. 2015a. "*Heavenly Myth*, Part 6; All That Story, Lee Hyun-Se." December. https://comic.naver.com/webtoon/list.nhn?titleId=670131&no=91&weekday=thu.

———. 2015b. "*Myth of Heaven*: Lee Hyun-Se; The Return of Painter Lee Hyun-See, the Myth of Korean Comics." July. https://comic.naver.com/webtoon/list.nhn?titleId=658823.

———. 2016. "Naver Webtoon Media Introduction ver 2.8." https://shared-comic.pstatic.net/fileShare/Webtoon_guide_ver2.8.7.pdf?.

Next Daily. 2009. "iRiver Placed in Webtoon" (Weptuneseo mannaneun airibeo). May 8. http://www.nextdaily.co.kr/news/article.html?id=20090508800004.

Nishimura, Yukiko. 2011. "Japanese Keitai Novels and Ideologies of Literacy." In *Digital Discourse: Language in the New Media*, edited by Crispin Thurlow and Kristine Mroczek, 86–109. New York: Oxford University Press.

Nyberg, Amy Kiste. 1998. *Seal of Approval: The History of the Comics Code*. Jackson: University Press of Mississippi.

Nye, Joseph S. 1990. *Bound to Lead: The Changing Nature of American Power*. New York: Basic Books.

Oh, Ingyu, and Bonwon Koo. 2018. "Japanese Webtoon: Marketing Manga Online Using South Korean Platform Designs." *Culture and Empathy* 1 (1–4): 49–69. https://culture-nempathy.org/wp-content/uploads/2018/10/Japanese-Webtoon-Marketing-Manga-Online-Using-South-Korean-Platform-Designs.pdf.

Oh, Sehwan, Hyunmi Baek, and JoongHo Ahn. 2013. "The Impact of YouTube on International Trade." Paper presented at Pacific Asia Conference on Information Systems (PACIS) 2013, Jeju Island, Korea, June 18–22, 2013. Text downloadable from http://aisel.aisnet.org/pacis2013/87 (paywall).

Organisation for Economic Co-operation and Development (OECD). 2004. *OECD Information Technology Outlook 2004*. Paris: OECD Publications. https://www.oecd.org/sti/ieconomy/37620123.pdf.

———. 2009. *OECD Communications Outlook 2009*. Paris: OECD Publications. https://read.oecd-ilibrary.org/science-and-technology/oecd-communications-outlook-2009_comms_outlook-2009-en - page1.

———. 2017. *OECD Digital Economy Outlook 2017*. Paris: OECD Publishing.

———. 2019. *Measuring the Digital Transformation: A Roadmap for the Future*. Paris: OECD Publishing. Text available from https://www.oecd.org/publications/measuring-the-digital-transformation-9789264311992-en.htm.

Osaki, Tomihiro. 2019. "South Korea's Booming 'Webtoons' Put Japan's Print Manga on Notice." *The Japan Times*, May 5. https://tinyurl.com/y4yq6cxx.

Otmazgin, Nissim. 2011. "A Tail that Wags the Dog? Cultural Industry and Cultural Policy in Japan and South Korea." *Journal of Comparative Policy Analysis: Research and Practice* 13 (3): 307–25.

Park, Chan-Ik. 2016. "Study the Phenomenon of Cross-Media between Video Media and Webtoon." *International Journal of Multimedia and Ubiquitous Engineering* 11 (5): 245–52.

Park, D. H. 2018. "Why Lezhin Artists Went to the Picket Lines" (rejinkomikseu jakgadeureun wae 1in siwie naseonna). *The Hankyoreh*, January 18. http://www.hani.co.kr/arti/culture/culture_general/828330.html.

Park, In-Ha. 2009. "The Story of the Copied Comics of the 1970s" (70 nyeondae bekkin manhwa iyagi). *ComixPark*, November 10. http://blog.naver.com/enterani/130073316109.

———. 2010. "The World Viewed through Manhwa: Byongmat Culture, Loser Culture, and Youth Culture" (Manhwaro Boneun Sesang: Byeongmasmanhwa, Rujeomunhwa, Cheongnyeonmunhwa). *ETNews*, April 23. http://www.etnews.com/201004210348.

———. 2012. "Comics Are Not a Problem, Stupid" (Baboya munjeneun manhwaga aniya). *The Hankyoreh* 21 (901), last updated March 8. http://h21.hani.co.kr/arti/culture/culture_general/31517.html.

Park, I. H., N. J. Hong, and H. J. Jeon. 2018. *A Study of Age-Rating Standards for the Self-Regulation of Webtoons*. Naju: KOCCA. https://bit.ly/2VMcTkl.

Park, J. H. 2018. "Lezhin Comics See Export Returns Exceeding 10 Billion KRW" (ejinkomikseu, weptun suchul eoneusae 100eog KRW dolpa). *Economic Review*, March 20. http://www.econovill.com/news/articleView.html?idxno=333975.

Park, Ji Hoon, Jeehyun Lee, and Yongsuk Lee. 2019. "Do Webtoon-Based TV Dramas Represent Transmedia Storytelling? Industrial Factors Leading to Webtoon-Based TV Dramas." *International Journal of Communication* 13: 2179–98. https://ijoc.org/index.php/ijoc/article/view/10010/2651.

Park, Kun-hyeong. 2009. "Book Rental Shop Closed: Success." *Seoul Newspaper*, October 13. https://www.seoul.co.kr/news/newsView.php?id=20091013006017.

Park, Seok-Hwan. 2013. "Manhwa Encyclopedia: Ko Woo-young." *Naver Cast*, September 27. https://terms.naver.com/entry.nhn?docId=3577132&cid=59065&categoryId=59074.

———. 2016. "Planning Article for Manga Day: November 3, 1996—20 Years After." *KOMACON Webzine*, October 25. http://dml.komacon.kr/webzine/cover/2541.

Park, Soo-ho. 2020. "Second Half of the Year's Biggest IPO Company KakaoPage, What Is CEO Lee Jin-su's Growth Strategy?" (Habangi IPO choedaeeo kakaopeiji, ijinsu daepyo seongjang jeollyageun?)" *MK Premium*, May 19. https://www.mk.co.kr/premium/behind-story/view/2020/05/28368/.

Park, S. Y. 2019. "Webtoons Abandoned in a Jungle Thick with Malicious Comments . . . I Am Stopping Uploading Webtoons" (Akpeul jeonggeure bangchidoen weptun . . . yeonjaereul jungdanhamnida). *Hankook Ilbo*, March 9. http://www.hankookilbo.com/News/Read/201911220085016129?did=NA&dtype=&dtypecode=&prnewsid=.

Poggi, Jeanine. 2018. "Here's How Much It Costs to Advertise in TV's Biggest Shows." *Adage.com*, October 2. https://adage.com/article/media/tv-pricing-chart/315120.

Rebagliati, Gabriele. 2016. "Autoethnography of Digital Fiction in Japan: A Case Study." *Journal of Organizational Ethnography* 5 (2): 139–51.

Ren, Xiang (Tony). 2019. "Publishing and Innovation: Disruption in the Chinese eBook Industry." In *Publishing and Culture*, edited by Dallas John Baker, Donna Lee Brien, and Jen Webb, 199–219. Newcastle-upon-Tyne, UK: Cambridge Scholars Publishing.

Research and Markets. 2019. "$44.7 Bn Virtual Reality Market—Global Forecast to 2024." *Globe Newswire*, February 25. https://www.globenewswire.com/news-release/2019/02/25/1741284/0/en/44-7-Bn-Virtual-Reality-Market-Global-Forecast-to-2024.html.

Rolling Stone. 2018. "10 K-Pop Artists to Watch in 2018." April 28. https://www.rollingstone.com/music/music lists/10-k-pop-artists-to-watch-in-2018-630096/chungha-630165/.

Rong, Rui. 2012. "Korean Internet Trend: The Emergence of the 'Tech Galapagos.'" *Btrax*, September 11. https://blog.btrax.com/korean-internet-trend/.

Scolari, Carlos Alberto. 2009. "Transmedia Storytelling: Implicit Consumers, Narrative Worlds, and Branding in Contemporary Media Production." *International Journal of Communication* 3: 586–606. https://ijoc.org/index.php/ijoc/article/view/477/336.

Serafino, Jason. 2015. "The YouTube of Comics: How Tapastic Offers New Publishing Opportunities for Creators and Fans." *Tech Times*, May 20. https://www.techtimes.com/articles/54294/20150520/youtube-comics-tapastic-creating-new-publishing-opportunities-creators-fans.htm.

See Noh, H. 2002. "Enterbiz: Enhanced by Moving Images, Sound Effects, Joy of Reading Comics Doubles" (Enteobijeu: Dongyeongsang.eumhyanghyogwa yangnyeom saljjakchini manhwaingneun jaemi dubae). *MK Kyungje*, December 2. https://entertain.naver.com/read?oid=009&aid=0000261053.

Seo, C. H. 2012. "How Come a Webtoon Given a Ministry of Culture Award Is Regarded as Having Harmful Content?" (Munhwabujanggwansang badeun weptuni yuhaemurirago?). *SisaIN*, March 17. http://www.sisain.co.kr/news/articleView.html?idxno=12574.

Seo, S. J. 2019. "Ground Breaking for Webtoon Convergence Center and Artists' Apartment within Bucheon Visual Complex" (bucheonyeongsangdanji nae weptunyunghapsenteo yesurinimdaejutaek cheot sap). *Sisa Journal*, December 17. https://www.sisajournal.com/news/articleView.html?idxno=193931.

Sheehan, Kim Bartel, and Deborah K. Morrison. 2009. "The Creativity Challenge: Media Confluence and Its Effects on the Evolving Advertising Industry." *Journal of Interactive Advertising* 9 (2): 40–43.

Shim, Ae-Gyung, and Brian Yecies. 2016. "Film Pioneer Lee Man-hee and the Creation of a Contemporary Korean Cinema Legend." *Korea Journal* 56 (3): 63–89. Available for download from https://ro.uow.edu.au/lhapapers/2736/.

Shim, Ae-Gyung, Brian Yecies, Xiang (Tony) Ren, and Dingkun Wang. 2020. "Cultural Intermediation and the Basis of Trust among Webtoon and Webnovel Communities." *Information, Communication & Society* 23 (6): 833–48.

Shim, W. S. 2018. "Lezhin Comics Blacklisted Artists Who Complained, According to Evidence" (Rejinkomikseu, jakga hanguihamyeon beullaengniseuteuro gwalli—jeunggeo ipsu). *SBS News*, January 11. http://news.sbs.co.kr/news/endPage.do?news_id=N1004570160&plink=ORI&cooper=NAVER.

Shin, J. 2018. "CEO of Lezhin, Top Webtoon Company, Admits the Existence of a Blacklist and Apologizes" (Weptun 1wi rejin daepyo weptunjakga beullaengniseuteu injeong/psagwa). *Oh My News*, July 12. http://www.ohmynews.com/NWS_Web/View/at_pg.aspx?CNTN_CD=A0002452022.

Shin, S. Y. 2012. "Goodbye Yahoo! Korea's Cartoon World . . . Shut Down at the End of June" (Gutbai, yahukoria katunsesangt2wolmal seobiseu jongnyo). *The Hankyoreh*, June 25. http://www.hani.co.kr/arti/culture/movie/539425.html.

Shu, Catherine. 2014. "Kakao and Daum to Merge, Creating one of South Korea's Largest Internet Companies." *TechCrunch*, May 25. https://techcrunch.com/2014/05/25/kakao-daum/.

Sim, Woo-seop 2018. "Exclusive: Lezin Comics, If the Author, Protests, It Is Managed as a Blacklist, Get Evidence." SBS News, January 11. https://news.sbs.co.kr/news/endPage.do?news_id=N1004570160.

Sohn, Ji-young. 2017. "Stepping into the Webtoon World, Literally." *The Korea Herald*, December 17. http://www.koreaherald.com/view.php?ud=20171217000267.

So, K. H. 1984. "So Kwang-hui's Essay: In Need of Cultural Space to Relieve Stress" (Sogwanghui esei seuteureseu pureojul munhwagonggan aswipda). *Kyunghyang Shinmun*, November 7, p. 5.

Song, Hyewon, Doyoung Kim, Hyuck Joo Kwon, and Sanghoon Lee. 2018. "Natural Scene Statistics Based Publication Classification Algorithm Using Convolutional Neural Network." In *Proceedings: Ninth Asia-Pacific Signal and Information Processing Association Annual Summit and Conferencei, APSIPA ASC 2017*, 1186–89. (December 12–15, 2017, Kuala Lumpur, Malaysia.) Kowloon, Hong Kong: APSIPA.

Song, K. W. 2014. "Gambling with Competitive Contents" (Chabyeolhwadoen kontencheuro seungbuhanda). *Cine21*, July 24. http://www.cine21.com/news/view/?mag_id=77482.

Song, T. H. 2001. "SK Has Successful Launch of Manhwa Portal Comic" (SK, manhwapoteol komik okei gaeseo). *Hanguk Kyungje*, February 5. https://news.naver.com/main/read.nhn?mode=LSD&mid=sec&sid1=101&oid=015&aid=0000331824.

Spangler, Todd. 2019. "BTS World Mobile Game from K-Pop Group Rockets to No. 1 Spot on App Charts Worldwide." *Variety*, June 26. https://variety.com/2019/digital/news/bts-world-no-1-app-spot-ranking-1203254316/.

Statista Research Department. 2020. "Number of Monthly Active LINE Users in Japan from 1st Quarter 2013 to 4th Quarter 2019." *Statista.com*, February 19. http://www.statista.com/statistics/560545/number-of-monthly-active-line-app-users-japan/.

Summers. 2013. "First Interview with Lezhin Comics: Lezhin and Guru Started Paid Webtoon Service" (Rejinkomikseu choecho inteobyu: Rejingwa guru, Yuryo weptun seobiseureul sijakada). *Slow News*, June 10. https://slownews.kr/11108.

Tassi, Paul. 2019. "Why on Earth Am I Still Playing 'BTS World'?" *Forbes*, July 1. http://www.forbes.com/sites/paultassi/2019/07/01/why-on-earth-am-i-still-playing-bts-world/ - 1e25fadb1167.

Tay, Daniel. 2014. "Daum and Kakao Merge, Massive Valuation Puts Them Head-to-Head with Naver Line." *Tech in Asia*, September 30. https://www.techinasia.com/daumkakao-merges-massive-valuation.

Taylor, Claire. 2019. *Electronic Literature in Latin America: From Text to Hypertext*. New York: Palgrave Macmillan.

10Asia. 2012. "Naver Webtoon Managers: Our Job Is to Discover Artists before They Give Up" (Neibeo weptun damdangja: Uriui yeokareun jakgadeuri pogihagi jeone balgulhaejuneun geot). May 6. http://tenasia.hankyung.com/archives/14304.

United Nations Conference on Trade and Development (UNCTAD). 2019. *Digital Economy Report 2019*. UNCTAD/DER/2019. UNCTAD: Geneva.

VR Research Center. 2018. "Introducing VR-toon Standard, SphereToon" (Vrweptunui Gijuneul Jesihada, Seupieotun). October 23. https://m.post.naver.com/viewer/postView.nhn?volumeNo=16937244&memberNo=29481007&vType=VERTICAL.

Vultaggio, Maria. 2019. "BTS Has an Unrivaled Twitter Fan Base." *Statista*, November 19. http://www.statista.com/chart/19998/bts-has-an-unrivaled-twitter-fan-base/.

Walatka, Pamela P. 1998. "How to Make a WebToon." NASA tech report NAS-98-014. https://www.nas.nasa.gov/assets/pdf/techreports/1998/nas-98-014.pdf.

Wardrip-Fruin, Noah. 2008. "Reading Digital Literature: Surface, Data, Interaction, and Expressive Processing." In *A Companion to Digital Literary Studies*, edited by Ray Siemens and Susan Schreibman, 163–82. Oxford: Blackwell.

Wee, Wills. 2013. "Kakao Launches KakaoPage, a Marketplace for Anyone to Publish Digital Content." *Tech in Asia*, April 12. http://www.techinasia.com/kakaotalk-launches-kakaopage-digital-content-marketplace.

Wi, G. W. 2018. "Wi Geun-wu's Reply: Lezhin Comics, Cultural Contents Distopia—Transforming Artists into Tools" (Wigeunuui ripeullei: jakgareul dogu-ro mandeuneun tmunhwa kontencheu diseutopiat rejinkomikseu). *Kyunghyang Shinmun*, January 5. http://news.khan.co.kr/kh_news/khan_art_view.html?artid=201801051718005&code=960100.

Wise, Damon. 2019. "After 2017's Cannes/Netflix Controversy, Bong Joon-Ho Moves On with His Genre-Bending 'Parasite'—Cannes." *Deadline Hollywood*, May 20. https://deadline.com/2019/05/bong-joon-ho-parasite-harvey-weinstein-cannes-interview-news-1202611001/.

Yamanaka, C. 2009. "Remember *Dragonball*" (Deuraegonboreul gieokara). *Platform*, May 12. http://platform.ifac.or.kr/webzine/view.php?cat=&sq=459&page=1&Q=w_no&S=15&sort=.

Yecies, Brian. 2008. "Planet Hallyuwood's Political Vulnerabilities: Censuring the Expression of Satire in *The President's Last Bang* (2005)." *International Review of Korean Studies* 5 (1): 37–64. https://www.researchgate.net/publication/228651551_Planet_Hallyuwood%27s_Political_Vulnerabilities_Censuring_the_Expression_of_Satire_in_The_President%27s_Last_Bang_2005.

Yecies, Brian. 2017a. "Informal Collaborations and Formal Agreements: Chinese-Korean Film Encounters." In *Reconceptualising Film Policies* (Routledge Studies in Media and Cultural Industries), edited by Nolwenn Mingant, and Cecilia Tirtaine, 83–95. New York: Routledge.

———. 2017b. "South Korea's International Culture Markets and the Rise of a New Creative Economy." In *2017 Report on International Cultural Markets*, 553–56. Beijing: Capital University of Economics and Business Press.

Yecies, Brian, and Ae-Gyung Shim. 2011. "Contemporary Korean Cinema: Challenges and the Transformation of 'Planet Hallyuwood.'" *Acta Koreana* 14 (1): 1–15. https://www.researchgate.net/publication/266347427_Contemporary_Korean_Cinema_Challenges_and_the_Transformation_of_%27Planet_Hallyuwood%27.

———. 2016. "At the Crossroads of Directing and Politics." In *The Changing Face of Korean Cinema: 1960 to 2015*, 42–61. London: Routledge.

Yecies, Brian, Ae-Gyung Shim, and Jack Yang. 2019. "Chinese Transcreators, Webtoons and the Korean Digital Wave." In *Digital Transactions in Asia: Economic, Informational, and Social Exchanges*, edited by Adrian Athique, and Emma Baulch, 224–24. London: Routledge.

Yecies, Brian, Ae-Gyung Shim, Jack (Jie) Yang, and Peter Yong Zhong. 2020. "Global Transcreators and the Extension of the Korean Webtoon IP-Engine." *Media, Culture & Society* 42 (1): 40–57.

Yeom, J. H. 2016. "The Rise of Webtoons and Web Dramas that Often Resemble Advertisements" (gwanggomyeonseo gwanggo anin deut weptuntpswepdeuramaga tteunda). *Joongang Sunday*, November 20. https://news.joins.com/article/20897607.

Yim, Haksoon. 2002. "Cultural Identity and Cultural Policy in South Korea." *International Journal of Cultural Policy* 8 (1): 37–48.

Yim, Hyun-su. 2018. "Emart to Make Film about Its Mascot Electro Man." *The Korea Herald*, July 24. http://www.koreaherald.com/view.php?ud=20180724000734.

Yonhap News Agency. 1991. "Comics Award to Be Launched to Encourage Sound Comics Culture" (Geonjeonmanhwa yukseongwihae manhwasang jejeongkiro). April 9. https://news.naver.com/main/read.nhn?mode=LSD&mid=sec&sid1=103&oid=001&aid=0003567918.

———. 1993. "Independence Day Special: Japan, an Unresolved Problem and a New Problem" (8.15 teukjip ilbon- motda pun munje, saeroun munje (3)). August 10. https://news.naver.com/main/read.nhn?mode=LSD&mid=sec&sid1=102&oid=001&aid=0003709013.

———. 2009. "Comic Industry Going against Free webtoon Contents" (manhwagye mobail muryo 'weptune bandae'). June 23. https://tinyurl.com/r7hz4mv.

———. 2019. "(LEAD) S. Korea to Spend Over 1 Tln Won to Nurture Content Creators." https://en.yna.co.kr/view/AEN20190917006451315.

Yoon, Hye-ji. 2014. "I Am Confident It Is the Cleanest Platform" (Gajang kkaekkeutan peullaetpomirago jabuhanda). *Cine21*, July 24. http://www.cine21.com/news/view/?mag_id=77480.

Yoon, Sung-won. 2016. "Kakao Separates Webtoon Business as Independent Subsidiary." *The Korea Times*, September 4. http://www.koreatimes.co.kr/www/news/tech/2016/11/129_213283.html.

Yu, B. S. 1999. "1,000 Won to Read Internet Comics All Day" (cheonwoneuro harujongil inteonet manhwabonda). *Maeil Kyungjae*, November 30, p. 14.

Yu, Chanmi. 2017. "Gan (Generative Adversarial Networks) Technology Applied to Naver Webtoon *Encountered*" (Neibeo weptun 'majuchyeossda'e jeogyongdoen gan gisul). *Naver Labs*, December 21. https://www.naverlabs.com/storyDetail/44.

Yuk, Y. S. 2017. "Planning and Distributing Branded Webtoons" (Beuraendeuweptunui gihoek mit yutong). Presentation at Bucheon International Comics Festival (BICOF) 2017, Korea Comics Agora, July 17–23, Bucheon, South Korea.

Yun, Hyeong-joon. 2013. "I Want to Challenge People Who Think of Comics as Free" (Manhwaneun gongjja'raneun sahoejeok insikgwa ssaugo sipda). *The Hankyoreh*, May 3. http://www.hani.co.kr/arti/culture/culture_general/585849.html.

Yun, Suh-young. 2013. "The Year in Movies." *The Korea Times*, December 30. http://www.koreatimes.co.kr/www/culture/2018/08/135_148864.html.

INDEX

ABOUT THE AUTHORS

Brian Yecies is associate professor in communication and media at the University of Wollongong, where he researches film and digital media, creative industries, cultural policy, and Big Data. He is chief investigator on two Australian Research Council Discovery Projects—Digital China: From Cultural Presence to Innovative Nation (2017–2020) and Mobile Korean Webtoons: Creative Innovation in a New Digital Economy (2018–2021). His books include *Korea's Occupied Cinemas, 1893–1948* (2011), *The Changing Face of Korean Cinema, 1960–2015* (2016), and *South Korea's Webtooniverse and the Digital Comic Revolution* (2021)—all coauthored with Ae-Gyung Shim. Yecies coedited *Willing Collaborators: Foreign Partners in Chinese Media* (2018) with Michael Keane and Terry Flew. Collaborative research supported by competitive funding from the Korea Foundation, the Australia-Korea Foundation, the Academy of Korean Studies, and the Asia Research Fund have facilitated the publication of his book chapters in *Big Data Recommender Systems: Recent Trends and Advances* (2019, with Jie Jack Yang), *Routledge Handbook of Cultural and Creative Industries in Asia* (2019, with Ae-Gyung Shim), *Asia-Pacific Film Coproductions: Theory, Industry and Aesthetics* (2019, with Luke Buckmaster), *Rediscovering Korean Cinema* (2019), *Digital Transactions in Asia: Economic, Informational, and Social Exchanges* (2019, with Ae-Gyung Shim and Jie Jack Yang), *Asian Cultural Flows: Creative Industries, Cultural Policies, and Media Consumers* (2018, with Michael Keane), *Reconceptualising Film Policies* (2017), *The Handbook of China's Cultural & Creative Industries* (2016), *Report on the International Cultural Mar-*

kets (2016, Beijing Capital University of Economics and Business, China), and *Creative Media in China* (2014). Academic journals featuring his research articles include *Acta Koreana, Asia-Pacific Journal, Asian Cinema, First Monday, Global Media & China, Information Communication and Society, International Journal of Cultural Policy, International Journal of Human-Computer Interaction, Journal of Big Data, Journal of Korean Studies, Korea Journal, Media, Culture and Society, Media International Australia, Participations: Journal of Audience & Reception Studies*, and *Studies in Australasian Cinema*.

Ae-Gyung Shim received her PhD in film studies, arts, and media from the University of New South Wales, and she presently researches transnational aspects of Asia's film, digital media, and entertainment industries. She is a past Korea Foundation Research Fellow and visiting scholar in the Institute for Social Transformation Research at the University of Wollongong and with Brian Yecies is coauthor of *Korea's Occupied Cinemas, 1893–1948* (2011), *The Changing Face of Korean Cinema, 1960–2015* (2016), and *South Korea's Webtooniverse and the Digital Comic Revolution* (2021).

www.ingramcontent.com/pod-product-compliance
Lightning Source LLC
Chambersburg PA
CBHW030647270326
41929CB00007B/238